D1363072

THE CLIA

THE CLIA GUIDE
to the Cruise Industry

Marc Mancini, Ph.D.
Professor of Travel
West Los Angeles College

DELMAR
CENGAGE Learning™

Australia • Brazil • Japan • Korea • Mexico • Singapore • Spain • United Kingdom • United States

The CLIA Guide to the Cruise Industry
Marc Mancini, Ph.D.

Vice President, Career and Professional
Editorial: Dave Garza

Director of Learning Solutions: Sandy Clark

Senior Acquisitions Editor: Jim Gish

Managing Editor: Larry Main

Product Manager: Anne Orgren

Editorial Assistant: Sarah Timm

Vice President Marketing, Career and
Professional: Jennifer Baker

Marketing Director: Wendy Mapstone

Senior Marketing Manager: Kristin McNary

Marketing Coordinator: Scott Chrysler

Associate Marketing Manager: Jonathan Sheehan

Production Director: Wendy Troeger

Content Project Management: Pre-Press PMG

Senior Art Director: Casey Kirchmayer

Technology Project Manager: Chris Catalina

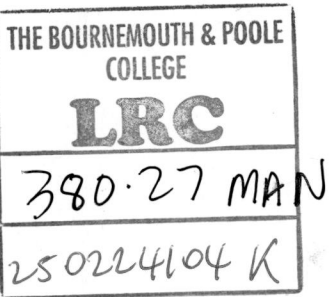
For product information and technology assistance, contact us at
Cengage Learning Customer & Sales Support, 1-800-354-9706

For permission to use material from this text or product,
submit all requests online at **cengage.com/permissions**
Further permissions questions can be emailed to
permissionrequest@cengage.com

Library of Congress Control Number: 2010924623

ISBN-13: 978-1-111-13089-3

ISBN-10: 1-111-13089-2

Delmar
5 Maxwell Drive
Clifton Park, NY 12065-2919
USA

Cengage Learning is a leading provider of customized learning solutions with office locations around the globe, including Singapore, the United Kingdom, Australia, Mexico, Brazil, and Japan. Locate your local office at: **international.cengage.com/region**

Cengage Learning products are represented in Canada by Nelson Education, Ltd.

To learn more about Delmar, visit **www.cengage.com/delmar**

Purchase any of our products at your local college store or at our preferred online store **www.cengagebrain.com**

Notice to the Reader

Publisher does not warrant or guarantee any of the products described herein or perform any independent analysis in connection with any of the product information contained herein. Publisher does not assume, and expressly disclaims, any obligation to obtain and include information other than that provided to it by the manufacturer. The reader is expressly warned to consider and adopt all safety precautions that might be indicated by the activities described herein and to avoid all potential hazards. By following the instructions contained herein, the reader willingly assumes all risks in connection with such instructions. The publisher makes no representations or warranties of any kind, including but not limited to, the warranties of fitness for particular purpose or merchantability, nor are any such representations implied with respect to the material set forth herein, and the publisher takes no responsibility with respect to such material. The publisher shall not be liable for any special, consequential, or exemplary damages resulting, in whole or part, from the readers' use of, or reliance upon, this material.

CONTENTS

PREFACE

Ask 100 people what makes a vacation getaway perfect, and you'll get 100 answers: relaxation, comfort, exploration, learning, great experiences in great places, plenty to do and plenty to see, great shopping, fabulous meals, constant pampering, and more. Some travel products feature *some* of these things. Cruises provide them *all*.

Cruising has become one of the most significant phenomena of our age. For that reason, it's something that almost certainly intrigues you. And if it does, then this edition of *The CLIA Guide to the Cruise Industry* is surely the right book for you. *The CLIA Guide to the Cruise Industry* is written for three kinds of readers:

- *Professionals,* such as travel agents and potential cruise line employees, who want to know more about the cruise experience.
- *Students of travel* who are contemplating careers as travel agents, cruise line employees, or other cruise-related professionals.
- *Members of the general public* who are interested in cruising and want to know more about it from an insider perspective.

If you fit any of these categories, then *The CLIA Guide to the Cruise Industry* is written with you in mind.

How This Book Is Unique

The CLIA Guide to the Cruise Industry is a unique sort of textbook:

- **It approaches its topic from the perspective of a working professional.** You'll get a true insider's look on how cruise sales, marketing, and operations unfold.
- **It makes reading about cruising fun.** Cruising *is* fun. A book—even a textbook— on cruises should be the same. *The CLIA Guide to the Cruise Industry* uses a breezy, magazine-like prose to make learning an enjoyable experience for you.
- **It uses many educational strategies to help you remember and understand what you read.** Highlighting, bullet points, headings, graphs, tables, photos, and application activities serve to clarify, magnify, and reinforce information. The result: You absorb a far greater percentage of what you read.
- **It's the official textbook of the Cruise Lines International Association.** Dozens of leading industry professionals—including several cruise line presidents—have reviewed its content. This ensures that what you read reflects real-world insights into the business.

How This Book Is Organized

The CLIA Guide to the Cruise Industry features 10 chapters. Each blends definitions, statistics, anecdotes, observations, and examples into what we hope is a definitive look at the cruise business.

- Each chapter begins with a list of *objectives*. They describe what you'll know and should be able to do by chapter's end.
- **Key terms** and **phrases** are boldfaced or italicized in the text to underscore their importance.
- *Photos*, *graphs*, and *sidebars* expand each chapter's content.
- *Questions for discussion* permit you to test your understanding of the material in that chapter.
- *Activities* close each chapter and challenge you to take a hypothetical situation and apply a creative solution to it.
- The book concludes with *appendices* (key addresses, port descriptions, and a bibliography), a *glossary* of cruise-related terms, and an *index.*

> Students:
>
> **Keep This Book!** Should you resell *The CLIA Guide to the Cruise Industry* after your course is over? Probably not. In the future, you may take a cruise—maybe many. It's then you'll want to revisit this book and be able to better appreciate your cruise experience. And if you go into the business, *The CLIA Guide to the Cruise Industry* will be doubly valuable. So, consider this book a lifetime investment. Someday, you'll be glad you kept it.

About CLIA Certification

If you're already a travel agent enrolled in the CLIA certification program, studying this book and passing a test available from CLIA and specific to this text will yield you 30 credits. To order your test or learn more about CLIA certification, visit its Web site at www.cruising.org.

To the Instructor or Trainer

The CLIA Guide to the Cruise Industry has been created with your pragmatic needs in mind. It can serve as your primary textbook in a course on cruising or it may be used as a supplement to other courses.

Its content was determined through a questionnaire sent to college and industry educators across North America. Ninety-three surveys were completed and returned to us, so we feel confident that our text reflects the needs of the educational community. The book was also thoroughly reviewed by the CLIA Marketing Committee, which is comprised of senior cruise line executives. Please keep in mind that because of the dynamic, evolving nature of the cruise industry, things can and do change.

An *Instructor's Manual* amplifies the book and will make your teaching much easier. Included in its content:

- Thematic outlines for all chapters
- Suggested answers to the Questions for Discussion

- Suggested solutions to the Activities
- A bank of quizzes, with answers, for each chapter

For your own copy of the *Instructor's Manual,* contact Delmar, Cengage Learning.

Acknowledgments

The author and publisher wish to acknowledge the following educators for serving as reviewers:

- Andrew O. Coggins. Jr., Virginia Tech, Blacksburg, Virginia
- Brenda Cook, Kings College, Charlotte, North Carolina
- Barbara Gallup, Parks Junior College, Denver, Colorado
- Joanne M. Giampa, College of DuPage, Glen Ellyn, Illinois
- Sherry A. Hine, Mid Florida Technical Institute, Orlando, Florida
- Chuck Laterza, Richland College, Dallas, Texas
- Beth O'Donnell, Edmonds Community College, Lynnwood, Washington.

We would also like to thank the CLIA member lines and their representatives to the marketing committee as well as the CLIA staff for their assistance, input, and support.

And special thanks to Rosalyn Gershell; Bob Sharak, CLIA's executive vice president of marketing and distribution; Tom Cogan, CLIA's director of training; Bernie Blomquist, CLIA's manager of training development; and to my assistant, Karen Fukushima , for her efficient, thorough, and enthusiastic support throughout this project.

About the Author

Marc Mancini, Ph.D., is one of the travel industry's most famous consultants and speakers. Over 300,000 people have attended seminars he's presented or designed, and nearly 100 companies and organizations—including CLIA, Holland America Line, Hurtigruten, Norwegian Cruise Line, and Silversea Cruises—have benefited from his consulting skills.

He has written four other textbooks (*Selling Destinations, Connecting with Customers, Conducting Tours,* and *Access*), published over 200 articles, and appeared on CNN and *Good Morning America.* He has a B.A. from Providence College and an M.A., M.S., and Ph.D. from the University of Southern California. He was named Teacher of the Year by the International Society of Travel and Tourism Educators. He lives in Brentwood, California.

Chapter **1**

Introduction

Courtesy of Seabourn Cruise Line

After reading this chapter, you'll be able to:

- Define the term *cruise*.
- Explain the history of cruising and how it affects today's cruise vacation experience.
- Describe the contemporary cruise experience.
- Distinguish among different types of itineraries.

When historians of the future look back to the way people of our time traveled, they'll almost certainly zero in on one remarkable phenomenon: the success of cruising. They'll cite the fact that the number of people who took a cruise vacation increased by more than 7% each year—a growth unmatched by any other segment of the travel industry. They'll note that the vast majority of cruisers said that they were very satisfied with the cruise experience. They'll marvel at the great, graceful vessels—both large and small— that carried just about every kind of person—married, single, young, old, wealthy, or just getting by—to virtually every place on the globe. And most of all, they'll be astonished by the level of service and spectrum of activities—both on and off the ship—that these passengers enjoyed. Once people have been on a cruise, they rate it higher than other types of vacations—and find the experience better than they thought it would be. See Figure 1-1.

We live in exciting times, when more and more people discover how truly wonderful a cruise vacation can be. And as a member—or a potential member—of the vast travel community that makes such cruise dreams come true, you should justifiably be proud.

Cruise Vacations Compared to Other Vacations (Q11)
% Much/Somewhat Better
BASE: *Cruisers and Vacationers*

	Rep. Sample (2002)	Rep. Sample (2004)	Rep. Sample (2006)	Rep. Sample (2008)	Cruisers	Non-Cruisers/ Vacationers
Chance to Visit Several Locations	67%	62%	63%	61%	73%	50%
Being Pampered	69%	63%	57%	53%	62%	45%
Fine Dining	70%	57%	54%	51%	62%	41%
Luxurious	67%	57%	52%	50%	58%	42%
Relax/Get Away From It All	61%	53%	48%	49%	63%	37%
Unique & Different		54%	50%	47%	56%	39%
Variety of Activities	50%	50%	46%	46%	58%	35%
Explore Vacation Area/Return Later	51%	44%	43%	45%	62%	30%
High Quality Entertainment	58%	51%	45%	45%	55%	36%
Hassle-free	54%	50%	46%	45%	58%	32%
Easy to Plan and Arrange	50%	46%	47%	44%	57%	33%
Offers Something for Everyone			45%	44%	59%	31%
Exciting and Adventurous	51%	45%	42%	42%	53%	32%
Fun Vacation	45%	40%	39%	40%	53%	28%
Romantic Getaway	55%	45%	42%	40%	46%	35%
Makes Me Feel Special -Rich & Famous			41%	38%	46%	30%
Good Value for the Money	42%	36%	35%	37%	53%	22%
Reliable	42%	34%	33%	35%	49%	22%
Good Vacation for Entire Family			32%	34%	46%	23%
Cultural Learning Experience	47%	34%	31%	32%	40%	24%
Safe	33%	29%	25%	31%	45%	18%
Comfortable Accommodations	37%	27%	28%	30%	38%	21%
Good Activities for Children	31%	26%	27%	30%	35%	24%
Participate in Sports You Enjoy	22%	19%	20%	18%	22%	16%

Q11. How do you think cruise vacations compare to other vacations you've taken? Are cruises much better, somewhat better, the same, somewhat worse, or much worse than your other vacations in terms of...

FIGURE 1-1 Cruise vacations compared to other vacations
Source: *CLIA's Cruise Market Profile Study*

However, as important as the present and future of cruising is, you should also know a little about its past. The cruise industry's genealogy is important. And it's a fascinating tale indeed.

Definitions and Beginnings

Before exploring cruising's ancestry, how about a definition for **cruising**? A **cruise** is a vacation trip by ship. It's that simple. This definition excludes traveling by water for purely business purposes (e.g., cargo ships), sailing on one's own small pleasure craft, or travel on a vessel for primarily transportational purposes (e.g., a short ferry ride). A cruise is primarily a leisure vacation experience, with the ship's staff doing all the work. Some cruise ships also transport cargo, and all of them carry people from place to place. But at the core of cruising—from the perspective of the traveler—is the desire to relax, to get away from it all, to experience, to learn, to be pampered, and to have fun. Today, that almost always takes place on a vessel custom-built to satisfy these goals, although it can also take place on a freighter, a ferrylike ship, or during a transatlantic sailing. As long as the emphasis is on the passenger's desire to have a great time, it's cruising.

And that's exactly what was going on in ancient times, to some extent, in the Mediterranean. Of course, ships sailed this legendary sea mostly for practical reasons: exploration, commerce, migration, and warfare. But there were always a few hardy souls who came aboard just to experience the far-flung ports that these vessels visited; the most famous of these people was Herodotus, who during his sailing compiled a list of the most interesting manmade things he saw. Today, we call them the Seven Wonders of the Ancient World (see box below). And there's a reason he did it: to provide other pleasure travelers of his time with a sort of guidebook to where to go and what to see. And, like him, most of them did it by boat.

The Seven Wonders of the Ancient World

- The Pyramids (Giza, Egypt)

- The Hanging Gardens of Babylon (near Baghdad, Iraq)

- The Statue of Zeus at Olympia (Greece)

- The Temple of Diana at Ephesus (Turkey)

- The Mausoleum (Halicarnassus, Turkey)

- The Colossus (Rhodes)

- The Pharos Lighthouse (Alexandria, Egypt)

After about A.D. 500, "leisure" travel virtually disappeared. Certainly, some awesome seagoing trips took place (e.g., people from Tahiti sailed 2,000 miles to Hawaii, the Vikings reached North America, and controversial evidence exists that the ancient Chinese crossed the Pacific all the way to California). But these and other sailings were to explore, to trade, to conquer, or to settle. "Tourists" aboard these ships were a rarity; pleasure was only an afterthought.

The Arrival of Leisure Sailing

In the 1800s, shipping companies rediscovered that they could increase their profits by booking passengers aboard their merchant ships. A few of these travelers were wealthy patrons looking for adventure in faraway lands. Most of the others were relatively poor people looking for a new place to live.

Eventually, shipping companies began building vessels ("steamships," they were called) whose primary purpose was to transport people, not cargo. Technology helped make it possible, as wooden ships with sails were replaced by steel-hulled vessels that were driven by coal, oil, and steam, not wind. The early steel ships also had sail riggings, which were only there to reassure passengers. These transports became larger and larger, with names like *Aquitania*, *Leviathan*, and, yes, *Titanic*. Surprisingly, a few of the steamship companies that built the great turn-of-the-century vessels are still around today: Cunard, P&O, and Holland America; all three are today owned by Carnival Corporation.

On July 5, 1961, seven luxury liners all happened to be in New York City at the same time. The vessel arriving is the *Queen Elizabeth*. Docked, from bottom to top, are the *Independence*, *America*, *United States*, *Olympia*, *Mauretania*, and *Sylvania*. Also in the shot is the aircraft carrier *USS Intrepid*.
Courtesy of CLIA

Ocean liners were among the most astonishing creations to appear in the early 1900s. Their exteriors were majestic and boastful, and their interiors were as lavish as the great hotels of Europe—or at least parts of them were.

The major purpose of the ocean liner of those times was to carry immigrants, not the well-to-do. That was where most of the money was made. Ships were usually divided into two or three "classes." In first class were the wealthy; second class accommodated people of modest but sufficient means; third class, or "steerage," was for the masses. On any given sailing, there might be 100 passengers in first, 100 in second, and 2,000 in third.

The contrast between first class and steerage was striking. In first class, passengers dined in elegant surroundings, were entertained by tuxedoed musicians, and slept in the poshest of staterooms. (Although there's controversy about this, the word *posh* is said to come from the words *Port Out, Starboard Home*, which described the best side of the ship to have your cabin on when sailing between England and India.) In steerage, passengers ate soup and boiled potatoes, were entertained by their fellow passengers, and slept in vast dormitories on cots bunked two or three high. Nowhere on the ship were the two groups allowed to mix.

Yet, these steerage passengers were so important to profitability that steamship lines actually designed their ship exteriors to appeal to immigrant beliefs. For example, steerage passengers would arrive at a port, dragging their ample baggage along, with no idea which ship they would take. They believed, naively, that the quality of a vessel could be judged by its number of smokestacks. So, the steamship lines would often put extra funnels atop their ships—funnels that had absolutely no function except to attract passengers.

This sort of travel seems alien to us today. But consider this: About one out of four North Americans has at least one ancestor who arrived via one of these ships. There's a good chance, then, that you wouldn't be here if it weren't for an ocean liner.

The Luxury Palaces

During World War I, most ocean-crossing vessels were converted into troop transport ships. After the war, they were joined by a new generation of ships: bigger, sleeker, and, above all, faster. Speed became the most important goal. Indeed, something called the Blue Riband was awarded regularly to whichever ship could cross the North Atlantic in the least amount of time. Transportation, not "cruising," continued to be what passenger ships were mostly about.

During the 1920s and 1930s, though, ocean liners did begin to provide more entertainment, attract more of the middle class, and provide much of the pampering we associate today with cruising. Even the Depression failed to dent the business. A key reason: During Prohibition, just about the only place for an American to drink liquor was on the high seas. (Onboard casinos, however, were still a rarity.) Being on an ocean liner became a fashionable thing. Newspapers regularly touted the names of celebrities who were sailing on ships.

Ships continued to become larger, with their costs often subsidized by governments. Nations used ocean liners as symbols of their prosperity, taste, and might. A prime example: The *Queen Mary*—now an attraction in Long Beach,

On a luxury cruise, staff go above and beyond to satisfy and impress.
Courtesy of Seabourn Cruise Line

California—was Britain's pride. Such ships were huge, floating cities, every bit as big as many of today's cruise vessels.

The Birth of Contemporary Cruising

Although plenty might be going on aboard ship, it would be wrong to call transoceanic crossings "cruising," as we know of cruising today. The primary purpose was transportation, with no intermediate stops to see what was along the way. But even in the early 1900s, a few (usually smaller) steamship lines devised a product that was closer to a "cruise." During winter (when ocean crossings were least popular), they would concede the transatlantic business to their bigger competitors and "reposition" their ships to warmer places, such as the Caribbean. (It was also a good way to avoid icebergs.) The experience—often called an *excursion*—became purely leisure. People would book a cruise to visit a series of exotic ports, to profit from the "health benefits" of bracing sea air, and to do interesting things while onboard their ship. Even a few around-the-world cruises appeared.

This vacation cruise business was a minor one—transoceanic transportation still dominated—until June 1958. During that month, airlines started the first commercial jet service across the Atlantic. Ocean crossings became a matter of hours, not days. And the cruise lines were instantly in trouble.

People bound for another continent suddenly found ships to be a slow, boring option. Within one year, more people were crossing the Atlantic by air than by sea. Only those who feared air travel or were looking for a very leisurely, away-from-the-ordinary experience continued to book transoceanic crossings. The joke was that ocean liners were only for "the newly wed and the nearly dead." Although they continued to market their ships as transoceanic transportation, steamship lines—or at least some of them—concluded that they had to dramatically rethink their business. Crossings diminished, and cruising was in.

Modern Cruising Develops

Those smaller ships cruising the Caribbean became the business model nearly every company pursued. Let's think of ships as floating resorts, they said, that offer pleasurable activities, great food, superb service, and—yes—convenient, no-packing-and-unpacking transportation from place to place. The Blue Riband no longer resonated in the minds of consumers; "fun ships" and "love boats" did.

A few new liners, built primarily for ocean crossings, appeared in the 1960s. There were still enough passengers to justify them, and it was believed that more "modern" vessels would bring the passengers back.

Huge ships have caused the dramatic growth of cruising.
Courtesy of Carnival Cruise Lines

But the emphasis on leisure cruising led to the rapid conversion of many existing ships into cruise vessels. The cruise lines tore out the bulkheads separating the classes, installed air conditioning, expanded pool areas, put in casinos, and converted staid function rooms into discos. Cruising became a major phenomenon, with cruise companies building new ships in the 1970s designed specifically for cruising.

Cruising gained even greater momentum in the 1980s and especially the 1990s. "Megaships" appeared that far exceeded the size and scope of the biggest ocean liners, while smaller super-luxury vessels targeted people who sought the very highest of experiences. There were also high-tech masted sailing ships and small expedition vessels that provided "soft" adventures. Massive paddlewheelers once again plied the Mississippi, while sleek modern vessels glided past the historic shores of Europe's Danube River. Soon, there was a cruise experience for just about everyone.

Cruising Today

Each year, millions of travelers choose to cruise. And far more intend to do so soon. One Cruise Lines International Association (CLIA) survey determined that 51 million North Americans intend to cruise within three years.

What are their choices? Many people try out cruising by selecting a short itinerary, such as a three-day Bahamas cruise out of Florida or a four-day journey from Los Angeles to Catalina and Ensenada, Mexico. Some may even sample a one-day "party cruise" before actually taking a multiday sailing. A few might book a three-month world cruise.

- A cruise company typically purchases over $600 million of food and beverages each year.
- Mass-market cruise lines spend about $10 per day per passenger for raw foodstuffs. For the most expensive lines, the average is about $40.
- On a weeklong cruise aboard a large vessel, about 5,000 cases of wine and champagne are used.
- Many ship gyms use air-resistance exercise machines. The kind that incorporate actual weights would be too heavy.
- A fully equipped ship-based gym and spa costs about a half-million dollars.
- One-third to one-half of the people onboard a ship are crew members.
- Large cruise ships typically carry $3 million of spare parts.
- The typical dining room server makes $25,000 to $30,000 a year in salary and tips (and crew members have few onboard living expenses).
- On most cruise lines, the main source of revenue onboard is beverage sales (so many places and opportunities to buy).
- People who gamble on a ship spend about $10 a day.
- In Bermuda, the typical cruise passenger spends $90 while in port.

Cruise factoids
Source: *Selling the Sea* by Bob Dickinson and Andy Vladimir

The most popular itineraries, however, are seven-day cruises. In cruise terminology, a Saturday-to-Saturday sailing is called a seven-day cruise, even though eight days are involved in the itinerary. Even more confusing: Because the ship probably leaves Saturday evening and arrives the following Saturday morning, passengers are actually sailing on the ship for six-and-a-half days!

The ship's agenda can be a **round-trip** or **circle itinerary**, with the vessel leaving from and returning to the same port. For example, a ship could sail from Vancouver, head northward through the Alaskan Inside Passage, turn back at, say, Skagway, and return to Vancouver (stopping, of course, at interesting ports along the way).

In other situations, the cruise might start at one port but finish at another. A ship could leave Vancouver but finish its trip in Anchorage. This is called a **one-way itinerary**. In all probability, the vessel would take on a whole new set of passengers in Anchorage and repeat the same itinerary, in reverse, to Vancouver. For an example of each, see Figure 1-2.

Round-Trip		Arrive	Depart
Day 0	Vancouver		5:00 P.M.
Day 1	Scenic Cruising: Inside Passage		
Day 2	Scenic Cruising: Tracy Arm and Sawyer Glaciers	8:00 A.M.	Noon
	Juneau	2:30 P.M.	10:30 P.M.
Day 3	Skagway	7:00 P.M.	9:00 P.M.
Day 4	Scenic Cruising: Glacier Bay National Park	7:00 A.M.	4:00 P.M.
Day 5	Ketchikan	10:00 A.M.	6:00 P.M.
Day 6	Cruising the Inside Passage		
Day 7	Vancouver	7:00 A.M.	
One-Way (Northbound)		**Arrive**	**Depart**
Day 0	Vancouver		5:00 P.M.
Day 1	Scenic Cruising: Inside Passage		
Day 2	Ketchikan	7:00 A.M.	3:00 P.M.
Day 3	Juneau	8:00 A.M.	10:30 P.M.
Day 4	Skagway	7:00 A.M.	9:00 P.M.
Day 5	Scenic Cruising: Glacier Bay National Park	7:00 A.M.	4:00 P.M.
Day 6	Scenic Cruising: College Fjord	5:00 P.M.	8:00 P.M.
Day 7	Seward (Anchorage)	6:00 A.M.	

FIGURE 1-2 Two possible Alaska itineraries
Source: *Holland America Line*

During the cruise, passengers experience a wealth of onboard activities (e.g., meals, shows, contests, lounging at the pool), which take place primarily on **at-sea days** (when the ship is traveling a long distance without stopping at any ports). On **port days** (usually the ship docks early in the morning and leaves in the evening), passengers have the option of going ashore (most do) or staying on the ship. During most itineraries, port days far outnumber at-sea days.

The cruise experience can extend well beyond the cruise itself. Cruise clients sometimes arrive at the cruise departure port a day or two early and/or stay at the port afterward. Their lodging can be purchased from the cruise line or booked separately; these are called **pre-** and **post-cruise packages**. In a few cases, the cruise line may even bundle and sell pre- and post-cruise hotel stays and at least some sightseeing for one price, as part of a larger cruise experience, or **cruise-tour**.

Cruising isn't just about ships; it's also about the people who anticipate your needs.
Courtesy of Windstar Cruises

For instance, a cruise line could start its cruise-tour in Istanbul, Turkey, with a two-night stay and one all-day city tour. The cruise itself would then begin, visit several Eastern Mediterranean islands, and finish in Athens, Greece, where another two-day hotel stay and city tour await the passengers. The entire experience would be sold at one price (although the option might be available to buy a cruise-only package at a lower price). Another example: A family could purchase a package that includes, among other things, a three-night stay at an Orlando hotel, several theme park admissions, transfer to Port Canaveral, and a three-day cruise to the Bahamas, with transfer back to Orlando.

There are four possibilities when it comes to passengers getting to their cruise. Let's say a couple living in New York City wants to take a cruise that follows a circle itinerary, departing from and returning to New Orleans. Their travel agent could book a flight for them to and from New Orleans; in airline terminology, a flight to and from the same city is called a **round-trip** or **closed-jaw itinerary**. Or the agent could purchase the flight directly from the cruise line; the cruise lines contract with the airlines for space and resell that space to passengers. In a few cases, the flight might even be included in the cruise price, but this is becoming less common.

What if this New York City couple wants to visit the Western Mediterranean? They would fly into, say, Rome, Italy. From Rome's port, their ship would sail

A grand ship visits a great city: Venice, Italy.
Courtesy of Seabourn Cruise Line

westward and finish a week later in Barcelona, Spain. The couple would then fly home from Barcelona or they could also continue on an extended land vacation in Spain. When an air itinerary features a return from a different city than the one first flown to, it's called an **open-jaw itinerary**.

There's a third possible scenario. A couple who resides in New York City decides to take a cruise to and from Bermuda. The cruise begins and ends in New York City, so there's no need for air travel.

A fourth possibility: That same New York couple decides instead to take a cruise into Canada. The cruise departs from and returns to Boston, so the New York couple drive to Boston—it takes about five hours—and leaves their car at a parking structure near the pier while on the cruise. When they return from the cruise, they pick up their car and drive back to New York.

These last two scenarios would be booked as a **cruise-only trip**.

This discussion of the various shapes a cruise experience can take may have triggered other questions in your mind: What other places do cruises go? How does a typical cruise unfold? What kind of people actually take cruises? All these and more are answered in chapters to come.

Questions for Discussion

1. How did a transoceanic sea voyage differ from a modern cruise?

2. Explain why a seven-day cruise might be viewed as either six, seven, or eight days long.

3. Define the following:

   - at-sea day

   - port day

   - circle itinerary

   - one-way itinerary

   - closed-jaw itinerary

   - open-jaw itinerary

 **Activity**

Obtain a brochure from one cruise line. Study it carefully and then answer these questions:

Cruise line: For which year?

Title of the brochure: For which geographic region?

1. Are there any cruises of four days or less? If yes, briefly describe one itinerary.

2. Are there any cruises of seven days or more? If yes, briefly describe one itinerary.

3. Does the cruise line offer pre- or post-cruise packages? If yes, give a brief description of one of them.

4. Does the cruise line offer air? If yes, describe how it is offered (e.g., as part of the cruise price? As an "extra" that can be booked separately? Anything else?).

5. What is the overall feeling you get about the cruise experiences described in the brochure? Would this be a cruise you would take? Why or why not?

6. If possible, visit this cruise line's Web site. Is the "feeling" you get about the cruise line the same or different from the brochure? What features does it have that the brochure doesn't?

Who Cruises— and Why

After reading this chapter, you'll be able to:

- Describe the typical clients onboard cruises of different lengths.
- Explain 20 reasons why people are drawn to cruising.
- Identify what's typically included in the cruise price and what isn't.
- Explain how cruises are priced.
- Recognize the 15 most common roadblocks to cruise purchase.

Imagine a huge wall map in an imaginary Museum of Cruising. On that map, little lights mark the spots where every cruise ship is currently located. The first surprise: There are lights just about everywhere there's water—hundreds of them: on the South China Sea, up the Amazon, around Hawaii, even along the coast of Antarctica.

Now press a button. Those lights disappear and are replaced by a new set of lights. These indicate the location of the cruise lines' headquarters. Fewer lights now, but again, they're spread across the map: Athens, Miami, Tokyo, and more. Press one more button. This time, you'll see where cruise passengers come from. Just about the whole map lights up.

Cruising is indeed a global phenomenon. People from everywhere take cruises to everywhere. One important statistic: Currently, only about 20% of all North American adults who can afford to take a cruise have done so, but about three times more say they would like to do so within the next three years.

Here are a few facts, based on research studies done by CLIA and other researchers:

- Twenty-nine percent of all cruisers are under 40 years old, 52% are between 40 and 59, and 20% are over 60. This clearly punctures the myth that "cruises are only for old people."
- On average, about 40% of the people onboard are taking their first cruise.
- Eighty-six percent of cruisers are married.
- People who take cruises earn about 18% more money in household income per year than do noncruisers. In general, they also travel more.
- About a quarter of all cruisers bring a child or children along.

Does this give you a clearer picture as to who cruises? Good. You should remember, though, that these statistics define the *average* cruiser. A wide variety of types make up each "average" statistic. The kind of cruise has a powerful bearing on which type within these statistics will be attracted to that cruise.

There are also many categories of cruisers (e.g., families, singles, and the physically challenged). We'll examine these in more detail later. For now, just remember that the category you fit in very much affects why you cruise.

For example, on a short cruise, passengers tend to:

- Be younger
- Have more modest incomes
- Have less education
- Be more likely to work full-time
- Be interested in a mass-market destination, such as the Caribbean
- Be new to cruising

Conversely, on a longer cruise, the passengers tend to:

- Be older
- Have higher incomes
- Be more educated
- Be more likely to be retired or semiretired

Romance is a major motivator for cruising.
Courtesy of Costa Cruises

- Be interested in a more exotic destination, such as South America
- Have already experienced cruising

Why People Cruise

It often seems that there are as many motives to cruise as there are people. Sometimes, the reason is pure curiosity. Other times, it's because of a travel agent's recommendation or, very often, positive word-of-mouth from a friend. Perhaps it's simply to fulfill a fantasy. Or maybe it's just to get away from a cold winter.

The cruise industry has intensely studied why people take cruises. Here are the 20 motives that seem to predominate:

1. **A cruise is a hassle-free vacation.** On a cruise, you pack and unpack only once. There's no driving around, looking for your hotel, or wondering where you should eat next. The cruise experience minimizes your concerns, melts away your stress, and maximizes your actual vacation time.

2. **A cruise takes you away from it all.** "It's different out there. . . ." So went one cruise line's promotional slogan. Smog, pollution, stress, traffic, alarm clocks, beepers, ringing telephones, chattering fax machines—these are *not* what a cruise is all about. Cruises are instead about water, sea, sky, and landscape—the simple things that touch us so deeply.

3. **You're pampered like nowhere else.** Breakfast in bed, lounging on deck, soaking in a hot tub, afternoon tea, perhaps champagne and caviar, and the most

ever-present and gracious service you're ever likely to experience; these are rare in our everyday life but commonplace on a cruise.

4. **You can do it all—or nothing at all.** Most cruises provide a vast series of choices, the kind that enable you to pick, choose, or pass up as you wish. Your day might start with morning exercises on deck, yoga in the gym, or dance lessons in the lounge, followed by breakfast. After eating, maybe it's a cooking class or a port lecture. You might choose to watch a new movie or learn a new sport—and all this before lunch. But no one will pressure you. You can sleep in until noon or snooze in a deck chair. It's all up to you. The level of planned activities also varies from ship to ship and from cruise line to cruise line. People who like plenty of things going on can certainly find a cruise that fits the bill. On the other hand, more independent types can select a cruise that features a very relaxed experience with very little structure.

5. **You can sample a broad geographic area.** A cruise usually covers a vast area, stopping at the most interesting places along the way. This is why the majority of cruisers, according to a CLIA study, consider a cruise vacation to be a good way to sample vacation spots that they may want to return to later for a more in-depth vacation. A number of destinations are in fact *best* visited via a ship. Some examples: Alaska, the Caribbean, the Mediterranean, the islands off Southeast Asia, and the fjords of Norway.

6. **A cruise is something "new."** Many people are tired of taking the same old trips, so they like trying out new vacation experiences. Because the vast majority of people have never been on a cruise, the desire to have a fresh "adventure" like a cruise can be powerfully motivating.

7. **Cruises offer a huge variety of events, activities, and meals.** See a show. Snooze lazily by the pool. Jog. Learn. Swim. Shop. Dine indoors or out, casual or elegant, seven times a day if you want. Explore a port or stay onboard. Cruises these days are about *choice*. Of course, the size and "personality" of the ship determine what choices you'll have, but you'll almost surely find it impossible to be bored on a cruise.

8. **A cruise facilitates shopping.** Each port has its own shopping opportunities (often duty-free), as does the ship itself. A wide selection of onboard boutiques is common. Plus, you don't have to haul your purchases around as you go from place to place.

9. **It's easy to make friends on a cruise.** Meeting new people on a cruise is simple. Opportunities to socialize are seemingly endless. Many of the people you meet will share your interests; that you chose the same ship, cruise, and destinations assures it. And some of these friendships may endure well beyond the cruise.

10. **Cruises lend themselves to groups.** If you take a cruise with people from an organization you belong to (e.g., a college alumni trip), you'll see old friends and meet new ones. If it's a theme cruise (e.g., a jazz-themed departure), you'll meet people you have plenty in common with. Family reunions are also easy to arrange and stage aboard a ship.

11. **A cruise is a romantic experience.** It's amazing how many films, plays, songs, and books use cruises as the setting for romance. Cruises have a way

of breathing new energy into an old relationship or of setting the stage for a new one. A *Cosmopolitan* survey concluded that 80% of cruisers feel more amorous at sea. It also concluded many other things that we will not go into here. . . .

12. **A cruise is a learning experience.** Even if your goal is merely to have a good time, you're almost sure to learn something new about the ports you visit. On many cruises, expert lecturers onboard give "enrichment" presentations that help you understand more fully the history and culture of places on the itinerary. Indeed, some specialty cruise lines make passenger education their primary goal—and that's precisely why their passengers select them. A few merge "soft" adventure experiences with education, offering what is called an *expedition* cruise product.

13. **There's a cruise that can satisfy virtually anyone.** As you've no doubt concluded by now, just about everyone—families, singles, clubs, church groups, young people, old people, lovers of sports, lovers of knowledge, and more—can find a cruise to be fulfilling. Few other vacation experiences can make that claim.

14. **It's a great way to celebrate a special event.** People on their honeymoon, couples celebrating their anniversary, or those enjoying a birthday all find a cruise to be especially fulfilling.

15. **Everybody's talking about how wonderful cruises are.** Cruising is an "in" thing. Everyone seems to talk about cruises—and that's being reinforced by many TV shows and movies. Several studies indicate that word-of-mouth from relatives, friends, and acquaintances is a prime reason consumers choose to cruise. And several experts argue that a "hidden" reason for people to go on cruises is so they can brag about it when they get back.

16. **Cruises represent a safe travel experience.** In an age when crime or terrorism happens far too easily, a cruise represents one of the safest vacation choices available. The ship's environment is highly managed. Anything out of the ordinary is swiftly noted. Passage onto and off the ship is strictly controlled. Professionals often check the vessel's hull while in port—even underwater. Luggage is scanned. And vessels have safety and construction features that make problems very unlikely.

17. **It's a fabulous value for the money.** When you compare what you get for your cruise dollar to what you'd pay for a similar land-based vacation, you quickly discover that a cruise is a remarkable bargain. Because consumers regularly rate cruises higher than other vacation choices, a cruise's value becomes keenly apparent.

18. **Cruises are ideal for family vacations.** Because they're a packaged product, in a controlled environment, and at a reasonable price, cruises appeal strongly to families. Many cruise lines have major facilities and programs to keep young people occupied and entertained.

19. **They provide an excellent context for extended business meetings.** Retreats, incentive programs, and similar away-from-the-office events are a growing option that the cruise lines can facilitate. Some companies charter the whole vessel.

20. **You know what you're paying in advance.** A cruise is generally an inclusive vacation. When people pay for their cruise experience, they know up front what the majority of their vacation will cost. Rarely is this so for other sorts of trips. For example, a family driving through southern Europe will probably know what the air, hotel, and car rental costs will be. But the cost for food, drinks, gas, tolls, and entertainment is quite unpredictable. These items could easily add 50% to the cost of the trip.

The degree of cruise "inclusiveness," however, varies from cruise line to cruise line, from ship to ship, and even from itinerary to itinerary:

- *Always or almost always* included are stateroom accommodations, stateroom amenities (e.g., shampoo), meals, certain beverages, entertainment, onboard activities, supervised children's programs, access to the exercise facility, and, of course, the ship transportation. In some cases, room service or dining at a special alternative onboard restaurant entails a relatively modest add-on charge.
- *Sometimes included but sometimes not* are port charges (what ports charge cruise lines to dock), government fees and taxes, and transfers between the airport and the dock when air travel is purchased from the cruise line.

Water slides: a popular attraction for young cruisers.
Courtesy of Carnival Cruise Lines

- *Usually not included* are airfares, shore excursions, gratuities to ship and shoreside personnel, alcoholic beverages and soft drinks (but they cost a little less than at a hotel), optional activities, laundry, certain special offerings (e.g., gourmet desserts at an onboard sweets shop), Internet connections, and pre-, post-, and/or land packages. As mentioned in Chapter 1, some cruise lines bundle pre- and/or post-cruise experiences, at one price, into a single package. Also noteworthy: Very upscale lines tend to include almost everything in their packages. Clients on such cruises get almost all drinks and maybe some shore excursions for the price they pay. Also, on such luxury cruises, the crew is not supposed to accept tips.

- *Never included* are the cost for meals ashore, parking at the departure port, shopping, gambling, photos, ship-to-shore phone calls, medical services, babysitting services, personal services (e.g., a massage or hairstyling), and insurance. The cruise line usually does sell trip cancellation, interruption, and lost/damaged luggage insurance.

The same reasons that account for the popularity of cruising among consumers also apply to travel agents, who make the vast majority of cruise sales. They also like the idea of a hassle-free, pampering, safe, diversified, and immensely satisfying vacation that can be offered to their clients—and that also represents a value. Moreover, cruise vacations are easy to book, they reinforce client loyalty, and are one of the most profitable products an agent can recommend.

Niche Cruising

As you've just seen, many motives account for the popularity of cruising. Some cruise lines, however, devote themselves primarily to satisfying only a few of these motives. They narrowly target the needs and special interests of only one segment of travelers. This is called *niche marketing*. (*Niche* means "nest" in French.) The cruise industry does an especially good job of serving the needs of five niche segments:

- **Families.** We've cited this niche, so you're already familiar with its attraction to cruising. "Families" who travel come in all sorts of configurations today (grandchild with grandparents, blended families, single parent with children, aunt with nephew, etc.), but here are what attracts most families to cruising:

  - Cruises can be a great value, an important factor for three or more people who are traveling together.

  - A cruise can reduce stress, simplify logistics, and save time compared to the most popular family form of travel: the family car.

  - Cruise ships provide facilities and activities tailored to different children's age groups. Some of these facilities are huge.

  - Kids on a cruise can have fun and learn at the same time.

- **Culture seekers.** This niche sees travel as a way to learn about history, people, and cultures, to grow intellectually, and to enrich their lives. For them, a cruise should be like a floating National Geographic channel. And some are.

- Culture seekers favor cruises that spend considerable time in ports and visit unusual or historic places.
- They favor cruises that offer educational seminars and programs.
- Many in this category are single travelers.
- They respect nature and are sensitive to the ecology of the places they visit.
- They favor smaller "expedition" ships that cater to this kind of travel.
- When on a conventional cruise, they use the ship as a base from which to explore on their own or to take shore excursions that reflect their interests.

- **Adventurers.** These travelers share some of the same traits as learners. The big difference: They want to do exciting, adventurous things at the places they visit.
  - They want a cruise with plenty of choices and energetic and/or participatory activities.
  - They favor exotic itineraries and smaller ships.
  - They expect that what they do will require at least some level of fitness.

Mirrors, windows, a balcony, and clever placement of furniture can make a stateroom seem even bigger.
Courtesy of Carnival Cruise Lines

- **Romantics.** This group includes all sorts of people: honeymooners, anniversary couples, etc.
  - They favor tropical cruises (e.g., Tahiti) or cultural ones (e.g., Italy, Greece).
  - They want minimal logistics and minimized stress.
  - Pampering and spas are very appealing to them.
- **The upscale.** They want the best but also want the best deal. They favor the most expensive cruise lines.
  - Quality cruising is vital to them.
  - A sophisticated environment is important.
  - They like itineraries that feature ports that are still relatively unknown to tourists.
  - Fine cuisine is an important part of their travel experience.

Cruise Prices

Cruise brochures spell out the prices for each sailing as well as what's included and what's not. The price is **basis two** or **double occupancy**—it's *per person,* based on two passengers to a room. Price depends on where the desired stateroom "category" is located on the ship. (The industry prefers the word *stateroom* to *cabin,* although consumers tend to use the words interchangeably.) In general:

- The higher the deck the stateroom is on, the higher the price.
- **Outside staterooms** (which have windows) are generally more expensive than **inside** or **interior staterooms** (generally without windows). Often, the industry calls an outside stateroom an "ocean-view" stateroom.
- Larger staterooms on a given ship are usually more expensive than smaller ones.
- Staterooms with balconies generally cost more than those without.
- Outside staterooms whose views are obstructed (e.g., by a lifeboat) often cost less than those with unobstructed views.

On many ships, it's possible to have three or four different stateroom price categories on a single deck: The smaller outside staterooms toward the front might be one price, larger outside staterooms another, inside ones another, a suite on that deck still another, etc.

Many other factors can affect price:

- Booking six to nine months or more in advance usually yields a savings. Advance bookings have another advantage: They give a better choice of stateroom type and location.
- A last-minute "sale" when the ship isn't fully booked also results in lower prices.
- To encourage early bookings or to energize slow sales, cruise lines often offer special promotional fares, such as two-for-one prices, 50% off the second passenger, and the like.

- Cruises on older ships usually cost less than those on more recently launched vessels.

- If there's a third or fourth person sharing the stateroom, their per-person price is often much less than for the first and second persons. Conversely, a **single occupancy**—one person in a stateroom designed for two or more—usually costs much more. For example: The first and second person pay $1,000 each and the third pays $500. A single, on the other hand, would pay $1,500. A few cruise ships have smaller staterooms designed especially for single travelers. To stay in such a room would cost a single traveler about $1,000.

"Seasonality" is also a factor. Cruise lines almost always price their itinerary according to seasonal demand. For example, summer is **high season** in the Mediterranean; that's when cruises there are most costly. Spring and fall are **shoulder seasons**, when prices are somewhat lower. Winter is **low season**. Prices for a Mediterranean cruise then are usually the lowest; the weather is windier and rainier. **Repositioning cruises**, when vessels are moving from one general cruise area to another, are almost always a bargain. You can learn more about repositioning cruises in Chapter 7.

Other factors that can reduce the cost of a cruise are special **alumni** or **past passenger rates** (rates given to people who have sailed on that cruise line before), group rates (group minimums vary by cruise line—some consider five passengers a group; others require at least 20; most are somewhere in between), and whether the cruise is bought through a travel agency that has specially negotiated prices. On occasion, cruise lines will substantially discount their brochure rates to increase slow bookings. The practice of adjusting price to supply and demand is called **yield management**.

Because cruise pricing is such an "elastic" thing, you should not consider the rate given in the brochure as set in stone. Instead, think of it as something more akin to a "suggested retail price."

Roadblocks to Purchase

You would think, with so many things *good* about cruising, that just about everyone would be ready to buy one! Not so. When average persons think about a cruise (especially if they've never been on one), they sometimes feel reluctant to commit. After all, it's hard to decide on something unknown. Their reasons are often based on misconceptions (although in some cases—e.g., extreme sensitivity to motion—their feelings may be valid).

Here are the 15 most commonly heard objections to cruising:

1. **Cruises are too expensive.** In most polls, this is the number one obstacle to purchasing a cruise. One reason: Consumers aren't accustomed to paying for their whole vacation experience at once, well in advance of departure. They forget that because a cruise is inclusive, it will *seem* to have a high price tag. This is why CLIA urges travel agents to do an analysis for clients that compares the cost of a cruise to a conventional land-based trip. When the clients see their costs spelled out, they realize that a cruise represents a remarkable value. See Figure 2-1.

		Typical land-based vacation vs. cruise vacation	
		Land-based resort package 7 Nights	**Cruise 8 days/7 nights 3 ports**
Fixed	Base price	$680 ($157/day)	$1,475 ($210/day)
	Air	$400	$400
	Transfers	$86	Included
	Meals	$620	Included
	Tips	$190	$150
	Taxes	$196	$109
Variable	Sightseeing	$135	$150
	Entertainment	$85	Included
	Beverages	$220	$140
	Total	$3,032	$2,424
	Per diem	$433	$346

FIGURE 2-1   Cost comparison
Source: *CLIA travel agency estimate for midrange vacation*

2. **Cruises are boring.** This objection comes from the days of transatlantic crossings, when the most some passengers did was sit on a deck chair bundled up in a blanket. Cruises are a different experience today. The problem isn't that there's too little to do but that there's often too much.

3. **Cruises are only for older people.** Here's another objection with roots in old-time cruising. A few cruise experiences do indeed skew toward a more *mature* passenger profile, but brochure descriptions make this bias very clear. Others tend toward *younger* passengers. The majority of cruises, however, feature passengers from just about every age group, with the *average* age being 46 years.

4. **Cruises are stuffy and too formal.** A cruise is largely an informal and relaxed experience. On certain ships, a dress code does prevail in the main dining room—sometimes for lunch; often for dinner. Formality is somewhat *more* frequent on upscale cruises but much *less* likely or even nonexistent on certain mass-market cruises, a sailing ship, or an adventure/education cruise.

5. **Cruises are too regimented.** To achieve the efficient flow of hundreds to thousands of passengers, cruise lines do try to organize things as best they can. But organization on a ship is far from rigid; there's plenty of freedom. Routines are especially relaxed on very large ships, upscale cruise lines, sailing ships, and adventure/education cruises.

Here's a typical dress code requirement (after 6 P.M.) on an upscale cruise.

Formal: Appropriate formal evening wear for women is an evening gown or cocktail dress; men wear tuxedos, dinner jackets, or dark suits. Sailings of eight days or less typically feature two formal nights, while longer cruises usually have three or four formal nights.

Informal: Ladies usually wear dresses or pantsuits; men wear jackets (tie optional).

Casual: Open-neck shirts, slacks, and sports outfits are appropriate.

Source: *Silversea Cruises*

6. **There's not enough time in ports.** It's true that cruise ships rarely stay in a port for more than 12 hours. At minor ports, this (or less time) may be all that's needed. And as we said earlier, one of the major goals of a cruise client is to *sample a region.*

   For example, a traveler might wish to visit the major ports of the western Mexican coast and then might return a few years later for a resort stay in the city that was most impressive. Moreover, it *is* possible—through a pre- or post-cruise package—to spend extended time at the departure and/or arrival port. And to satisfy those clients who want a more extended port experience, some cruise lines are now spending more than a day in certain intermediate ports or building faster ships that will get from place to place more quickly, thus permitting a longer port stay.

7. **The ship environment is too confining.** Cruise ship designers have become increasingly adept at creating a sense of spaciousness aboard ship. Vast windows in public spaces, pale colors, and other tricks of the architectural trade "expand" the environment. The actual space that each client has is fairly well expressed by something called *space ratio.* More about that in Chapter 3.

8. **Aren't you forced to socialize with people?** As mentioned earlier, meeting interesting fellow passengers aboard ship is perceived as a *benefit* by many cruisers. The likelihood that you'll meet people you have plenty in common with is great. Some people, though, find socializing uncomfortable. To address this, cruise lines organize all sorts of optional events to make mixing comfortable and easy. In theory, though, someone who wants to be alone could very well do that aboard a ship. Reading while in a deck chair, dining in one's stateroom, watching the scenery go by from a private veranda, opting for a ship with an unregimented approach—these and more can enable someone to enjoy a cruise without a whole lot of socializing.

9. **I was in the Navy, and the last thing I want to do is take my vacation on a ship.** You'd be surprised how often this one comes up. But a pleasure cruise is dramatically different from the Navy experience. Virtually everyone who cites this objection discovers quite rapidly that this is a silly preconception.

10. **I'll eat too much and put on weight.** Cruise veterans jokingly refer to "five-pound cruises" and "ten-pound cruises." The reality today is this: Low-calorie, healthy dining choices are increasingly available on ships, plus exercise opportunities allow you to work off all those calories. Or at least some of them.

11. **Are ships really safe?** The *Titanic* still looms large in the minds of the public—witness the immense box office success this 1998 film achieved. But a *Titanic*-like catastrophe is virtually impossible today. Modern safety regulation requirements and radar have seen to that. Fires aboard ships have occurred, but they're rare and easily contained. Pirates have sometimes tried to seize cruise ships—without success.

12. **I'm worried about terrorism.** After 9/11, the cruise lines took very forceful steps to guard against acts of terrorism. Passenger and staff names are checked against government alert lists, luggage is scanned, photo IDs are often required of everyone—indeed, in some cases, the procedures followed are more rigorous than those at airports. Also, cruise lines swiftly alter itineraries to adjust for potential political flare-ups.

13. **It's too far to fly to the port.** This is a problem voiced by those who live far inland (e.g., North Dakota or Saskatchewan) and whose ship is leaving from, say, San Juan, Puerto Rico. Make them realize it's worth it for such a great experience (e.g., "It's only a half-day to one of the greatest vacations of your life") or sell them on a closer port destination—one that requires less flying time and/or fewer connections or perhaps is within a reasonable driving distance.

14. **I'm worried about getting sick.** Some people are especially vulnerable to motion discomfort. But ship **stabilizers** (underwater wing-like devices that reduce a ship's roll) and other design features have minimized this problem. Cruise vessels also tend to sail in protected waters, where motion is less likely to occur. Many cruisers use Sea Bands®, wrist bracelets that, through accupressure, apparently reduce the effect of ship motion. Physicians can also prescribe pills or skin patches that, for most people, relieve motion sickness. Alcohol and lack of sleep can worsen seasickness. People who are prone to motion discomfort should avoid drinking too much or sleeping too little. Another sickness concern: "Will I catch something onboard?" Press coverage sometimes makes it seem that stomach-attacking germs lurk everywhere on a cruise or that every ship railing hosts the norovirus. Yet, the U.S. government's Centers for Disease Control and Prevention (CDC), which regularly assesses shipboard sanitation conditions, has stressed that such viruses exist everywhere and that they may be the second-most common thing people catch in any situation (the common cold is first). To allay fears, however, cruise lines now take intense precautions to keep their vessels extra clean and sanitized. A question allied to all this: "What happens if I get ill while onboard?" Almost all cruise ships have a medical facility and health care professionals on staff to deal with problems. No hotel can offer that.

15. **I don't know enough about cruises.** Although this objection is not commonly voiced, it's behind almost all the others. Many people are afraid to try something they've never experienced. More information usually resolves their reluctance, since this objection often implies that the client wants to know more. Your job is to make them visualize themselves on a ship and feel—in advance—how wonderful it will be.

In sum, the reasons to take a cruise vacation are many. The reasons *not* to take a cruise are often bogus. The key to cruise client satisfaction: A person must take

Fine dining: an important element of the cruise experience.
Courtesy of Avalon Waterways

the right cruise, on the right ship, and to the right destination for them. That's why travel agents—familiar with both cruises and their clients—are so critical to the cruise-buying process. When the personalities of the traveler and the cruise match, then all the objections a client may conceive will probably—and simply—melt away.

Questions for Discussion

1. You're going on a three-day cruise out of Florida. What can you predict about the passengers?

2. You've "graduated" to a ten-day cruise of Northern Europe. What can you anticipate about the passengers this time?

3. Give the six most important reasons why, in *your* opinion, the cruise experience is so successful.

4. What's typically included on a cruise? What isn't?

5. List at least six objections that people might have about a cruise vacation.

 **Activity**

Do you know at least one person who has taken a cruise? Interview that person by using the questions below. Summarize that person's answers in the spaces given. It doesn't matter whether you've cruised or not. The purpose of this exercise is to explore *someone else's* perceptions.

1. What cruise or cruises have you taken?

2. What was the most important reason you decided to try cruising?

3. What were the other motives you had for cruising?

4. Were you reluctant in any way about taking a cruise? What caused this reluctance? Did the actual cruise change your mind?

5. Now that you've tried cruising, what's the best thing about it?

6. Do you plan to take another cruise? If yes, what kind of cruise will it be? (Destination, cruise line, number of days.)

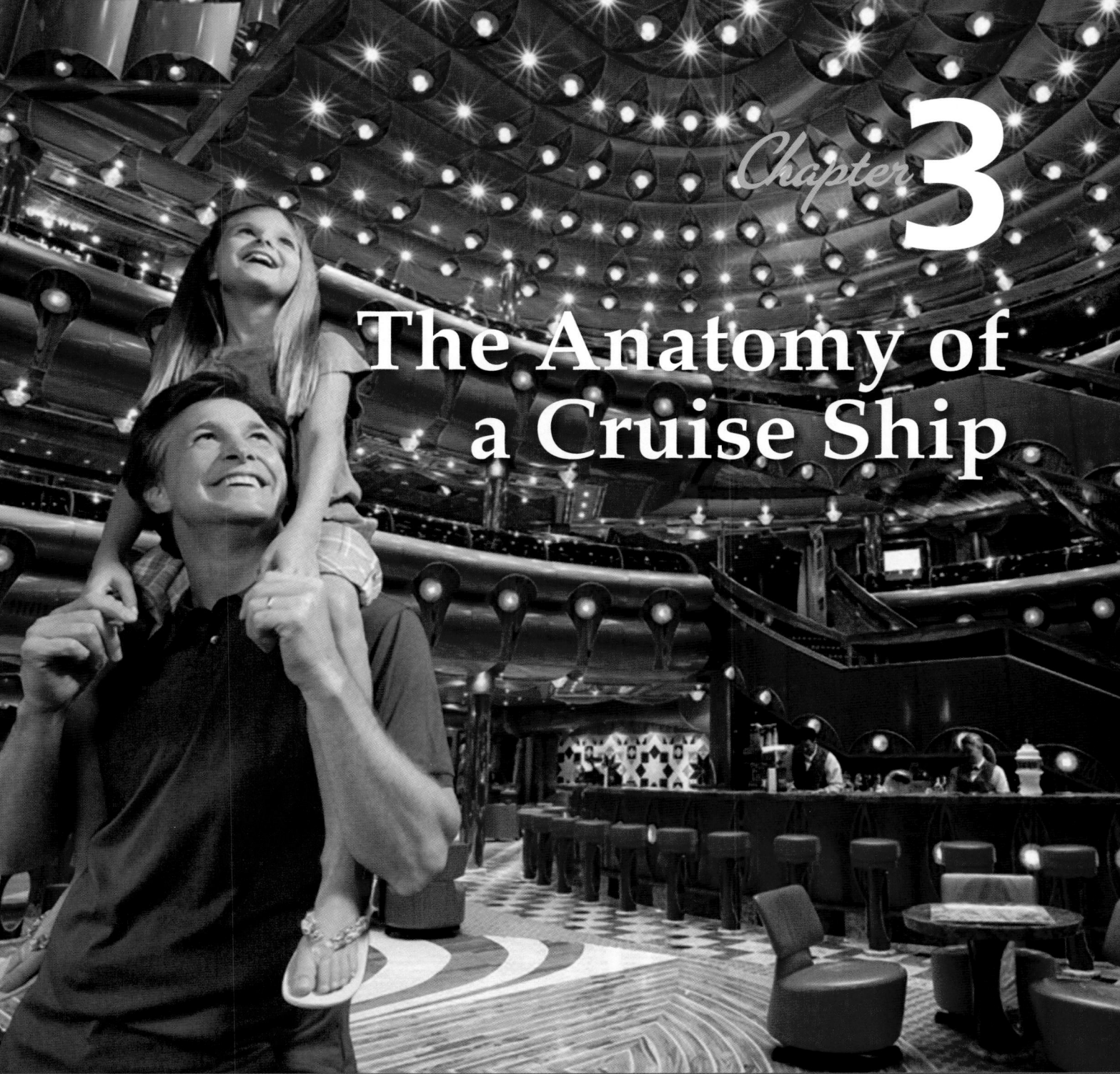

Chapter 3

The Anatomy of a Cruise Ship

Courtesy of Carnival Cruise Lines

After reading this chapter, you'll be able to:

- Classify ships according to their "style."
- Compare older ship styles to newer ones.
- Explain how ship size and space are measured.
- List the facilities found on most cruise vessels.
- Interpret a deck plan.

Think of a cruise ship. What have you pictured in your mind? A great ocean liner slicing through the Atlantic? A floating resort-like palace sliding from tropical isle to tropical isle? Did you think of a ship with sails? A Mississippi paddle wheeler? An overgrown yacht? All these and more can be found in the cruise industry.

Styles of Ships

Over 350 cruise ships—all sizes and all types—sail the world's waters today. Let's take a quick look at the types of vessels that cruisers can choose from.

- **The classic ocean liner.** These ships—a few of which are still in service today— epitomize the first Golden Age of cruising. Primarily used for transatlantic crossings or world voyages, and mostly built before 1970, they're sleek, stream-lined, and built to knife their way through open ocean waves. Most are rather small by today's cruise standards and are operated by European companies.

- **The contemporary cruise ship.** In the 1970s, ship designers began to redefine what a cruise ship should be. Speed was no longer of prime consideration. Tapered, knife-like hulls gave way to broader, boxier, still attractive vessels built to accommodate uniformly sized staterooms and the numerous activity venues that the modern cruise vacation experience requires. These ships have grown larger and larger, eventually surpassing the size and capacity of the mid-twentieth-century behemoths, such as the *Queen Mary* and the original *Queen Elizabeth*. The industry generally calls these giant-sized ships **megaships**. They can accommodate 2,000 passengers or more and have 12 or more decks (a **deck** is the equivalent of a story in a building). The very largest carry more than 5,000 passengers on 16 or more decks.

- **Small ships.** In contrast to megaships are much smaller vessels, most of which accommodate fewer than 300 passengers. Here, the emphasis is on an up-close,

Not all cruise vessels are alike.
Courtesy of Windstar Cruises

more intimate cruise vacation. The cruise lines that rely on small-ship cruising often stress education, soft adventure, and/or luxury experiences. Their ships often look like cruise ships in miniature or oversized yachts.

- **Masted sailing ships.** Yes, there are still cruise ships that have masts and sails and are partly or almost entirely powered by the wind. In some cases, these vessels are technologically sophisticated, with computers controlling the sails. In other instances, the crew and even passenger volunteers rig the sails. The ships have motors, just in case the wind dies down. People who sail on such ships want an experience rooted in other times, when billowing cloth and the romance of the sea were what sailing was all about.

- **River vessels.** Two kinds of vessels carry passengers along the great rivers of the world. The first type are modern-style ships that can be found on the Rhine, the Danube, and the Nile, to name just a few. The second type, modeled after the great steamboats of the nineteenth century, permit passengers to experience America's great rivers in a style memorialized in the works of Mark Twain.

- **Barges.** Whether it's a twelve-passenger barge drifting along a French canal or a much larger vessel floating down the Mississippi, barge travel is far less

The era when a ship was built has a direct impact on the cruise experience. So, let's compare older ships with newer ships. Remember: Some clients prefer older vessels; others newer ones. It's just a matter of taste. Also, the descriptions given are *generally* true. Exceptions do exist.

Older, "classic" ships	Newer, "modern" ships
• Much use of wood, brass, and other natural materials	• Synthetic materials more common
• Modest-sized public areas	• Large public areas (especially atriums, showrooms, malls, and casinos)
• Can travel up to 30 knots	• Travel at 20–25 knots
• Nostalgic appearance	• Modern appearance
• Hulls have deep drafts; some ports are therefore inaccessible and/or require tendering	• Hulls have shallow drafts; ports more accessible (except for truly huge ships)
• Small windows or portholes	• Larger windows
• More obstructed stateroom views	• Fewer obstructed stateroom views
• "Pedestrian" flow through ship sometimes awkward	• Easy "pedestrian" flow through ship
• Stateroom verandas more rare	• Stateroom verandas more likely
• Smaller swimming pools	• Larger swimming pools
• "Promenade" decks common	• "Promenade" decks less common
• Many different-sized staterooms; staterooms are relatively large rooms	• More standardized stateroom size; some staterooms may be small

spartan than you might think. In fact, it's usually quite the opposite. Passenger barges are usually luxurious, affording a pampered and leisurely discovery of the countryside.

- **Ferries.** We don't usually think of a ferry trip as a cruise. Yet, in Europe (especially in Northern Europe), many ferries provide an overnight or even multi-day, cruise-like experience, with private staterooms, glitzy entertainment, and bountiful dining.

- **Multipurpose ships.** Some vessels, such as those that sail the fjord-lined west coast of Norway, serve many functions. They carry cargo, transport passengers between close-by villages, and—yes—serve as cruise ships for leisure travelers too.

- **Miscellaneous.** Many unusual forms of water transportation provide cruise-like vacations. It's possible, for example, for a leisure traveler to book passage on a freighter. The itineraries are unpredictable and the entertainment nonexistent (except for videos), but the food is usually excellent and the staterooms are large. It's also possible to charter your own yacht, either with or without a crew. (The latter is called a **bare boat charter**.) Similarly, many people rent houseboats, often with family and usually to vacation on a lake or a river.

Sizing Ships

How does the cruise industry measure its ships? One way is by the number of staterooms. Another is by how many passengers the ship accommodates. (The cruise business often uses the word *guests* instead of *passengers*.) For example, any vessel that carries 2,000 passengers or more is usually considered a megaship. This passenger count doesn't include the crew members. The average ship staffs one crew member per two or three passengers. So, a 3,000-passenger ship also would carry 1,000 to 1,500 crew members.

A third way to measure is by something called **gross registered tonnage** (GRT). Gross registered tonnage is determined by a formula that gauges the volume of the public spaces on a ship. It measures only enclosed space available to passengers. It doesn't factor in open areas, such as the promenade decks, or private spaces used only by the crew (e.g., the engine room). Because it deals only with parts of the vessel, the actual ship's weight is probably much more than the GRT. And, no, there are no huge scales to test it out.

How the formula works is unimportant. What the resulting number means, however, is important. Here's how the industry generally interprets GRT, with a rough idea of how many passengers each ship size accommodates. (**Pax** is an industry abbreviation for "passengers.")

- **Very small:** Under 10,000 GRT; under 200 pax
- **Small:** 10,000–20,000 GRT; 200–500 pax
- **Medium:** 20,000–50,000 GRT; 500–1,200 pax
- **Large:** 50,000–70,000 GRT; 1,200–2,000 pax
- **Megaship:** 70,000 GRT or more; 2,000 pax or more; the very largest megaships are now over 200,000 GRT and carry more than 5,000 passengers.

Some cruisers like smaller ships; others prefer larger ones. What are the benefits of each?

Larger ships:

- Offer many more facilities, activities, choices, and options
- Are often more dramatic-looking
- Are able to serve a wider spectrum of guest types
- Easily accommodate groups
- Are generally quite stable in the water

Smaller ships:

- Offer a more intimate atmosphere
- Can sail into smaller places
- Permit easier **embarkation** and **debarkation**
- Make it simple for passengers to get to know the ship and others onboard

Although two ships may be about the same size and carry approximately the same number of passengers, each will have a very different ambiance, style, and "personality."

One other function of ship size is something called the **space ratio**. The space ratio of a vessel is determined by dividing the GRT by passenger capacity. For instance, if a vessel has a 30,000 GRT and can carry 1,000 passengers, its space ratio is 30.

The space ratio number conveys the "space" or "elbow room" each person will have. The higher the space ratio, the more passengers will have a sense of the ship's "roominess"; the hallways and stairs will be less crowded, and there will be more space between tables in the dining room.

A few things about space ratio:

- Most ships have a space ratio between 25 and 40. The lowest is about 8; the highest is about 70.
- The space ratio doesn't necessarily correlate to size. Small ships can have high space ratios, and megaships can have low space ratios. It all depends on how many passengers a certain-size ship carries.
- A ship's space ratio isn't the only thing that conveys roominess. Light colors and ample windows can make a ship with a low space ratio seem more spacious.
- If a vessel with a low space ratio isn't full (say, 80% of the staterooms are occupied), the passengers will probably feel less crowded than they would if it were fully booked. Note, though, that ships today go out at full capacity on almost every sailing.
- Space ratio doesn't necessarily correlate to stateroom size. A ship with small staterooms may have huge public areas, yielding a higher space ratio number. Remember: The space ratio is derived from the *entire* ship's noncrew volume, or GRT.
- The more expensive a cruise is per day, the more likely the ship will have a high space ratio. One of the features that an upscale cruise offers is roominess.

Pool areas serve multiple functions on modern ships.
Courtesy of Costa Cruises

How can you find out a ship's space ratio? Most reference sources and many brochures give passenger capacity and tonnage. Just plug them into the formula to find the space ratio. Indeed, some references actually give you the space ratio, already calculated, for every ship afloat.

One final point: A high space ratio isn't necessarily critical to the enjoyment of the cruise experience. Some people prefer the cozy feeling that ships with low space ratios convey. Others feel that if they've saved money by booking a vessel with a low space ratio, then the tradeoff was worth it. The bottom line: If the passengers see interesting ports, experience wonderful food and entertainment, meet interesting people, and have a great time, then the space ratio will probably be a minor consideration.

Ship Facilities

Space on a ship can be divided into three types: stateroom space, private (or crew) space, and public space.

Passengers almost never see the spaces that serve the ship's crew. (They're usually on decks below those of the passengers.) These include crew cabins, dining areas, and recreational facilities. Other private spaces are the **bridge** (where the vessel is controlled), the **galley** or kitchen (where food is prepared), and mechanical areas (such as the engine room). On certain cruises, passengers are permitted to visit the bridge and/or the galley on a special "behind-the-scenes" tour.

Public spaces are those where passengers mingle. Here are the most common:

- **The reception area.** All ships have a lobby-like area where the **purser's office** (also known as the **front desk**, **hotel desk**, **reception desk**, or **information desk**) is located. The purser's office is the direct equivalent of a hotel's front desk (although, unlike hotels, cruise passengers do *not* need to check in at this desk to get their rooms). Nearby is usually the shore excursion office or tour desk, where passengers can inquire about and/or book port tours and activities. On newer ships, the reception area may be in a multistory space called an **atrium**. Some vessels have interior **malls** that run the length of the ship.

- **The dining room.** Guests eat dinner here, and, often, also breakfast and lunch. Larger ships typically feature several main dining rooms.

- **Alternate dining areas.** Informal, buffet-like dining usually takes place on the pool deck for some or all meals. Guests can dine indoors or, in good weather, outdoors. (This area is often called the **lido deck** or cafe.) Many ships also have alternate restaurants—such as pizzerias or specialty dining facilities—that are open part or even all of the day. Small facilities dispensing fast food (e.g., hot dogs and hamburgers) are often located on the pool deck. (Outdoor dining is often referred to as **al fresco** dining.)

A dramatic atrium: what guests often see first when embarking.
Courtesy of Carnival Cruise Lines

- **The showroom.** Entertainment events usually take place here each night. During the day, the showroom may host orientation meetings, port lectures, games (e.g., bingo), movies, or other special events. Most ships usually feature one or more additional entertainment areas, bars, and discos.

- **The pool area.** The majority of ships today have one or more swimming pools, perhaps with hot tubs nearby. However, these pools aren't usually very big. Imagine how much such a volume of water weighs! Because the pool is usually on an upper deck, a massive pool would destabilize the ship. A deck with many lounge chairs and (perhaps) tables usually surrounds the pool. There may be a shallow wading pool for kids. On some ships, a retractable glass skylight—sometimes called a **magrodome**—can cover the pool area. In warm weather, it slides away, permitting passengers to feel the cool sea breeze in an open environment. In cold or rainy weather, it slides shut. Increasingly, the pool area contains all sorts of novelties, such as elaborate water slides, waves in the pool (for surfing!), and similar features.

- **The health club.** Most cruise vessels provide an area for guests to exercise, with an aerobics area, stationary bicycles, treadmills, and weight machines. The health club frequently adjoins a **spa** that offers massages, facials, saunas, whirlpools, aromatherapy, and other beauty or relaxation-related services. In addition to the customary shuffleboard and ping-pong, ships may also offer jogging tracks, basketball courts, and other exercise-related facilities.

- **The children's area.** Family cruise vacations have become important for many cruise lines. Facilities for children—supervised by specially trained staff— have therefore become common. Their features and activities are often tailored to multiple age groups (e.g., young children, older children, and teens).

- **The gift shop.** On some ships, it's just a little store where you can buy sundries. On many others, it's a more extensive place that sells souvenirs, duty-free goods, T-shirts, and the like—often themed to the ship. Some vessels feature many places to buy things, arranged in mini-mall fashion.

- **The medical facility.** Maritime law requires any vessel that carries more than 100 passengers to have a physician onboard, often assisted by one or more nurses. These health care professionals work out of a small, hospital-like facility.

- **The movie theater.** Many ships feature screenings of recent movies in a theater. These theaters often serve double-duty as meeting spaces. In-cabin video, however, is—on some ships—eliminating the need for an onboard movie theater.

- **The photo gallery.** At key moments and picturesque spots, professional photographers take photos of passengers. These photos are then displayed in a photo gallery on the ship. Passengers can purchase the ones they like for a reasonable price. (Passengers can drop off their own film or memory cards for developing here too.)

- **The art auction gallery.** This area exhibits paintings and other fine art that will be sold during the cruise.

- **The casino.** Because gambling is usually legal on ships, most cruise vessels boast casinos where clients can play blackjack, roulette, slot machines, and other games. (Gambling *is* prohibited on ships calling only on U.S. ports.)

The casino—either for legal reasons or so as not to compete with shoreside facilities—is usually closed when the ship is in port.

- **The Internet center.** Here, for a time-based fee, passengers can send and receive e-mail and surf the Web.

The above list represents the most common and important public spaces found on a ship. Here are other facilities—some common; some unusual—that a guest will find on some of today's cruise ships.

conference/business center	drugstore	miniature golf course
tuxedo rental shop	tennis courts	florist shop
card rooms	function rooms	climbing wall
cigar/smoking lounges	game/video game rooms	zip line
ATMs	golf simulation areas	water slide
launderette	libraries (books and/or videos)	watersport platforms
chapel (for weddings and nondenominational services)		ice skating rink

Large cruise lines with many ships often divide them into classes, based on similar design. (The ships in each class resemble one another.)

Most vessels today feature a main dining room and several alternate restaurants.
Courtesy of Costa Cruises

Cruise Staterooms

A **stateroom**—also called a **cabin**—is to a ship what a guest room is to a hotel. There's one big difference: Ship staterooms are usually extremely compact. Author Douglas Ward has an evocative name for them: "hotel rooms in miniature." The average hotel room in America today is about 350 to 450 square feet. Some staterooms are as small as 100 square feet, and few exceed 250 square feet.

However, staterooms are astonishingly efficient. Ship designers manage to fit all manner of cabinets, drawers, and shelves into the typical stateroom, making it often as functional as a hotel room twice the size.

Three types of ship staterooms exist:

- *Outside staterooms* (also called *ocean-view staterooms*) have windows. Because you can look outside, these accommodations feel more open. They're ideal for clients who worry about feeling cramped. Older ships have portholes. Newer ships have larger windows. Some staterooms feature a full-wall sliding glass door that leads to a veranda, which enables guests to go outside and experience the environment in a direct and private way. (Believe it or not, some first-time cruisers conclude that outside accommodations must be out on deck or even off the ship!)

- *Inside staterooms* are in the ship's interior. Usually, they have no windows but often use mirrors, pastel colors, bright lighting, and even false window drapes to make the room feel more open (a few ships do have inside staterooms with windows that look out on an interior atrium or mall). Many cruisers prefer inside staterooms because these rooms are usually the least expensive on the ship. They may also feel that a stateroom "is only a place to sleep." Late sleepers like inside staterooms because early daylight won't disturb them.

- *Suites* are the most expensive accommodations on a ship. Some vessels have only a few; others boast entire upper decks composed of larger staterooms and/or suites. By the traditional definition, a suite should feature a living room, a sleeping room, and a bathroom. This is not necessarily so on a ship. Shipboard suites typically feature, in the same rectangular space, a sitting area and a sleeping area, often divided by a curtain and featuring just under 300 square feet of living area. Suites can usually accommodate more than two people, making such accommodations popular for families (the sofa often converts into a bed). On certain vessels, an entire deck may be made up of suites and be called a **concierge level**. Guests on this deck may have access to a concierge who helps arrange certain services for them. They may even have a butler at their call. Some vessels feature suites that resemble a suite in a luxury hotel. A few ships have suites that approach 5,000 square feet. (At this size, they're sometimes called *villas*.)

Here's what you find in a typical stateroom:

- Two single **lower beds**, either parallel to each other or at right angles. Sometimes, the beds can be pushed together by staff to create a double or queen-sized bed. Larger staterooms boast double, queen, or even king-size beds. Staterooms with **upper beds** can accommodate three or four passengers; these uppers are recessed into the wall or ceiling during the day. In cruise jargon, a bed is often called a **berth**. (*Berth* also can refer to the docking space of a ship.)

- A bed stand between the beds or on each side

- A vanity, often with a chair, along with built-in drawers, cabinets, and the like

- A closet, perhaps with multiple levels and storage places
- A television that feeds live or repeated broadcasts of shipboard events, movies, port talks, and satellite transmission of regular TV programming
- Extensive lighting, wall-to-wall carpeting, and everything else you'd associate with a hotel

For examples of stateroom floor plans, see the diagrams given in Figure 3-1.

FLOOR PLANS & STATEROOM DIAGRAMS

OWNER'S SUITE WITH PRIVATE BALCONY

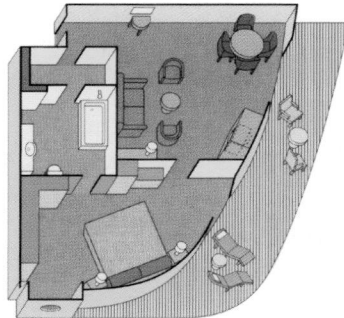

(Category OS) Queen-size bed. Separate sitting room with dining area. Large private balcony. Sofa or sofa bed. Two televisions. Refrigerator. Spacious closet. Large bathroom with whirlpool tub. Guest bathroom. Approximately 786–962 square feet including balcony.

MINI-SUITE WITH PRIVATE BALCONY

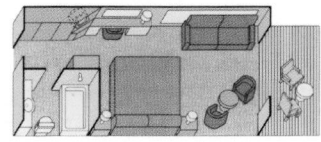

(Categories AA, AB & AC) Twin beds that make up into a comfortable queen-size bed. Separate sitting area with sofa or sofa bed. Private balcony. TV and desk. Refrigerator. Spacious closet. Bath with tub and shower. Approximately 322 square feet including balcony.

OUTSIDE DOUBLE

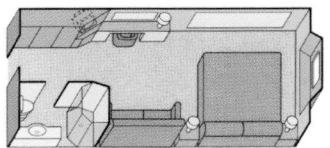

(Categories CC, C, D, E, F, GG & G) Twin beds that make up into a comfortable queen-size bed. Sofa or sofa bed. Picture window. TV and desk. Spacious closet. Bath with shower. Views obstructed in category F. Portholes categories GG and G. Approximately 146 to 206 square feet.

OUTSIDE DOUBLE WITH PRIVATE BALCONY

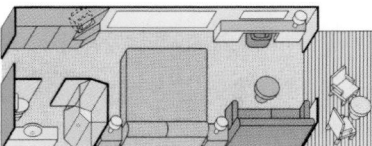

(Categories BA, BB, BC, BD, BE & BF) Twin beds that make up into a comfortable queen-size bed. Private balcony. Sofa or sofa bed. TV and desk. Spacious closet. Bath with shower. Approximately 216 square feet including balcony.

INSIDE DOUBLE

(Categories II, I, J, K & L) Twin beds that make up into a comfortable queen-size bed. Sofa. TV and desk. Spacious closet. Bath and shower. Approximately 158 square feet.

FIGURE 3-1   Stateroom floor plans
Courtesy of Princess Cruises

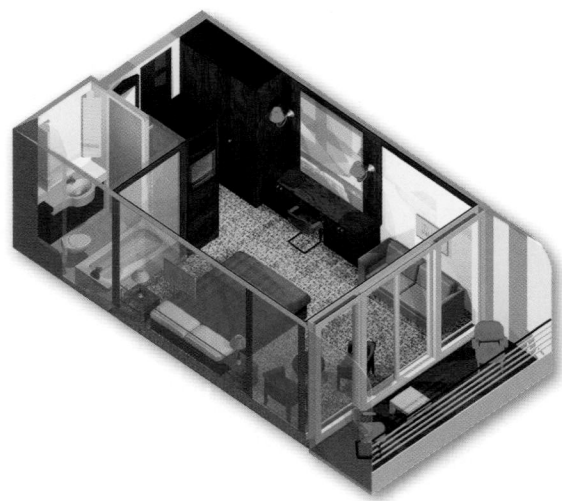

Some floor plans are shown in 3-D.
Courtesy of Oceania Cruises

A stateroom on today's ships almost always has a bathroom. It's usually very compact but, again, well-conceived, with a sink, toilet, and shower. Larger staterooms may have a full tub and shower, while suites sometimes have a little vanity area between the stateroom and its bathroom.

Reading a Deck Plan

Every cruise brochure, cruise line Web site, and many reference resources (such as the *CLIA Cruise Manual*) reproduce the plans of ships. A ship plan usually consists of two elements: the **deck plan** (or floor plan) and a cross-section of the ship, with each "layer" shown (only those decks that are "public" are indicated). Sometimes, accompanying the deck plan are floor plans of various kinds of staterooms. See Figure 3-2 for an example of a deck plan.

Here are a few things you need to know about ships' plans:

- **Deck plans are important.** Unlike at hotels, guests can often select the exact staterooms they want when the cruise is booked. But there are exceptions. These will be explained in Chapter 9.

- **In brochures and Web sites, color coding makes a deck plan easy to read.** Colors help indicate which price categories apply to which staterooms. (A **stateroom category** is the price that a certain kind or level of stateroom represents.) However, other reference resources usually reproduce deck plans in black and white.

- **Usually, the higher the deck is on the ship, the higher the category and price.** Suites and larger staterooms are generally located on the highest decks. There are, however, many exceptions.

- **Deck plans often note certain special stateroom circumstances.** Examples include obstructed views from windows (a lifeboat may be in the way), staterooms specially equipped for the physically challenged, or those that can accommodate three or four passengers.

- **Deck plans are also posted aboard ship.** They're usually located in the elevator/staircase areas. These deck plans help guests orient themselves onboard. (For the record, the front of the ship is called the *bow* and the back is called the *stern*. Facing forward, the left side is labeled the *port side* and the right side is *starboard*.) To further help passengers find their way around, each deck usually has a name and/or number.

When cruise clients and travel agents study a deck plan, they should carefully examine the relationship of a stateroom to the ship's public spaces. Here's how a location can be an asset or a drawback depending on the client's needs.

Location	Potential advantage(s)	Potential disadvantage(s)
Near elevators	Not far to walk to elevators	Pedestrian "traffic" and noise in hallway
Near bow or stern	Usually less expensive; possibly dramatic views; quiet	Far from everything; greater feeling of ship motion
Near public spaces	Close to where things are happening	Potential noise (e.g., if the public space is below or above the stateroom)
Lower deck	Less expensive; less motion felt	Possibly far from public spaces; may be smaller staterooms
Higher deck	Possibly closer to public areas; closer to "sun" deck and pool; feels more prestigious; often larger staterooms	More expensive; possibly more "traffic"; potential to feel more ship motion

Miscellaneous Considerations

What else should you know about cruise ships? Here are some thoughts:

- **A ship's "registry" usually has nothing to do with where the line is headquartered.** Financial, legal, labor, and routing concerns tend to dictate the ship's registry. The name of the country where the ship is registered is usually painted on the exterior of the vessel's stern and the ship flies that country's flag. (This is called its *flag of convenience.*)
- **On some ships, smoking is permitted almost everywhere onboard.** On most, it's limited to certain officially designated places. One or two ships are smoke-free.
- **Where do ships go when they "retire"?** Some are turned into scrap metal (mostly in India). Others are "parked" at ports (especially in Greece and the Bahamas), with the hope that someone will buy, refurbish, and return them to active cruising.
- **Each year, the CDC conducts about two unannounced inspections of any cruise vessel that carries 13 or more passengers and that calls on U.S. ports.** The inspectors look for potentially hazardous conditions, such as improperly stored food, poor food preparation and display procedures, and the like.

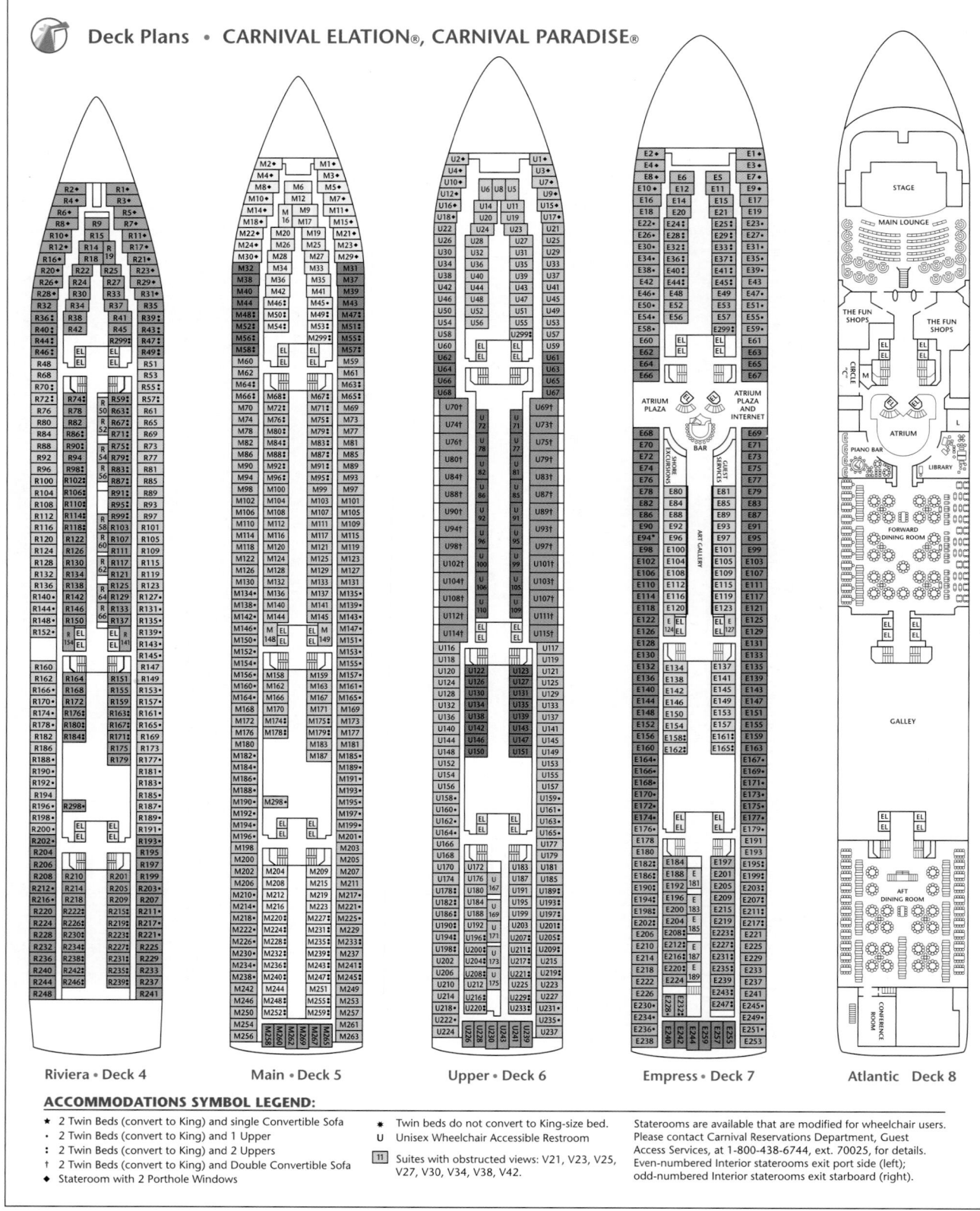

Deck Plans • CARNIVAL ELATION®, CARNIVAL PARADISE®

Riviera • Deck 4   Main • Deck 5   Upper • Deck 6   Empress • Deck 7   Atlantic Deck 8

ACCOMMODATIONS SYMBOL LEGEND:

★ 2 Twin Beds (convert to King) and single Convertible Sofa
• 2 Twin Beds (convert to King) and 1 Upper
‡ 2 Twin Beds (convert to King) and 2 Uppers
† 2 Twin Beds (convert to King) and Double Convertible Sofa
◆ Stateroom with 2 Porthole Windows

✳ Twin beds do not convert to King-size bed.
U Unisex Wheelchair Accessible Restroom
11 Suites with obstructed views: V21, V23, V25, V27, V30, V34, V38, V42.

Staterooms are available that are modified for wheelchair users. Please contact Carnival Reservations Department, Guest Access Services, at 1-800-438-6744, ext. 70025, for details. Even-numbered Interior staterooms exit port side (left); odd-numbered Interior staterooms exit starboard (right).

FIGURE 3-2 A sample deck plan
Courtesy of Carnival Cruise Lines

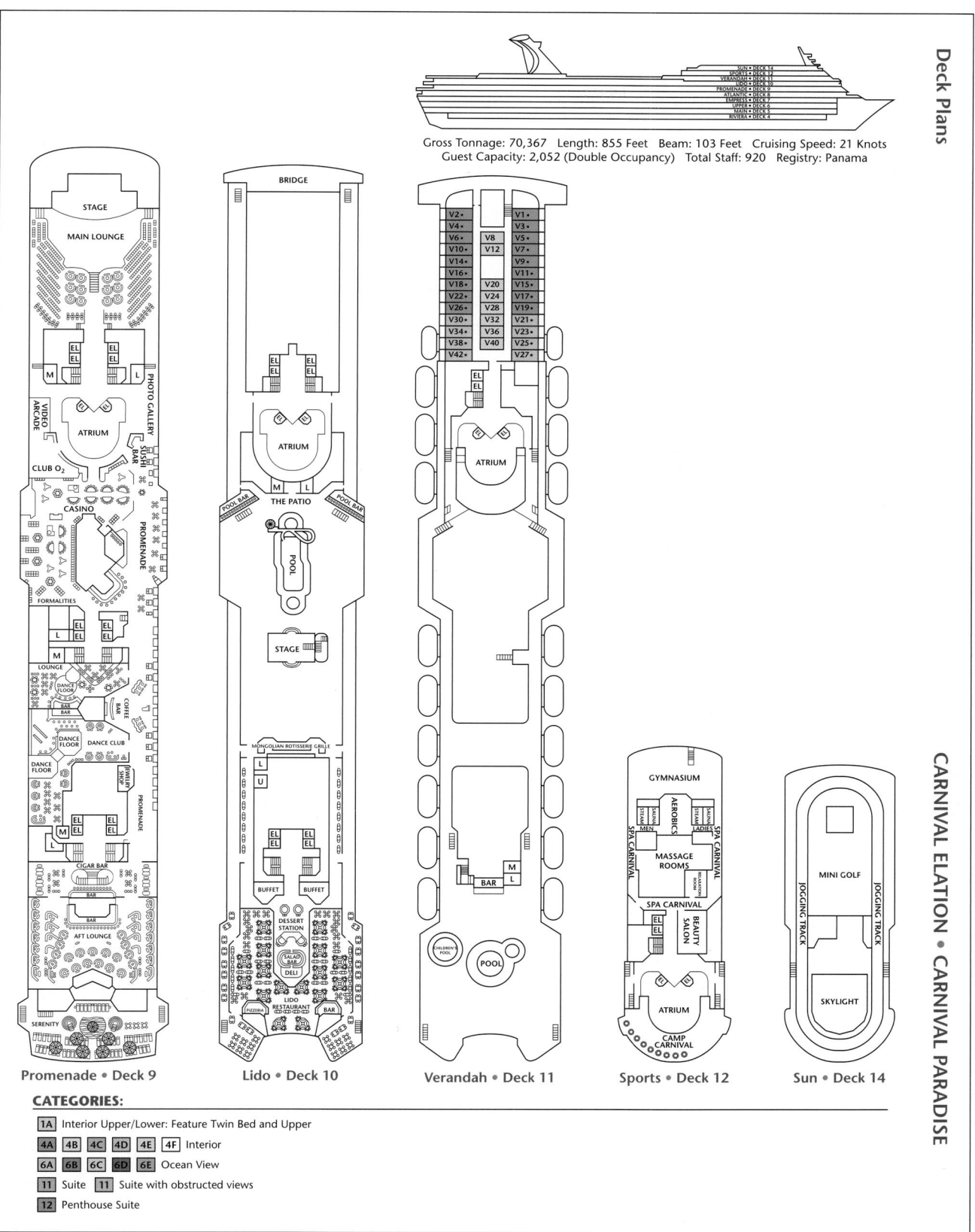

Gross Tonnage: 70,367   Length: 855 Feet   Beam: 103 Feet   Cruising Speed: 21 Knots
Guest Capacity: 2,052 (Double Occupancy)   Total Staff: 920   Registry: Panama

Promenade • Deck 9   Lido • Deck 10   Verandah • Deck 11   Sports • Deck 12   Sun • Deck 14

CARNIVAL ELATION • CARNIVAL PARADISE

CATEGORIES:

1A   Interior Upper/Lower: Feature Twin Bed and Upper

4A 4B 4C 4D 4E 4F   Interior

6A 6B 6C 6D 6E   Ocean View

11   Suite   11   Suite with obstructed views

12   Penthouse Suite

FIGURE 3-2   (Continued)

The CDC gives each ship a score (85 or below out of 100 is considered failing) and publishes the results via print circulars and on its Web site. A cruise line whose ship fails an inspection is given the opportunity to rectify the shortcomings.

 # Questions for Discussion

1. Give at least five ways in which a "classic" ship differs from a "modern" ship.

2. Explain GRT and space ratio.

3. List at least four advantages of larger ships. List at least four advantages of smaller ships.

4. Name eight public facilities that are typically found on cruise ships.

5. Define or describe the following:

   - magrodome

   - atrium

   - lido deck

   - purser's office

   - spa

   - inside stateroom

   - suite

   - stateroom category

   - bow

- stern

- port side

- starboard

- galley

- bridge

Activity

Examine Figure 3-3 and then answer the following questions:

1. Which is the only deck that has no staterooms?

2. How many inside staterooms are there?

3. How many dining facilities are there onboard? What are they and on which decks?

4. How many elevators does this vessel have? Why?

5. Deck 1 is not indicated. What could be a possible reason?

6. Which two staterooms are the closest to the ship's bow?

7. A potential passenger is worried about the ship's motion. In which two staterooms would she probably sense the least motion?

8. Do any staterooms have obstructed views? Why?

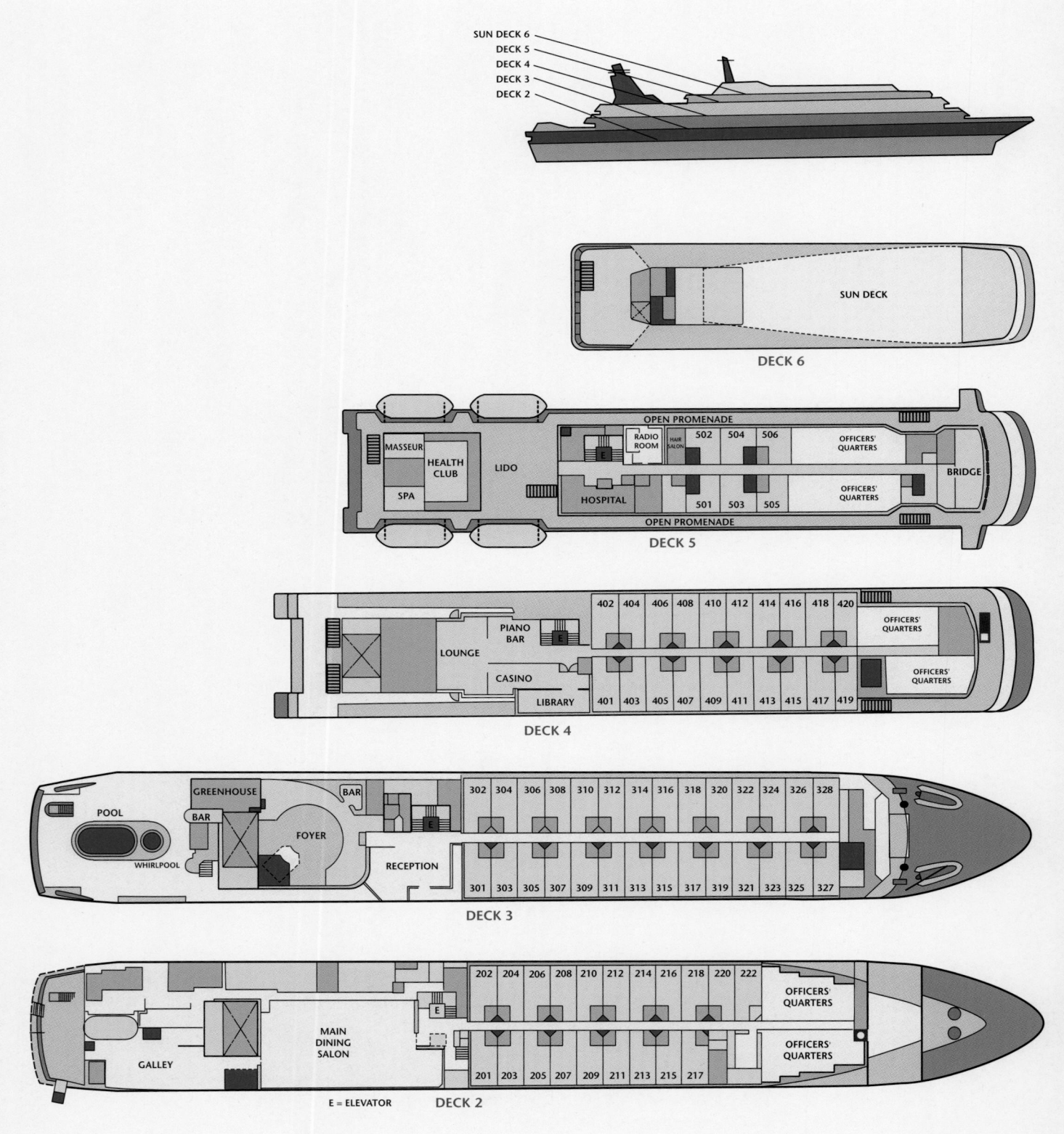

FIGURE 3-3

Chapter 4

The Cruise Experience

After reading this chapter, you'll be able to:

- Describe what occurs before a passenger actually sails.
- Explain dining patterns and options.
- Relate what typically takes place on a day at sea and a day in port.

Ⅰf only we could take you on a cruise right now. So much of what this book covers would become immediately apparent in a direct and compelling way.

But, sorry, we don't have that luxury. So, let's take an imaginary, first-time cruise vacation instead. Let's say it's to the Bahamas and the Caribbean. If you've never been on a cruise, much of this will be fresh and new. If you're a cruise veteran, our imaginary trip will bring back pleasant memories. Remember: It portrays a *typical* cruise. (About half of all cruises are to the Bahamas and the Caribbean.) All sorts of variations—both minor and major—are possible on the scenario that you're about to read.

Before You Buy

If you're typical, you almost surely found out about cruising from ads, commercials, or a friend. Your interest ignited, you perhaps did some preliminary research on the Internet and then probably contacted a travel agent. This is, after all, an important decision—the kind that requires the insight, analysis, and opinions of someone who knows cruising well. To see how far in advance cruise clients plan their vacation, see Figure 4-1. You may have even approached the travel agent with only vague ideas of your travel plans and then the agent brought up the idea of a cruise.

The travel agent asks you a series of questions to discover your needs. He or she understands that many types of cruises are available, and to be satisfied, it's critical that you travel on the ship, itinerary, and line that's right for you. The recommendation of a Caribbean cruise sounds great. "Go ahead. Let's do it,"

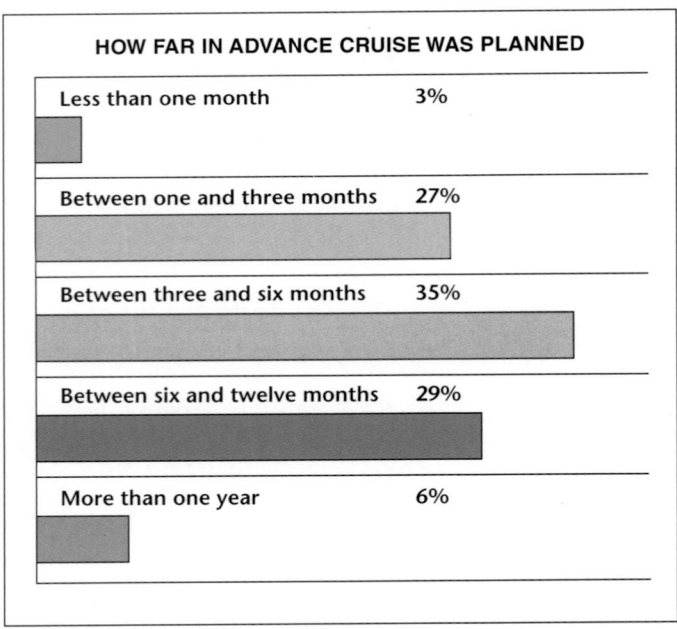

FIGURE 4-1   Planning ahead for a cruise
Source: *CLIA's 2008 Cruise Market Profile Study*

you say. You give your deposit, with the balance due later. (This whole process is explored in detail in Chapter 9.)

A few weeks before departure, your travel agent calls. Your cruise documents have arrived. You pick them up. You'll find some or all of the following in the documents folder:

- An invoice, confirmation, ticket, or voucher that verifies you're on the trip, probably also listing such information as embarkation date and hours, pier location, cabin number, which dining room seating you have, your booking ID number, and the terms and conditions of your voyage

- A booklet summarizing important information on such topics as dress requirements, onboard credit policies, and what clothes to bring

- A list of the documents you'll need (e.g., passport)

- An identification button

- A document on tuxedo rentals

- A gift order form (e.g., for champagne available in your cabin upon arrival)

- Color-coded luggage tags (usually two for each person)

- Immigration and customs forms, if needed

- An explanation/signup form for travel insurance (not necessary if you've already purchased insurance from your travel agent)

A modern cruise offers a wider variety of sports activities than ever before.
Courtesy of Costa Cruises

- An itinerary
- Air tickets and hotel information (if arranged through the cruise line)
- Embarkation port information (the cruise line or your travel agent may have also given you a map of your embarkation port)
- A leaflet on how ship-to-shore communication works, which may also list important telephone and fax numbers; make a copy of this document for friends or family in case there's an emergency back home
- A list of shore excursions and how to sign up for them
- A card that will serve as your identification throughout the trip in order to charge things, to get on the ship, etc.; you might not get this card until you get to the ship.

Increasingly, some or all of these will be sent to you or to your agent in electronic form. The printouts will replace what would have been in the folder.

On the Way to Your Cruise

On the day of your cruise, you fly to Miami. (If you live in or near Miami, you can drive to the port.) You could have flown in a day or two before to take advantage of a pre-cruise package. However, you've visited the Miami area several times, so you passed on that option.

Because the flight was booked through the cruise line, a company representative meets you at the airline terminal, along with others bound for the same ship. (If you had booked your flight separately, no **meet-and-greet** person from the cruise line would be there for you, and the cruise line transfer service wouldn't be part of your package. You could, however, purchase a transfer from the cruise line.)

With your fellow passengers, you board a motorcoach for the transfer to the port of Miami. Your luggage is placed in the bus or on another vehicle. You probably won't see it again until you get to your stateroom. The cruise line will take care of everything. It's the first of many hassle-saving benefits of a cruise.

Your bus arrives at the port terminal. Embarkation began at 2 P.M., and it's now 3:30 P.M. So, you check in with a cruise line representative, who reviews your documents, takes your credit card imprint to cover onboard charges, and gives you any materials you need. (This is the equivalent of checking in at a hotel front desk.) You then usually pass through some sort of security procedure and carry-on luggage screening, similar to those at airports. You make your way up the **gangway**—the walkway that connects the ship with the dock. Perhaps the ship's photographer takes your picture. It will be the first of many photo opportunities. (The pictures will be available for your inspection and purchase later, if you like, at the ship's photo gallery or via a computer screen.)

As you enter the ship, you pass through another security screening checkpoint. As you enter, several smiling ship staff members greet you. A trio of musicians may be playing too. You're finally finding out what others have told you: Once you're on a cruise ship, boredom is left behind on the dock.

Onboard the Ship

You now find your way to your stateroom, escorted by a crew member. The stateroom door is open. You settle in and review any in-room literature, such as the daily activities log, to find out what happens next. See Figure 4-2. Some cruise lines even provide daily "children-only" activities logs in addition to the regular one. You're eager to explore the ship—maybe stopping by the dining room to confirm your seating. You may also go to the purser's desk to register your credit card, if you didn't do so at the port. Most ships today operate on a "cashless" basis. You sign to your account all onboard expenses not included in the cruise price. On the last day, they'll be charged to your credit card.

Upon return to your stateroom, you find that your luggage has arrived. At this time, your **cabin steward**—the person who maintains your stateroom—introduces him or herself to you. You sense already that the level of service on a ship exceeds what hotels provide. The last time you stayed at a hotel, was the maid there to say hello?

On every ship, a lifeboat drill must take place within 24 hours of departure. It often happens before you even set sail. You knew it was going to happen: The ship's activities log gave you the time and details. Now a public address announcement reminds you it's about to occur. You put on the orange life vest you found in your stateroom—*fumble with* are better words. Like most people, you have to figure out how it goes on. (Of course, that's the point!) You then report to

Shipboard alternate dining: a Japanese Teppanyaki restaurant.
Courtesy of Norwegian Cruise Line

Stuff for "morning people"...

Early Morning Stretching	Fitness Center, Deck 12, Fwd.	7:00am
Total Body Conditioning Class	Fitness Center, Deck 12, Fwd.	7:30am
Indoor Cycling ($12 fee)	Fitness Center, Deck 12, Fwd.	8:00am
Adult Tennis Play	Sports Court, Deck 13, Aft.	8:00am-10:00am
Shuffleboard equipment is available	Deck 7, Mid. Starboard side	8:00am-2:00pm
Golf Clubs are available	Golf Cage, Deck 13, Aft.	8:00am-8:00pm
Seminar: A Life Changing Introduction - Acupuncture	Crystal Atrium, Deck 7, Mid	8:30am
Pathway to Yoga ($12 fee)	Fitness Center, Deck 12, Fwd.	9:00am
Rock Climbing Wall (6 yrs. or older, weather permitting)	Rock Climbing Wall, Deck 14, Aft.	9:00am-1:00pm
Under 2 Zoo Playroom	Behind Kiddy Pool, Deck 12, Mid.	9:00am-7:00pm
Bowling Alley (Must be 6 years or older to play)	Bliss Ultra Lounge, Deck 7, Aft.	9:00am-Whenever
Good Morning Trivia with your Cruise Director's Staff	Bar City, Deck 6, Mid.	9:15am
Juneau & Gemstones - 3 Free Gemstone Pendants	Crystal Atrium, Deck 7, Mid.	9:30am
Library is Open	Library, Deck 12, Fwd.	9:30am-11:30am
Darts Men vs. Ladies with your Cruise Director's Staff	Bar City, Deck 6, Mid.	9:45am
NCL "U" - Glaciers and Fjords with Robert Morrow	**Spinnaker Lounge, Deck 13, Fwd.**	**10:00am**
Sports Court is Available	Sports Court, Deck 13, Aft.	10:00am-5:00pm
Seminar: Eat More to Weigh Less	Fitness Center, Deck 12, Fwd.	10:30am
Golf Chipping with your Cruise Director's Staff	Bar City, Deck 6, Mid.	10:30am
Art Seminar - 30k years of Art History	Crystal Atrium, Deck 7, Mid.	11:00am
$5,000 Mega Jackpot Bingo	Spinnaker Lounge, Deck 13, Fwd.	11:15am
Australian Airbrushed Tattoos (Fees Apply)	Spinnaker Lounge, Deck 13, Fwd.	11:30am-12:30pm
Look 10 Years Younger with Dr. Cardona	Fitness Center, Deck 12, Fwd.	11:45am
Interactive Trivia with your Cruise Director's Staff	Bliss Ultra Lounge, Deck 7, Aft.	11:45am

Add pizzazz to your afternoon...

Singles Mingle Luncheon	Meet in Bliss Ultra Lounge, Deck 7, Aft.	Noon
Preview: Norwegian Epic and Cruise Reward Talk	Crystal Atrium, Deck 7, Mid.	12:15pm
LEGO Family Hour	Aqua Kid's Club, Deck 12, Mid	1:00pm-2:00pm
Nintendo Wii for all - on the Giant Screen	Crystal Atrium, Deck 7, Mid.	1:15pm-2:30pm
Meet your fellow guests for card play	Card Room, Deck 12, Fwd.	1:30pm
Arrival in Juneau, Alaska	Listen For Announcements	2:00pm (Approx.)
Port Play for Kids (Fees Apply)	Aqua Kids Club, Deck 12, Mid.	2:00pm-7:00pm
Indoor Bowls with your Cruise Director's Staff	Bar City, Deck 6, Mid.	2:30pm
Fun Trivia with your Cruise Director's Staff	Bar City, Deck 6, Mid.	3:15pm
Library is Open	Library, Deck 12, Fwd.	4:00pm-5:00pm
Rock Climbing Wall (6 yrs. or older, weather permitting)	Rock Climbing Wall, Deck 14, Aft.	4:00pm-6:00pm

Everything's hotter when the sun goes down...

Karaoke Madness with your Cruise Director's Staff	Bliss Ultra Lounge, Deck 7, Aft.	6:30pm-8:30pm
Ballroom Dance Music with Norwegian Pearl Show Band	Spinnaker Lounge, Deck 13, Fwd.	7:00pm
Friends Of Bill W.	The Chapel, Deck 13, Fwd.	7:00pm
Folkloric Entertainment: The Alaska String Band	Spinnaker Lounge, Deck 13, Fwd.	8:00pm
The Great Sounds of Wildfire	Bliss Ultra Lounge, Deck 7, Aft.	8:30pm-10:00pm
Sailing Solo & Ready To Mingle	Bliss Ultra Lounge, Deck 7, Aft.	9:00pm
Instant Wins: A chance to Win $2000 Instantly	Stardust Theater, Decks 6 & 7, Fwd.	9:00pm-9:15pm
Showtime: Sea Legs, A Showgirl Revue	Stardust Theater, Decks 6 & 7, Fwd.	9:15pm
All Aboard	Welcome back	9:30pm
Late Movie: Pirates of the Caribbean-Curse of the Black Pearl	Crystal Atrium, Deck 7, Mid.	10:00pm
Friendly Feud with your Cruise Director's Staff	Spinnaker Lounge, Deck 13, Fwd.	10:15pm
50's & 60's Sock Hop Party with Wildfire	Bliss Ultra Lounge, Deck 7, Aft.	10:15pm-11:00pm
Friends Of Dorothy - A Gathering for our LGBT Guests	Bliss Ultra Lounge, Deck 7, Aft. (VIP Area)	10:30pm
Music with Roots Link	Spinnaker Lounge, Deck 13, Fwd.	10:45pm-Whenever
Bowling Tournament with your Cruise Director's Staff	Bliss Ultra Lounge, Deck 7, Aft.	11:00pm
Disco with DJ Patrick (18 yrs. & Older)	Bliss Ultra Lounge, Deck 7, Aft.	11:00pm-Whenever

Ok, we know this looks like a schedule (gasp!) but remember, you're free to whatever!

FIGURE 4-2   Daily activities
Source: *Norwegian Cruise Line*

Bar Services

Java Café Deck 7, Mid.	7:00am-Whenever
Great Outdoors Bar Deck 12, Aft.	7:00am-Whenever
Topsiders Bar Deck 12, Mid.	7:30am-Whenever
Sky High Bar Deck 13, Fwd.	Weather Permitting
Bliss Ultra Lounge Deck 7, Aft.	10:00am-Whenever
Spinnaker Bar Deck 13, Fwd.	10:00am-3:00pm
	6:00pm-Whenever
Bar City Deck 6, Mid.	4:00pm-Whenever
Maltings Bar Deck 6, Mid.	4:00pm-Whenever
Star Bar Deck 13, Mid.	Noon-2:00pm
	6:00pm-Whenever
Casino Bar Deck 6, Fwd.	9:00am-1:00pm
	10:00pm-Whenever

Guest Services

Guest Service Desk Deck 7, Mid (#00)	Always Open
Internet Café Deck 7, Aft.	Always Open
Metro Video Arcade Deck 12, Mid.	Always Open
Body Waves Fitness Deck 12, Fwd. (Dial #12300)	Always Open
Quiet Zones Deck 14, Fwd & Aft.	Always Open
Shore Excursions Desk Deck 7, Mid.	9:00am-12:30pm
	8:00pm-9:00pm
Onboard Credit Desk Deck 7, Mid.	9:00am-Noon
	6:00pm-8:00pm
Pool Towel Exchange Deck 12, Mid.	7:00am-10:00pm
Internet Manager Deck 7, Aft.	9:00am-Noon
	5:00pm-6:00pm
	7:00pm-10:00pm
South Pacific Spa Deck 12, Fwd. (Dial #12200)	8:00am-10:00pm
Tahitian Pool* Deck 12, Mid.	8:00am-10:00pm
Jacuzzis* Deck 12, Mid.	8:00am-Midnight
Medical Center Deck 4, Mid.	8:30am-10:00am
	4:00pm-5:00pm
Library Open Deck 12, Fwd.	9:30am-11:30am
	4:00pm-5:00pm
Aqua Kid's Club Deck 12, Mid	9:00am-2:00pm
	7:00pm-10:30pm
Water Slide* Deck 12, Mid.	10:00am-6:00pm
Rock Climbing Wall Deck 14, Aft.	9:00am-2:00pm
	4:00pm-6:00pm
Cruise Consultant Deck 7, Mid.	9:00am-2:00pm
	8:00pm-9:00pm
Photo Gallery Deck 7, Aft.	9:00am-Arrival
	7:00pm-11:00pm
Tax & Duty Free Shops Deck 7, Fwd.	9:00am-Arrival
Pearl Club Casino Deck 6, Fwd.	9:00am-Close &
	10:00 pm-Close

Walking, Jogging & Sports Activities: Deck 13 is a walking/jogging track open 24/7. Deck 7 is a walking-only track; it's open 9am-9pm. All sports play is at your own risk, including our own island.
Jacuzzis & Pools: Will be open weather permitting. Forward Jacuzzis and Pool, Deck 12, are for adults only. Please, no reserving of deck chairs. Items left on deck chairs for more than 30 minutes will be removed & placed at the Reception. Glass & bottles can't be brought into any of the pools or hot tubs; neither can children in diapers or pull-ups, including swimmers. Pool towels & outdoor blankets are available in the Dive In Window, Pool Deck, Deck 12, Portside Fwd.
Water Slide: Children under 6 years old must be accompanied by an adult.
Casino: You have to be 18 (and have ID) to gamble or be in the casino. Sorry, but no winnings can be paid to any person or bets in violation. Also, drinks or glassware can't be taken out; pipes or cigars can't be taken in, but cigarette smoking is ok. Slot winnings of $1200 and above could be subject to W2-G tax withholding.
Alcohol Policy: On NCL cruises the minimum age for the consumption of any kind of alcohol is 21 years of age.
Liquor Purchased Ashore: Any liquor purchased in our ports of call will be collected and returned to you at the end of the voyage.
Smoking Policy: Public areas are smoke free. If you want to smoke, we've set aside spots just for you. If you smoke cigarettes, you can smoke in your stateroom, on your balcony, in the casino or cigar bar. If you prefer pipes or cigars, you can smoke in the cigar bar. You can smoke cigarettes, pipes and cigars outside on open decks, (just please don't smoke around food venues, sports decks or jogging areas, kids' pool areas and other designated non-smoking areas).
Please do not throw cigarettes overboard And please remember to never smoke in bed. **Please do not store towels on your balcony.**

Freestyle Dining

Getting Started

Early Risers Deck 12, Mid.	5:30am
Garden Café Deck 12, Mid.	7:00am-10:00am
Summer Palace Deck 7, Aft.	7:30am-9:00am
Great Outdoors** Deck 12, Aft.	7:30am-11:30am

Satisfy Your Afternoon Appetite

Garden Café Deck 12, Mid.	11:00am-2:30pm
Sushi Bar Deck 7 Mid. (Cover Charge applies)	11:30am-1:00pm
Topsiders Grill** Poolside, Deck 12, Mid.	11:30am-Whenever
Summer Palace Deck 7, Aft.	11:30-1:30pm
Great Outdoors** Deck 12, Aft.	Noon-2:30pm

What Are You In The Mood For?

Garden Café Deck 12, Mid.	5:30pm-10:30pm
Main Dining Rooms:	
Summer Palace Deck 7, Aft.	5:30pm-9:30pm
Indigo Deck 6, Mid.	6:00pm-10:30pm

Specialty Restaurants

Mambo's ($10)* Deck 8, Mid.	6:00pm-10:30pm
La Cucina ($10)* Deck 12, Aft., Portside	6:00pm-10:30pm
Lotus Garden ($15)* Deck 7, Mid.	6:00pm-10:30pm
Shabu-Shabu ($15)* Deck 7, Mid.	6:00pm-10:30pm
Sushi Bar ($15)* Deck 7, Mid.	6:00pm-10:30pm
Le Bistro ($15)* Deck 6, Mid.	6:00pm-10:30pm
Cagney's ($25)* Deck 13, Mid	6:00pm-10:30pm
T Teppanyaki ($25)* Deck 7, Mid.	6:00pm, 6:30pm
	7:30pm, 8:00pm, 9:00pm, 9:30pm

For Whenever You Are Hungry

Room Service Dial #6500	Always Open
Blue Lagoon Café Deck 8, Mid.	Always Open
BBQ-The Grill** Deck 12, Mid (Weather Permitting)	12:00am-Whenever
Garden Café Late Night Snacks Deck 12, Mid.	10:30pm-Midnight
Casino Snacks Deck 6, Fwd.	11:00pm-1:00am

****Weather Permitting
*These restaurants charge a cover, but the costs are really minimal (and for what you get, you'll find it's well worth it.)
It's time to try Mambos: Come up for dinner & the first Margarita's on the house! Wake up your taste buds and mosey up to Mambos Restaurant.

Onboard Flowers: Everyday is a special day to let that person in your life know you care. Roses & Diamonds are a girl's best friend; so make your love one smile with a single touch of rose, just dial 050.

Restaurants Reservations: Reservations can be made for the day of or the next day before dinner time. To make your reservations, call extension number 050 until 9:30pm or visit us at the reservation's desk located in Guest Service Desk, Deck 7, Mid from 7:30am-4:30pm and in the Garden Café, Deck 12, Mid, 7:30am-9:30pm.

Restaurant Cancellations: To ensure each of our guests receive our best service, we can only hold your dinner reservation for 15 minutes. If you need to cancel, please do so by 5:00pm on the day of your reservation to avoid having the cover charge for up to two guests applied to your account.

What to wear: You'll always find a place for your style, no matter what you want to wear. Resort casual, including jeans, is welcome in any of our restaurants, except the Summer Palace, our designated "dress up" restaurant. No shorts are permitted in any of our restaurants (except Garden Café) after 5:00pm.

Door Decorations: Be safe — overly decorated stateroom doors can pose a fire hazard, so please keep your decorations inside your room.
Environmental Hotline: You can report environmental incidents by calling 1-877-501-5976, the ship's Guest Service Desk, Deck 7, Mid or via e-mail EnvironmentalHotline@ncl.com. Reports are confidential.
Customer Advisory: Eat Smart: In case you didn't know, there's a certain level of danger to eating raw or undercooked animal products. It's also risky to drink juices that haven't been pasteurized. So if you have any immune system disorders, you should talk with your doctor. If you are allergic to nuts or have any other food allergies please call 050.
Safety Equipment: Please don't remove or meddle with any safety equipment onboard (such as smoke detectors or fire extinguishers). And, please follow safety instructions from the crew members.
Announcements: All announcements can be heard on channel 24.
Open Flames: Open flames (burning candles and incense) are strictly forbidden.
Sharps Containers: If you've got needles to throw away, please ask for a special container from Guest Service Desk, your Room Steward or Medical Center
Customer Relations: Got a service problem? We'll do our best to solve it! Dial '00'.

the lifeboat station that was pre-assigned to you. The ship's crew members inspect you and your fellow passengers, check to make sure everyone is there, explain procedures, and then dismiss you. It's back to your stateroom to prepare for the upcoming festivities.

Departure

A ship's departure is one of the most energetic moments on a cruise. You notice it's 6 P.M.—departure time—so you head for the pool deck, where a Caribbean steel drum band performs, staff members serve you tropical beverages with hors d'oeuvres, and everyone watches as the ship dramatically glides from its dock. The sky is blue, the breeze is warm and wonderful, and the sense of fun and excitement is everywhere.

After enjoying some activities, you return to your stateroom. A cocktail reception is next. But the big departure-day event is your first dinner at sea.

When you booked your cruise, your travel agent asked you which "seating" you wanted for the voyage. **First seating** is the earlier of two meal times (e.g., 6:30 P.M.); **second seating** is the later one (e.g., 8:30 P.M.). You opted for first. The maitre d' escorts you to your assigned table—it happens to be a table for eight. There you meet your companions for this meal and for subsequent dining room meals. They certainly seem congenial.

Your table captain, waiter, and other dining staff introduce themselves. You order wine. (This cost isn't included in the cruise price.) The waiter presents the menu. It's extensive. And there will be a different menu at each meal. For a sample, see Figure 4-3. You order the lobster. Each course is served with a flourish. Yes, you can get used to this.

Dinner on most ships is followed by entertainment in the main showroom. Tonight, it's a Las Vegas–style revue. And there are plenty of choices, now or later: a drink at the lounge, a little shopping perhaps, a try at the casino slot machines. And this is only the first night.

The traditional first seating/second seating dinner format at tables assigned for the entire cruise is still offered. But others are becoming increasingly common. Smaller ships may have only one seating. Some have **open seating**—passengers sit where they wish during extended times, much like a restaurant. One cruise line has three dining rooms, each themed uniquely. Guests eat in a different one each night—but with the same fellow guests, at a similarly placed table, with the same waiters. Passengers, though, have other choices. Most ships today also feature alternate dining facilities, like pizzerias and lido deck buffets, which offer extended hours and open seating. Many larger ships have multiple specialty restaurants, which require reservations (passengers book them when they board the ship or as the cruise progresses). A few offer a land resort approach, with a dozen or more dining options, open seating, and extended hours. And there's always room service.

RESTAURANT DINNER MENU
SUNDAY, OCTOBER 18, 2009

First Course

MALOSSOL CAVIAR
potato shallot cake, remoulade, spiced greens

SEARED VEAL CARPACCIO
young spinach, pesto vinaigrette, pecorino romano shavings

SAUTÉED ESCALOPE OF FOIE GRAS
roasted apples, caramelized honey

PUFF PASTRY BAKED PARMESAN & PROSCIUTTO CONSOMMÉ
navy beans, black truffle essence

WHITE ASPARAGUS SOUP
tarragon foam, smoked fish tortellini

THREE PEA SALAD
red wine dressing

TOSSED TOMATO & GRILLED BREAD
cucumber and toasted pine nuts

Main Course

PAN SAUTÉED DORADE FILLET, WHITE BEAN PUREE, BRAISED ARTICHOKES
slivered olives and tomato confit

BUTTER POACHED LOBSTER
cepes and chanteralles mushroom risotto, asparagus, lemon beurre blanc

HERB CRUSTED LAMB CHOPS
fondant potatoes in mustard jus, peas and wilted lettuce

CHATEAUBRIAND
roast filet of beef tenderloin, glazed vegetables, potato sticks, sauce bearnaise

VEGETARIAN – CRISP POLENTA WITH EGGPLANT & OLIVE RELISH
braised fennel and oven dried tomatoes

PULIGNY MONTRACHET, BOUCHARD PÉRE ET FILS 2006 $ 108.00
CHATEAU PAVILLON ROUGE, MARGAUX 2004 $ 158.00

The United States Public Health Service has determined that eating uncooked or partially cooked meat, poultry, fish, seafood or eggs may present a health risk to the consumer.

FIGURE 4-3   A sample menu
Courtesy of Seabourn Cruise Line

A Day at Sea

Basically, cruise days come in two varieties: *days at sea* and *days in port*. Except when a ship is doing an ocean crossing, days in port far outnumber days at sea. Let's assume, though, that your first full day is at sea.

Your wakeup call—which you set up the night before—reminds you it's time to get going. A condensed, faxed news summary was slid under your door overnight. You read it to catch up on what's going on in the world (which seems so far removed).

Breakfast may be on the lido deck or in the main dining room. It's your choice. In either place, there's almost too much to choose from. The cuisine quality, you note, is high, and the presentation is refined. Seating this time is open. (Assigned seating usually applies only to dinner in the main dining room.) You decide that tomorrow you'll order room service and have breakfast in bed instead.

What to do now? Again, the choices seem endless. You attend an orientation lecture that explains all you need to know about this cruise. (You could also watch it via your in-room TV.) You then decide that you want to read a book and work on a tan. So, you change and head for the pool.

Guests get the opportunity to work with a master chef in a culinary class.
Courtesy of Holland America Line

Before you know it, it's time for lunch! You opt again for the lido cafe and its seemingly endless buffet. You feel guilty. So much food! It's time to burn off some of those calories, so you jog for about 20 minutes on a track that encircles the ship, finishing off with a workout at the health club. Next door, an aerobics class is going through the paces. You remind yourself to do that tomorrow.

Down now to your stateroom. It's already been spiffed up by your cabin steward. You shower, change, and then attend a "port talk" that will prepare you for tomorrow's stop at St. Thomas. The cruise director describes St. Thomas, the **shore excursions** (port-based tours) available, and what you might wish to buy while there. The cruise line even gives you a list of approved shops. If you buy from one of these, you'll get a discount and a guarantee that if anything goes wrong, the cruise line will help resolve the problem. You decide to sign up for one of the shore excursions. Then back to your stateroom for a snooze—it's been freshened up *again* by your steward. How does he or she know when you come and go? It's one of the great mysteries of the cruise experience.

Tonight, it's formal night. You dress well, head for the dining room's first seating, and enjoy an elegant four-course meal. Then, it's off to see a spectacular magic show, followed by a few drinks with newly made friends. And some people think a cruise is boring!

A Day in Port

You're up early. The ship docks at Charlotte Amalie, the capital city, at 8 A.M. You want to take the 9 A.M. shore excursion—a two-hour tour of St. Thomas. You spend the afternoon strolling Main Street to do some shopping. Then, it's back to the ship for—yes—dinner. But this time, you're a bit tired from all that sun. You decide to have dinner in your stateroom, selecting from the room service menu. You feel re-energized, so you head down to the ship's theater to watch a movie. Then, you realize that there's a midnight buffet tonight! And it's a grand one too. You sample a few things as a late snack and then return to your stateroom. The sound of the sea outside lulls you into a perfect night's rest.

Here are some of the possible shore excursions in St. Thomas:

- Accessible Scenic Island Drive
- The Best of St. Thomas
- BOSS Underwater Adventure
- Butterflies Galore Anytime
- Captain Nautica's Power Raft Snorkeling
- Caribbean Amber Museum
- Caribbean Sail to Christmas & Honeymoon Coves

- St. John Eco Hike and Beach
- St. John Island Tour
- St. John Sea Safari by PowerCat
- St. Thomas Helmet Dive
- St. Thomas Island Tour
- St. Thomas Jeep and Beach Tour
- St. Thomas Mini Boat Adventure

(Continued)

• Catamaran Sailing & Snorkeling Tour	• St. Thomas Ocean Racing Challenge
• Champagne Sunset Harbor Cruise	• St. Thomas Panoramic Drive
• Coral Land & Coral Sea	• St. Thomas Scuba
• Discover Scuba Diving	• St. Thomas Spotlight 5 Star Island Tour
• Emerald Beach Resort Day	• Sapphire Beach & Island Drive
• Historic Blackbeard Castle & Recommended Shopping	• Screamin' Eagle
• Jost Van Dyke – Best of the British Virgin Islands	• Scuba Dive With Equipment
• Kayak, Hike & Snorkel on Cas Cay	• Scuba Dive Without Equipment
• Legends & Lore of St. Thomas	• Sea Blaster Marine Snorkel Tour
• Magen's Bay & Coral World	• Skyride to Paradise Point
• Magen's Bay Beach Getaway	• Tortola Dolphin Swim Adventure
• Mahogany Run Golf Course	• Turtle Cove Sail & Snorkel
• Parasail	• Turtle Cove Sail With Power Snorkel
• Red Sails in the Sunset Schooner Cocktail Cruise	• Ultimate Island Experience
• St. John 1/2 Day Champagne Cat Sail	• Water Island Bike Trip
• St. John Beach and Cays by Classic Schooner	• Yacht Adventures Sail & Snorkel
• St. John Beach and Snorkel Tour	

Source: *Royal Caribbean International*

The Last Night and the Following Day

After several more ports, countless events, and some genuinely memorable meals (during one, the waiters—dressed in red, white, and blue—marched out to a tune of John Philip Sousa while carrying Baked Alaska lit with sparklers), it's time for your great vacation to draw to a close. Dinner, a pleasant show, and back to the stateroom to do some packing. As per directions, you keep a few overnight things with you and put all the rest in your luggage. You place the suitcase outside your stateroom door. A staff member will pick it up and store it for the night.

You've already left a gratuity for your cabin steward and presented your table staff with tips too. The cruise line gives a guideline for what those gratuities generally are. See the box on page 61 for an example.

You fill out a customs form and a comment card. See Figure 4-4. You then settle your outstanding bills at the purser's office.

The next day, there's an early breakfast. You head with your overnight things to a public area, where you await the announcement of your turn to **disembark** (exit the ship). As with most events on a ship, disembarkation runs like clockwork.

Suggested guidelines for offering gratuities (per person per day):

Restaurant service	Stateroom service
Waiter: $3.50	Butler (Suites Only): $3.50
Assistant Waiter: $2.00	Stateroom Attendant $3.50
Maitre d': $.75	Chief Housekeeper $.50

Source: *Celebrity Cruises*

Luggage tags are color-coded. Twenty percent of the passengers have red tags, 20% yellow, and so forth. Each color is called sequentially. (A few cruise lines allow passengers to disembark at their leisure.) You leave the ship, claim your luggage (it's in one big room), go through immigration and customs, and board your motorcoach to Miami International Airport. Your cruise has been all you had hoped for—and more. And the only thought going through your mind is this: "Why didn't I do this sooner?"

Entertainment in the main showroom.
Courtesy of Norwegian Cruise Line

Guest Satisfaction Survey

Thank you for cruising with us. It has been our pleasure to serve you. Your thoughts are important to us, so please take a few moments to fill out this survey. We hope that your Holland America Line vacation will be a source of many happy memories for years to come, and look forward to welcoming you back in the near future.

Stein Kruse, President and CEO

Please fill circle completely
Do not use an ✗ or ✓ to mark your answer   ●   ⑧   ⑦   ⑥   ⑤   ④   ③   ②   ①   ⊗

Fill-in questions are read by computer, so please do not fold, roll or bend.
Use a black ball-point pen and do not attempt to cross-out or change an answer once it has been marked.

Please Rate	Excellent								Poor	N/A
AIRPORT MEET AND GREET STAFF (HAL TRANSFER ONLY)	⑨	⑧	⑦	⑥	⑤	④	③	②	①	⊗
AIRPORT/HOTEL TO PIER TRANSFER (HAL TRANSFER ONLY)	⑨	⑧	⑦	⑥	⑤	④	③	②	①	⊗
PIER CHECK-IN STAFF	⑨	⑧	⑦	⑥	⑤	④	③	②	①	⊗
BAGGAGE HANDLING (SHORE)	⑨	⑧	⑦	⑥	⑤	④	③	②	①	⊗
BAGGAGE HANDLING (ON BOARD)	⑨	⑧	⑦	⑥	⑤	④	③	②	①	⊗
TENDER SERVICES	⑨	⑧	⑦	⑥	⑤	④	③	②	①	⊗

Comments

Service of Personnel	Excellent								Poor	N/A
HELPFULNESS/FRIENDLINESS OF CREW	⑨	⑧	⑦	⑥	⑤	④	③	②	①	⊗
STATEROOM STEWARDS	⑨	⑧	⑦	⑥	⑤	④	③	②	①	⊗
ONBOARD SIGNATURE SHOP STAFF	⑨	⑧	⑦	⑥	⑤	④	③	②	①	⊗
PHOTO SHOP STAFF	⑨	⑧	⑦	⑥	⑤	④	③	②	①	⊗
CASINO STAFF	⑨	⑧	⑦	⑥	⑤	④	③	②	①	⊗
THE GREENHOUSE SALON STAFF	⑨	⑧	⑦	⑥	⑤	④	③	②	①	⊗
THE GREENHOUSE SPA STAFF	⑨	⑧	⑦	⑥	⑤	④	③	②	①	⊗
FRONT OFFICE STAFF	⑨	⑧	⑦	⑥	⑤	④	③	②	①	⊗
SHORE EXCURSION STAFF	⑨	⑧	⑦	⑥	⑤	④	③	②	①	⊗
LAUNDRY AND VALET SERVICE	⑨	⑧	⑦	⑥	⑤	④	③	②	①	⊗
RELIGIOUS SERVICES	⑨	⑧	⑦	⑥	⑤	④	③	②	①	⊗

Comments

FIGURE 4-4   Passenger comment card
Source: *Courtesy of Holland America Line*

Food & Beverage	Excellent	←						→	Poor	N/A
DINING ROOM STEWARD	⑨	⑧	⑦	⑥	⑤	④	③	②	①	⊗
DINING ROOM WINE STEWARD	⑨	⑧	⑦	⑥	⑤	④	③	②	①	⊗
DINING ROOM FOOD TASTE	⑨	⑧	⑦	⑥	⑤	④	③	②	①	⊗
DINING ROOM MENU SELECTION	⑨	⑧	⑦	⑥	⑤	④	③	②	①	⊗
DINING ROOM FOOD PRESENTATION	⑨	⑧	⑦	⑥	⑤	④	③	②	①	⊗
LIDO STAFF	⑨	⑧	⑦	⑥	⑤	④	③	②	①	⊗
LIDO FOOD TASTE	⑨	⑧	⑦	⑥	⑤	④	③	②	①	⊗
LIDO FOOD SELECTION	⑨	⑧	⑦	⑥	⑤	④	③	②	①	⊗
LIDO FOOD PRESENTATION	⑨	⑧	⑦	⑥	⑤	④	③	②	①	⊗
IN-ROOM DINING FOOD TASTE	⑨	⑧	⑦	⑥	⑤	④	③	②	①	⊗
IN-ROOM DINING FOOD PRESENTATION	⑨	⑧	⑦	⑥	⑤	④	③	②	①	⊗
PINNACLE GRILL WAITSTAFF	⑨	⑧	⑦	⑥	⑤	④	③	②	①	⊗
PINNACLE GRILL FOOD TASTE	⑨	⑧	⑦	⑥	⑤	④	③	②	①	⊗
PINNACLE GRILL MENU SELECTION	⑨	⑧	⑦	⑥	⑤	④	③	②	①	⊗
BEVERAGES BAR AND LOUNGE SERVICE	⑨	⑧	⑦	⑥	⑤	④	③	②	①	⊗
BEVERAGES POOLSIDE SERVICE	⑨	⑧	⑦	⑥	⑤	④	③	②	①	⊗

If any of the items listed to the right need improvement, please fill in the appropriate circle.

○ lamb   ○ beef   ○ salads   ○ desserts
○ veal   ○ poultry   ○ soups   ○ appetizers
○ pork   ○ seafood/fish   ○ coffee   ○ vegetables
○ pastas

Comments

Port & Shore Excursions	Excellent	←						→	Poor	N/A
SHORE EXCURSIONS	⑨	⑧	⑦	⑥	⑤	④	③	②	①	⊗
INFORMATION PROVIDED ABOUT PORTS OF CALL	⑨	⑧	⑦	⑥	⑤	④	③	②	①	⊗

Comments

FIGURE 4-4 *(Continued)*

Entertainment	Excellent								Poor	N/A
SHOWTIME ENTERTAINMENT	⑨	⑧	⑦	⑥	⑤	④	③	②	①	⊗
PIANO BAR	⑨	⑧	⑦	⑥	⑤	④	③	②	①	⊗
EXPLORATIONS TEAM ACTIVITIES	⑨	⑧	⑦	⑥	⑤	④	③	②	①	⊗
HELPFULNESS AND FRIENDLINESS OF STAFF	⑨	⑧	⑦	⑥	⑤	④	③	②	①	⊗
KIDS AND TEEN PROGRAMS	⑨	⑧	⑦	⑥	⑤	④	③	②	①	⊗

Comments

Facilities	Excellent								Poor	N/A
CLEANLINESS OF SHIP	⑨	⑧	⑦	⑥	⑤	④	③	②	①	⊗
STATEROOM ACCOMODATIONS	⑨	⑧	⑦	⑥	⑤	④	③	②	①	⊗
THE GREENHOUSE SPA AND SALON	⑨	⑧	⑦	⑥	⑤	④	③	②	①	⊗
EXPLORATIONS CAFÉ	⑨	⑧	⑦	⑥	⑤	④	③	②	①	⊗

Comments

Please also rate	Excellent								Poor	N/A
	⑨	⑧	⑦	⑥	⑤	④	③	②	①	⊗
	⑨	⑧	⑦	⑥	⑤	④	③	②	①	⊗
	⑨	⑧	⑦	⑥	⑤	④	③	②	①	⊗
	⑨	⑧	⑦	⑥	⑤	④	③	②	①	⊗
	⑨	⑧	⑦	⑥	⑤	④	③	②	①	⊗
	⑨	⑧	⑦	⑥	⑤	④	③	②	①	⊗
	⑨	⑧	⑦	⑥	⑤	④	③	②	①	⊗
	⑨	⑧	⑦	⑥	⑤	④	③	②	①	⊗
	⑨	⑧	⑦	⑥	⑤	④	③	②	①	⊗
	⑨	⑧	⑦	⑥	⑤	④	③	②	①	⊗
	⑨	⑧	⑦	⑥	⑤	④	③	②	①	⊗
	⑨	⑧	⑦	⑥	⑤	④	③	②	①	⊗

	Excellent								Poor
How would you rate your overall experience on this cruise?	⑨	⑧	⑦	⑥	⑤	④	③	②	①
Would you recommend a Holland America Line cruise to a friend or relative?	○ yes	○ no							

FIGURE 4-4 *(Continued)*

General Information (for classification purposes only)

You are:	○ male ○ female
Is this your first cruise ever?	○ yes ○ no
Before this cruise, have you ever cruised with Holland America Line?	○ yes ○ no
Which one of the following statements best describes why you cruise?	○ I mainly cruise to relax and get away from it all ○ I mainly cruise to visit interesting places and experience different cultures ○ I mainly cruise to enjoy the cuisine and onboard dining experiences
What is your marital status?	○ married ○ divorced/separated ○ single ○ widowed
You are currently:	○ retired ○ employed full/part time ○ not employed
When do you think your next cruise with Holland America Line will most likely occur?	○ within 6 months ○ 24 months ○ 12 months ○ longer than 24 months ○ I don't plan to cruise with HAL again
If you are likely to take another cruise in the next two years, in which destinations are you most interested?	○ Alaska ○ Africa ○ Australia/N. Zealand ○ Caribbean ○ Hawaii ○ Canada/N. England ○ Mexico ○ South Pacific ○ China/Japan/SE Asia ○ Panama Canal ○ South America ○ Around the World ○ Mediterranean ○ N. Europe/Baltic
What is your approximate total annual household income before taxes?	○ under $20,000 ○ $75,000-99,999 ○ $175,000-199,999 ○ $20,000-34,999 ○ $100,000-124,999 ○ $200,000 and over ○ $35,000-54,999 ○ $125,000-149,999 ○ $55,000-74,999 ○ $150,000-174,999

If you would like more information on cruises and tours with Holland America Line, please visit our website at www.hollandamerica.com

FIGURE 4-4 *(Continued)*

Miscellaneous Thoughts

Yes, that's the typical cruise vacation experience. But as we've noted all along, *all manner of variations are possible*. Small ships may offer a more intimate experience, with only a few, well-selected options. Cruises on sailing ships, ferrylike vessels, riverboats, and barges will certainly stray from the scenario we've portrayed. So, too, will cruises that strongly emphasize education, adventure, or exploration.

The cruise scenario we've described was flawless. But nothing is ever entirely perfect. Sometimes, a few things do go wrong. Yet, on a cruise, these glitches are rare.

A few miscellaneous bits of information about the cruise experience:

- In a few cases, an itinerary may feature only a half day in port (e.g., 7 A.M. to 1 P.M.), with the rest of the day at sea or on the river.

- When ships are in exotic or adventurous places, such as Antarctica, you may have to take **zodiac boats** to go ashore. (A *zodiac* is a large rubber boat.) In other places, a ship may be too large or have too deep a **draft** to tie up to the dock. The ship will instead anchor offshore. Small boats, called **tenders**, will ferry passengers between port and ship.

- On most cruises, you can dine far more than three times a day. In addition to breakfast, lunch, and dinner, there may be snacks or afternoon tea served between meals and an all-day buffet. Room service is usually available 24 hours a day.

- A **spa** or **lean-and-light menu** often refers to a low-calorie, low-fat dining alternative. Because so many passengers now watch what they eat, such healthy choices are becoming more common.

- "Themes" add an interesting spin to some cruises. A certain departure might focus on, say, basketball, with current and former basketball stars onboard. They mingle with guests, sign autographs, and teach volunteers how to improve their foul shooting. Other possible themes: jazz, filmmaking, finance, murder mysteries, and eclipse watching.

- Shore excursions are rarely included in the cruise price. It's not necessary to book a shore excursion through the cruise line, either. You can buy one from a shoreside company, rent a car, stroll around, or do just about anything you please. But remember: If the cruise line–sponsored shore excursion is late getting back, the ship will almost surely wait. If you're on your own and you return late, though, you may have to wave goodbye to your fellow passengers as they sail off into the horizon.

- It's not unusual for a ship's officer to occasionally join passengers at their table. The most prestigious table to sit at, of course, is the captain's table (although this custom is becoming somewhat passé).

- In some cases, room service or dining at a special alternate venue requires a modest extra charge.

- Once all passengers have left the ship, staff rapidly prepares the vessel for the next cruise and its passengers. Amazingly, they often can "turn around" the ship within a matter of hours.

- Traditionally, passengers gave cash gratuities to their dining and stateroom crew on the last evening of the cruise. Increasingly, though, passengers may charge to their onboard account gratuities covering all service staff (many lines charge these tips to the passenger's cruise bill automatically). Many cruise lines allow passengers to prepay gratuities along with their cruise fare. (The amount can be adjusted during the cruise if you're unhappy with the service.) Most lines add an automatic gratuity (usually 15–18%) to beverage charges and spa services. A few upscale cruise lines have a "tipping not required" policy, which means that the guest need not feel obligated to tip. The super-luxury lines forbid tipping.

- Can a cruise be canceled? Yes, although it's rare. Among the possible reasons: mechanical problems on the ship, dangerous weather at the port (e.g., a hurricane), or the failure of a shipbuilding facility to deliver a new ship on time. Invariably, the cruise line will make every effort to reassign passengers to a later cruise or provide a credit toward a future sailing.

- Are itineraries ever changed at the last minute? It can happen, either because of, say, weather conditions or political turmoil. Cruise lines are adept at making quick adjustments, substituting certain ports for others.

Passenger Questions
Yes, passengers really have asked the following:

- How will we know which photos are ours?
- Will trapshooting be held outside?
- Does the crew sleep onboard?
- (To the waiter) Is the fish caught each day by the crew?
- (To the featured entertainer) Do you hope to go into show business some day?
- Do these stairs go up as well as down?
- How far are we above sea level?
- Is there water all around the island?
- What do you do with the ice carvings after they melt?
- Why does the ship rock only when we are at sea?
- Does the ship generate its own electricity?
- Does the elevator go to the front of the ship?
- Will I get wet if I go snorkeling?
- What time is the midnight buffet?

Questions for Discussion

1. Name at least six items that make up the cruise documents sent to a client before he or she leaves.

2. Outline briefly what happens on the first night of a cruise.

3. You're on a day at sea. What would *you* probably do? Name at least 10 activities.

4. What goes on during the last evening of the cruise and the following day?

Activity

Obtain a cruise brochure. It should be a different one from the brochure you used in Chapter 1. After reading it carefully, describe below how the cruise and line you chose might offer cruise experiences that are different from the one given in this chapter. For example, does it have open-seating meals? Is there a casino? Look carefully for clues to what does—and doesn't—go on.

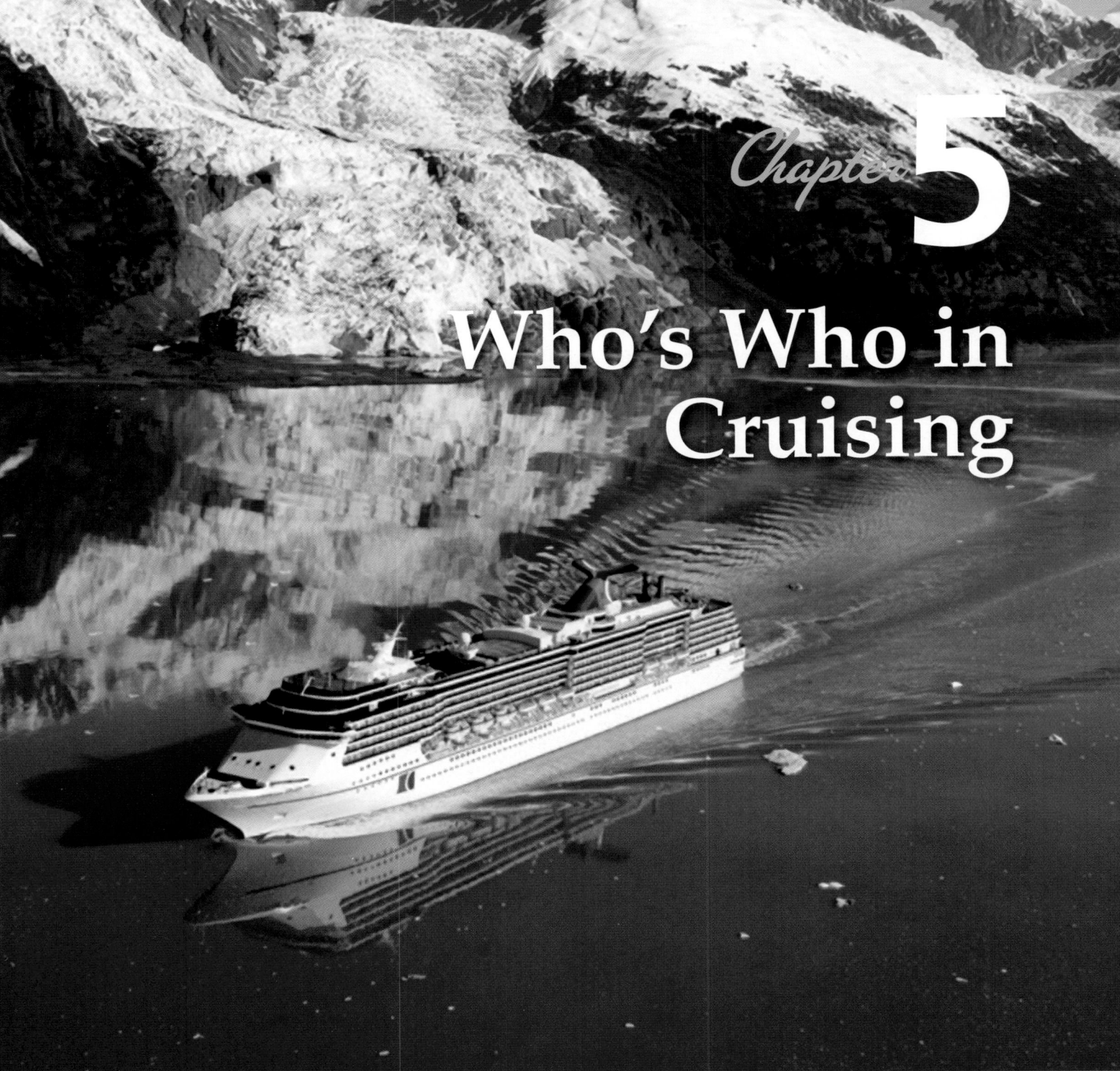

Chapter 5

Who's Who in Cruising

After reading this chapter, you'll be able to:

- Explain what sea-based cruise staff do.
- Relate the responsibilities of land-based management and staff.
- Describe how travel agents are a vital link to the cruise sales process.
- Explain how and where professionals learn about the cruise vacation experience.

Ever wonder what it would be like to be part of the cruise industry? In this chapter, we're going to explore three occupational areas that you could consider: sea-based operations, land-based operations, and the segment that sells over 90% of all cruises—the travel agency community.

Sea-Based Operations

You may be surprised to discover how many people work onboard a ship. Most vessels have *at least* one crew member for every three passengers. On some luxury ships, the ratio is closer to 1.5 to 1. The largest megaships may have more than 2,000 workers onboard.

Cruise lines divide operations onboard their ships into two broad categories: sailing operations and hotel operations. The captain is in charge of both operational sectors. He also attends certain social functions onboard so passengers can get to know him better.

A team of officers supervises those factors that directly relate to the ship's sailing operations:

- The *staff*, *deputy captain*, or *first officer* is in charge when the captain is busy or not onboard (e.g., at a port). On large ships, the staff captain supervises a team of senior and junior officers. Among his or her special duties is overseeing ship safety and security.

- The *chief engineer* oversees all mechanical operations, including the engines, electrical systems, lighting, plumbing, waste management, onboard climate control, and the maintenance or repair of the ship itself. The larger the ship, the more specialist tradespeople work under the chief engineer.

- The *chief medical officer*, or *doctor*, tends to the health of passengers and crew. (All ships with 100 or more passengers onboard must have a doctor.) He or she may have a nurse and/or orderly to help out with medical concerns. Medical services on a ship are not free of charge. Billings are handled as with any hospital or doctor's office.

- In today's world, the responsibilities of *chief radio* or *communications officer* are complex. He or she oversees in-room satellite TV programming, ship-to-shore phone calls, Internet service, and all other shipboard communication systems.

The team of people who compose hotel operations is equally diversified:

- The *hotel manager*, or *hotel director* (also sometimes called the *chief purser*), conducts his or her business very much like the manager of a land-based hotel or resort but with a specialized understanding of the cruise experience. Prime areas of responsibility include guest satisfaction and comfort, human resources, security, expenditures, and revenues.

- The *purser* is much like a hotel front desk manager or assistant manager. Unlike the hotel manager—who tends to larger operational issues—the purser administers day-to-day affairs. Some examples include management of passenger accounts, mail, messages, printing, the storing of valuables, and immigration and customs requirements. On larger vessels, the purser has two assistants: the crew purser (who deals with crew issues) and the hotel purser (who tends

The professionals who make a great cruise possible.
Courtesy of AMAWATERWAYS

to passenger matters). The purser may have a large team of assistants who staff the purser's desk, coordinate publications, deliver messages, and handle other concerns.

- The *shore excursion manager* orchestrates the operation and booking of port-based packages. On certain lines, he or she is sometimes called the *concierge,* with broader responsibilities such as booking customized port experiences, changing flights, etc. On larger ships, a team of people tend to shore excursions, including an onboard travel agent who can book a passenger's future cruise needs. (If a sale occurs, the passenger's travel agent will usually still get the commission for that sale.)

- The *cruise director* coordinates all entertainment and informational activities that take place as part of the cruise experience. Part host, part entertainer, gregarious, and always gracious, the cruise director serves as a critical link between passengers and crew. He or she presides over many functions, including passenger orientation and disembarkation meetings. The cruise director also manages the musicians, entertainers, *onboard lecturers* (experts who provide their services in exchange for a free cruise), *social hosts* (who converse and dance with single women onboard), health club staff, photographers, and, in some cases, the shore excursion manager.

- The *executive chef* controls the preparation and serving of all food and beverages. He or she supervises the *assistant* or *sous chef*, the pastry chef, food preparers, and other kitchen staff.

- The *head housekeeper* or *chief steward* manages all stateroom, public space, and other shipboard cleaning. He or she supervises a squad of *cabin* or *room stewards* who tend to the passengers' stateroom needs. (Cabin stewards have a much more active, personal, and round-the-clock relationship with guests than do maids at hotels.)

- The *food and beverage manager* oversees the serving of meals and drinks. (On smaller ships, this may be handled by the *executive chef.*) The food and beverage manager watches over the *dining room maitre d'*, *table captains*, *waiters*, and *busboys*. The food and beverage manager also oversees the *bartenders*, *drink servers*, and *wine steward*.

Responsibilities onboard a ship often overlap. The smaller the vessel, the more likely this is, especially when it comes to entertainment: The shore excursion director, the cruise director, and even the waiters may do double-duty as performers at the evening show. And on many ships, entertainers may serve in numerous other capacities. Note, however, that not all those working on a cruise ship are necessarily employees of the cruise line.

> To serve certain passenger needs, cruise lines contract with independent concessioners, contractors, or vendors. This is often true with shore excursion tour operators, onboard entertainer groups, onboard lecturers, and port operations staff. Casino and beauty salon workers, photographers, shop salespeople, and spa staff (e.g., aerobic instructors or masseuses) may also be independent contractors.

Land-Based Operations

To summarize a cruise line's land-based operations is no easy task. Some cruise lines are relatively small, with fewer than 100 off-ship employees. Others are huge, with thousands of employees. What do they have in common?

Surprisingly, the layers of management are often similar. They parallel the standard structure employed in other North American corporations. See Figure 5-1.

Let's take a look first at the hierarchy of the typical large cruise line. At the top may be a *chairman* who presides over a *board of directors*. The chairman may be the principal or sole owner of the cruise line or may be responsible to the stockholders. He or she may also be referred to as the *CEO, or chief executive officer.* (Sometimes, it's the president, not the chairman, who's referred to as the CEO.)

Reporting to the chairman and board is the line's *president.* He or she sets the company's direction in all areas: sales, marketing, operations, finance, and the like. Reporting to the president may be one or two *executive* or *senior vice presidents.*

In turn, there are a number of vice presidents, each with a set of responsibilities in a specific segment of the company's operations. A few possibilities:

- The *vice president of marketing* orchestrates the research, development, promotion, and follow-up of the cruise line's products.

- The *vice president of sales* oversees the actual selling of cruises, either through travel agencies or directly to the public. Below him or her are *business development managers* (also called district sales managers, regional sales managers, district sales representatives, regional sales representatives, or by some other title—it depends on the cruise line), who are the spokespersons for the cruise line at

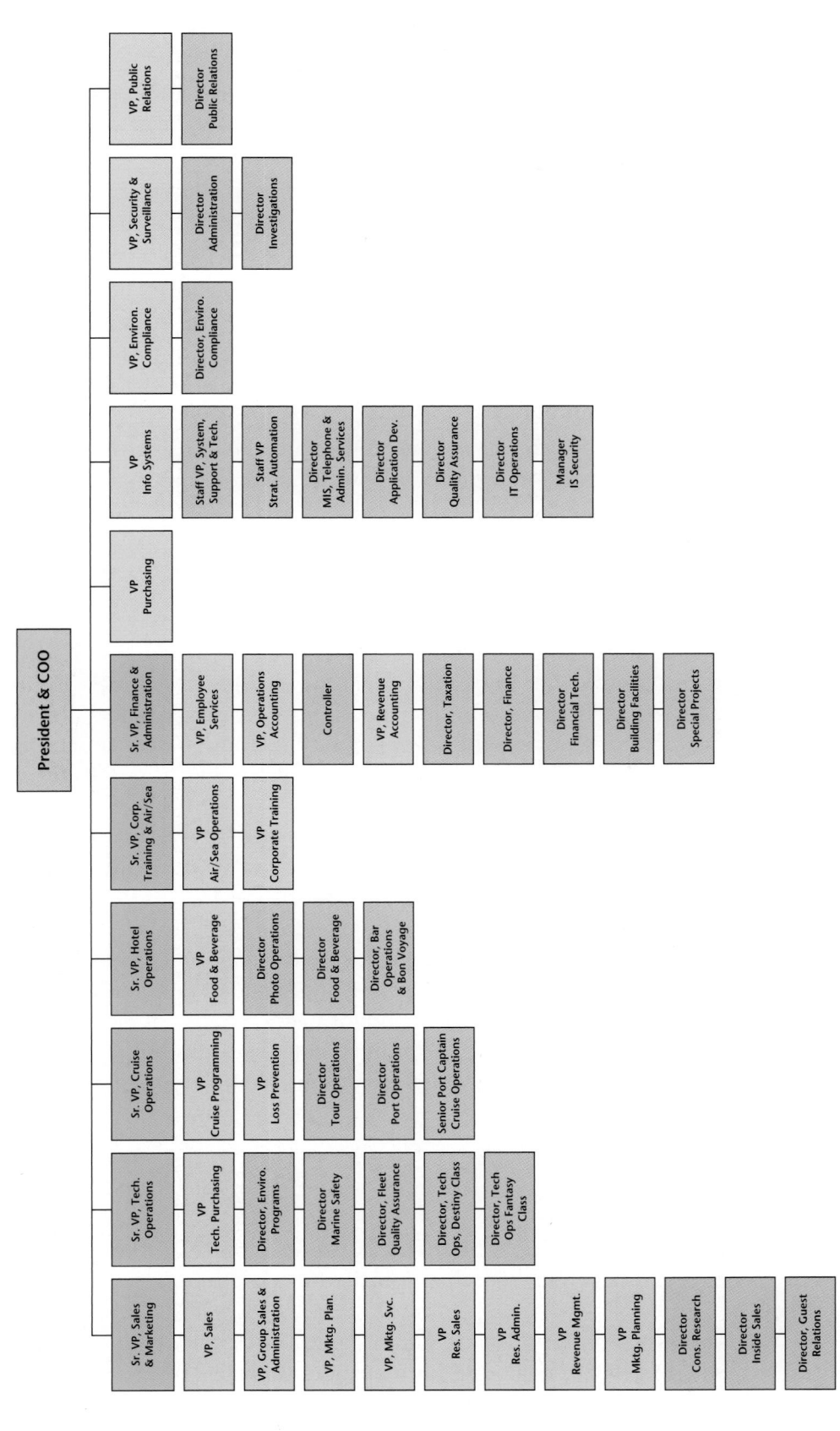

FIGURE 5-1   Organization chart
Source: *Courtesy of Carnival Cruise Line*

trade shows and communicate with travel agents in their assigned geographic area. The vice president of sales is also in charge of the people who take calls from agents and clients as well as those who supervise them.

- The *vice president of finance* administers and addresses all financial issues. If he or she is the company's CFO, or chief financial officer, he or she may well be a senior vice president.

- The *vice president of operations or passenger services* is responsible for all onboard and shore-side activities. This job is sometimes divided into two: a vice president of hotel operations (who manages shipboard hotel-type services) and a vice president of marine operations (who handles logistic and technical factors, such as ship and port considerations).

- At very large cruise lines, a third vice president might be in charge of shore excursion tour companies that the line itself owns and of staff that checks in passengers at major embarkation and debarkation ports.

- The *vice president of national accounts* represents the cruise line to major agency chains, usually those in a preferred supplier relationship. (More about this soon.)

- The *vice president of groups and incentives* orchestrates all group sales, marketing, and operational activities.

Only the very largest cruise lines would have this many vice presidents. At smaller cruise lines, some positions might meld the functions of several vice presidents into one. Other lines might feel that the responsibility doesn't merit a vice presidency. The person in charge of, say, groups might have a "lower" title (e.g., director). What are the layers of management below that of vice president? As in the rest of the business world, they are, in order, *director, manager,* and *supervisor.*

A vice president might have one or two directors to oversee (or perhaps one assistant director who reports to a director). They in turn would have managers beneath them, the managers would have supervisors, and the supervisors would have staff.

One last point: At large cruise lines, business development managers (BDMs) usually work exclusively for one cruise line. For smaller companies, the business development managers may be independent, working for not only the cruise line but also for other, noncompeting suppliers, such as tour companies and tourist bureaus. These independent sales representatives are called **multiline reps**.

Travel Agencies

Why are travel agents so important to the cruise sales process? The reason is simple: Purchasing a cruise is a far more complicated matter than, say, buying an airline ticket.

A cruise isn't a commodity. It's an *experience.* All cruises *aren't* alike. To decide which cruise is the right one for a particular person is a complex and sensitive task—one that requires the analysis, advice, and experience of a professional travel agent. That's why travel agents are often called *travel counselors.*

People who purchase a cruise want to make sure that they'll fully enjoy and profit from it. They want one that will provide destinations, food, activities, entertainment, and an environment that matches their style. Perhaps they could do the research themselves and book the cruise directly (either by phone or the Internet) through the cruise line or some other sales entity. But wouldn't it be easier, quicker, safer, and perhaps cheaper to let an expert guide that choice? After all, cruises often cost thousands of dollars—they're investments, not transactions. And the cruise ship isn't just a way to get from Point A to Point B. It represents an experience, not a commodity.

Travel agents are therefore integral to the cruise sales process. Let's briefly explore how their industry operates.

The Travel Agency Business

Thousands of travel agencies serve the North American market today. Many of them are full-service outlets, providing air, rail, car, lodging, tours, cruises, and other travel products.

At one time, commissions on air tickets fueled agency profitability. However, in 1996, the airlines began a series of steps to severely cap the amount of commissions an agency could earn from selling air travel. Eventually, most airlines eliminated commissions altogether (except for very large agency chains). Since then, many travel agencies have treated air sales as "loss leaders." They've begun charging fees for their services and have redirected their efforts to selling cruises, tours, and all-inclusive resorts. The reason: These products are comprehensive packages, yielding commissions on virtually everything that a client does while on vacation. Cruises generally require only one phone call or computer entry in order to book. A cruise produces extremely high satisfaction in clients, helping to ensure loyalty and repeat business. And most cruise lines treat travel agents as valued partners in the sales process. No wonder agents love selling cruises.

Kinds of Travel Agencies

Here are the kinds of travel agencies that are likely to sell cruises:

- **Independent agencies.** These agencies are privately owned and unaffiliated with any larger institution. Often called *mom & pops,* they're the "corner store" of travel retailers, usually with small staffs and a keen sense of the communities they serve. However, independent agencies have limited economic leverage with suppliers and often find it a challenge to negotiate higher override commissions and preferred status.

  Yet some independent agencies have flourished in the current competitive business environment. Their strategy: Focus on very specialized travel products, establish a reputation for excellence, operate super efficiently, and/or provide a high level of personal service. This is no easy task, however, so the number of mom & pop agencies—once the mainstay of the travel agency industry—has rapidly diminished.

- **Agency chains.** As with most other retail industries, large groups of regionally or nationally branded agencies have developed in North America. Some embrace a dozen or more locations in a defined geographic area. Others count hundreds in their organization. Still others—usually called *mega-agency chains*—have a thousand or more.

    Many of these chains have well-known names (e.g., American Express and AAA), creating public recognition and inspiring buyer confidence. Their size and reputation provide them with economic clout too. It permits them to negotiate favored status with carefully selected "preferred" suppliers. In turn, these preferreds provide the chains with many advantages. (More about that soon.)

    Within a chain may be two kinds of agencies: wholly owned and franchises. *Wholly owned agencies* are what the name implies—the chain owns them. *Franchises* are semi-independent agencies who pay for the right to use a chain's name, preferred products, and services. They sign on, hoping that the fees they pay for franchise status will result in such benefits as brand recognition (which will attract more customers), training support, business guidance, higher commissions, and greater profitability.

- **Consortium-affiliated agencies.** Consortia promise agencies greater independence than they would have if they were an agency franchise, with the leverage that a large national organization brings. (However, there's no public brand name involved.) For a relatively modest fee (sometimes pegged to sales volume), an independent agency can affiliate itself with a consortium organization. In turn, the consortium forges preferred-supplier relationships on behalf of its member agencies and provides them with marketing aid, training support, financial advice, and possibly a 24-hour backup reservation service. Some small or medium-sized chains also join consortia to further leverage their position in the industry. Some examples of large consortia: Vacation.com, Signature Travel Network, Ensemble, and Virtuoso.

Not all travel agencies are full service. A few only sell tours or ski packages. Some concentrate almost exclusively on business travel. And a good number sell only cruises.

Cruise-only agencies (sometimes called *cruise-oriented agencies*) are specialists. They pride themselves on their especially deep knowledge of ships, cruise lines, and ports. They may sell air and lodging but only in conjunction with cruises. (They usually tap into the cruise line's air and hotel inventory.) Cruise-onlys can be independent, belong to a consortium, or be part of a chain. There are even cruise-only consortia and chains.

Although travel agencies powerfully dominate cruise sales, other sellers of cruises exist. *Online* companies sell cruises via the Internet. *Tour companies* sell cruises through their catalogs and other promotional avenues. They may even offer special group activities for their clients onboard, fold shore excursions into their package, and provide a tour director to tend to the group's shipboard needs. *Cruise consolidators* buy blocks of staterooms from the lines, often for resale at a discounted price and at the last minute (when a cruise line is trying to sell remaining inventory). Cruise consolidators generally sell through toll-free numbers or the Internet. *Incentive companies* buy space from cruise lines for special cruise experiences they arrange for major corporations. (Incentives will be explained in Chapter 10.) And *intermediary companies* (especially in Canada) buy cruises in volume, package them with air, tours, and other components, and then resell them to travel agencies, sometimes offering a higher commission than the agency could get directly from the cruise line.

The cruise lines do sell direct to the public too, but most carefully avoid letting this erode their relationship with the travel agency community. A few don't permit the public to buy from them directly at all. Some omit their toll-free numbers from their brochures, directing the reader to "see your professional travel agent." Still others list their toll-free numbers and Web site addresses but only as an information source for consumers or to reach those who would never use the services of a travel agent, no matter what. Cruise lines also provide group space directly to groups, clubs, and associations, who in turn sell special cruise departures to their members. Such special group cruises are also often arranged through travel agencies.

In general, travel agencies sell a cruise for the same price as the cruise line does. However, rarely is the price identical to what the brochure indicates. Early booking incentives, two-for-one offers, and other promotional discount strategies often lead to a lower price (which further underscores buying a cruise as a "deal"). If the cruise line is offering such a deal, the travel agency can offer the very same one too.

Or better, they can offer "preferred" deals to their clients. Cruise lines routinely identify those agencies, consortia, or chains that sell—or whom they *wish* to sell—a large volume of their products. These productive agencies—through a negotiated process—become preferred sellers of the cruise line products. In turn, the agencies refer to the cruise line with whom they have a special relationship as a "preferred" vendor.

What are the advantages of being a preferred agency?

- The agency may be capable of offering its clients a *better cruise deal* than their competitors.

- The agency may be able to offer the client certain *value-added benefits,* such as an automatic two-class stateroom upgrade at no extra charge.

- The cruise line may provide promotional items and **co-op funds** (money that goes toward advertising) to help the agency promote its offerings.

- The cruise line may allow access to *inventory* that others cannot readily get. (In cruise lingo, inventory represents staterooms available.)

- Because agents have to *master only a few products* (typically, an agency will have only a few preferred cruise lines), they can better explain those products to their customers.

- *If a problem occurs, it's easier to resolve* the issue with someone you know—the preferred cruise line.
- The agency typically gets a *higher commission* for their sales performance.

This brings us to an important topic: How do travel agencies make money? When a travel agency sells a cruise, it receives a commission for its efforts. The minimum base commission is 10% of the stateroom sale price. So, if an agent sells a $2,000 cruise, the agency will receive $200 from the cruise line. Excluded are add-on costs, such as port charges and taxes, which yield no commission. Air transportation provided by the cruise line may generate 5%.

If they enjoy a preferred arrangement, the cruise line will give the agency a commission over and above the base commission, known as an **override commission**. The greater the agency's productivity (or perhaps that of its consortium or chain), the greater the override might be. Sometimes, the commission structure is based on productivity levels. For instance, an agency might receive 10% for the first 10 staterooms it sells in a given year, 12% on the next 10, and so on, up to as high as 18%. In other cases, the agency or chain's proven productivity level results in a 15% to 18% commission on all sales during the given year.

In 1996, most airlines capped at $50 the commissions that a travel agency could receive from selling air tickets. Prior to 1996, for example, a $2,000 ticket would have yielded $200 to the agency. After the policy change, that same ticket generated only $50. The lifeblood of agency profitability had been cut severely. It got worse in 2001, when most airlines totally eliminated commissions.

Agencies immediately searched for new profit centers. Cruises were an obvious choice. To sell a cruise was to receive at least 10% commission on most of what a client bought on vacation: lodging, transportation, meals, entertainment, pre- and post-cruise packages, and more. Air bought from the cruise lines (to get the client to and from the port) might also yield 5% on the cost of the ticket. (Usually, the maximum commission applies only to the cruise package itself, not the air.) The most successful agencies, therefore, weaned themselves off their dependency on air tickets and shifted their attention toward selling the much more lucrative cruise experiences.

Travel agencies typically have two kinds of salespersons: *inside* and *outside* sales representatives. An inside salesperson works at the agency, fielding calls, responding to e-mail, and dealing with walk-in business. They may be paid straight salary or a percentage of their commissions. In many cases, agents receive a base salary *and* a percentage of commissions.

Outside salespersons—also called *home-based agents*—are allied to an agency and sell to the general public, often—but not necessarily—to friends, acquaintances, or customers referred by them. Paid a percentage of the commission, they usually work out of their homes, although they may come into the agency to access its resources or to have an inside agent complete the transaction for them. In some cases, these outside salespeople are part of a chain-like enterprise composed entirely of home-based agents, called a *host agency*. Typically, the agent—like all agents—asks the client questions and then makes a recommendation based on that client's travel needs. He or she then turns over the client to the host agency's central phone booking center or Web site to handle the actual details of the trip.

Associations and Training

How does a travel agent learn about cruise products and how to sell them most efficiently? Cruise lines may offer agents individualized print materials, videos, CD-ROMs, DVDs, Internet training sites, visits to agencies by their sales representatives, seminars at key city locations, presentations at conferences, and inspections of their ships. See Figure 5-2 for a ship inspection form. Cruise lines also make it easy for travel agents to take cruises at a very reduced price—sometimes individually; sometimes with a group of other agents. These are called **familiarization cruises**, or **fams**, and they permit agents to have firsthand experience with the cruise product—the kind that helps them to better sell cruise vacations to their customers.

The Cruise Lines International Association (CLIA), which represents the vast majority of cruise companies, also makes available a highly diversified mix of training products and events. Indeed, CLIA's training program is regularly rated as the best in the travel business. Travel agents employed by CLIA-affiliated agencies may enroll in its Cruise Counsellor certification program. They can achieve three levels of certification: Accredited Cruise Counsellor (ACC), Master Cruise Counsellor (MCC), or Elite Cruise Counsellor (ECC). Credits are earned via a combination of classroom, Internet, and/or video training; cruise experience; attendance at CLIA-endorsed conferences; ship inspections; analysis of case studies; cabins sales; and even by studying this book. After completion of each training component, the certification candidate must pass an exam. For more details, you may contact CLIA at the address given in Appendix B.

In 2006, CLIA merged with the International Council of Cruise Lines (ICCL), which participates in the regulatory and policy development process on matters having to do with the environment, medical facilities, passenger protection, public health, safety, and security. Also, the Niche Cruise Marketing Alliance (NCMA) represents cruise lines with unusual and distinct cruise products. Some lines belong to both CLIA and the NCMA.

Here are some other North American organizations that offer education in cruise-related topics:

- The Association of Canadian Travel Associations (ACTA) is a nonprofit trade association of travel agencies and suppliers who work together for the promotion, improvement, and advancement of the travel industry, while safeguarding the interests of the traveling public.

- The American Society of Travel Agents (ASTA) is a trade association that enhances the professionalism and profitability of member agents through effective representation in industry and government affairs, education, and training and by identifying and meeting the needs of the traveling public.

Name of Ship _____

Date of Inspection _____

Inspected by _____

In Port _____

At Sea _____

Checklist for Shipboard Inspections

Instructions: Identify each stateroom, restaurant or other facility inspected in the space provided and make appropriate comments. Review completed checklist with colleagues and insert into your travel agents' Cruise Manual.

1. Passengers' accommodations	Cabin ___	Cabin ___	Cabin ___	Cabin ___
Size of room ___				
Berth arrangement (upper/lower/sofa, etc.) ___				
Furniture comfort & arrangement ___				
Windows and portholes (sealed at sea) ___				
Floor covering ___				
Decor ___				
Self-controlled air temp. ___				
Television/radio ___				
Lighting ___				
Drawer space ___				
Wardrobe space ___				
Bathroom facilities ___				
Convenience Items				
Clothes hangers ___				
Clothes hooks ___				
Writing shelf ___				
Night light ___				
Reading light ___				
110 v electricity for hair blowers ___				
Refrigerator ___				
Potable water ___				
Bottle opener ___				
Clothes line ___				
2. Cabin service				
Promptness ___				
Courtesy ___				
Professionalism ___				
Efficiency ___				
Food and beverages ___				
Quality ___				
Quantity ___				
Eye appeal ___				
Hot/cold ___				

3. Entertainment	Professional	Movies	Semi-professional	Crew sponsored
Quality ___				
Frequency ___				
Variety ___				
Audience reaction ___				

FIGURE 5-2   CLIA's ship inspection form
Source: *Courtesy of CLIA*

4. **Restaurant**
    Seating arrangements
    Tables for two _____
                    four _____
                    six _____
                    eight _____
                    twelve _____
    Cleanliness _____
    Lighting _____
    Air conditioning _____
    Seating comfort _____
    Noise level _____
    Service
        Promptness _____
        Courtesy _____
        Professionalism _____
        Efficiency _____
    Food
        Quality _____
        Quantity _____
        Eye appeal _____
        Served hot (cold) _____
        Special diets available _____

5. **Lounges & other public rooms**
    Seating arrangements _____
    Seating comfort _____
    Cleanliness _____
    Lighting _____
    Air conditioning _____
    Acoustics _____
    Dance areas _____
    Bar accessibility _____
    View of sea _____

6. **Lido and deck area**
    Size _____
    Spaciousness _____
    Shaded areas _____
    Deck chairs _____
    Food & beverage service _____
    Deck surface _____
    Pool features _____
    Handrails _____

7. **Theater**
    Obstruction of view _____
    Air conditioning _____
    Acoustics _____
    Lighting _____

Seating comfort _____
Accessibility _____
_____
_____

8. **Passageways**
    Lighting _____
    Handrails _____
    Ashtrays _____
    Floor covering _____
    Width _____
    Height _____
    _____
    _____

9. **Service areas**
    Shops _____
    Drug store _____
    Beauty & barber shop _____
    Photo shop _____
    Tour office _____
    Purser's office _____
    _____

10. **Miscellaneous**
    Medical facilities _____
    Chapel facilities _____
    Casino
        Slots only _____
        Full casino _____
    Health club _____
    Sauna _____
    Indoor pool _____
    Children's playroom _____

11. **Pier facilities**
    Lighting _____
    Heating _____
    Ventilation _____
    Cleanliness _____
    Baggage handling
    areas _____
    Customs inspection
    facilities _____
    Parking facilities
    (indoor/outdoor) _____
    _____
    _____

FIGURE 5-2 (Continued)
Source: *Courtesy of CLIA*

- The Association of Retail Travel Agents (ARTA) is an organization that provides a forum for travel agents (especially at small- and medium-sized agencies) to emphasize to both the consumer and the supplier the important role they play in providing professional, unbiased travel information.

- The Canadian Institute of Travel Counsellors (CITC) encourages education and professionalism in the travel industry through support services, such as seminars, courses, agent education trips, newsletters, and special events.

- The International Airlines Travel Agent Network (IATAN), a wholly owned subsidiary of the International Air Transport Association (IATA), is a not-for-profit organization committed to upholding professional travel business standards. Among other things, it provides education and identifies travel professionals who are entitled to industry benefits.

- The National Association of Career Travel Agents (NACTA) is an association of travel industry cruise-oriented travel agencies, independent travel agencies, and other agencies that work with outside sales and independent contractors.

- The National Association of Cruise-Oriented Agencies (NACOA) is a nonprofit trade association of travel agencies whose members have made significant professional commitment to the cruise vacation product. It is the only agency association dedicated to cruise specialists.

- The National Tour Association (NTA) is a professional trade association for the packaged travel industry, made up of tour operators, destination marketing organizations, and the suppliers (including cruise lines) that service them.

Gracious service and pampering are high on a cruiser's wish list.
Courtesy of Windstar Cruises

- The Outside Sales Support Network (OSSN) is an association established to represent independent travel contractor needs, providing education, fam training programs, and marketing directives to help sell and promote travel products for the outside travel agent.

- The Society of Incentive and Travel Executives (SITE) is a worldwide organization of business professionals dedicated to the recognition development of motivational and performance improvement strategies involving, among other things, cruises.

- The Travel Institute (formerly the Institute of Certified Travel Agents) is a non-profit organization that has educated travel industry professionals for more than 40 years. Through quality training and certification programs, the Travel Institute ensures that travel agents are skilled professionals who can expertly satisfy their clients' travel needs.

- The University of Travel is an association that has provided training to thousands of travel professionals. It makes available a wide variety of courses via video, audio, and live seminars, usually as part of a fam cruise. Well-known trainers and speakers, some from CLIA, deliver many of the courses.

Working for the Cruise Lines

How easy is it to get a job in the cruise industry? For land-based employment, it's certainly feasible. Like any major company, a big cruise line employs hundreds or thousands of people at all levels—from receptionists through reservationists on up to executives—but you generally need to live near its headquarters. Most cruise lines are located in the Miami–Fort Lauderdale area. A few large cruise lines have home offices in the Seattle, Los Angeles, or New York City areas.

It's easier to work your way up in the cruise industry than in many other businesses. Most cruise executives started in entry-level positions. Talent is very much cultivated from within.

If you don't live near a cruise line's home office location, three other kinds of land-based jobs are possible. Most cruise lines employ a limited number of people—usually part-time—at their pier embarkation facilities. In Alaska, many cruise companies own tour operators, hotels, and rail services, providing a substantial number of seasonal jobs. Business development managers (BDM) and multiline reps, of course, can represent their cruise lines in any of a number of major North American cities. BDM jobs, though, are hard to get. Many BDMs are former travel agents.

Working at sea is more problematic. Most U.S.-headquartered cruise line staff comes from non-English-speaking countries (although they're expected to be relatively fluent in English). The best job opportunities for English speakers are staff positions in shops, the spa, the casino, the children's activity area, the purser's office, and the medical facility. Sports personnel, shore excursion staff, hairdressers, photographers, entertainers, and the cruise director are also likely to come from English-speaking countries. Officers generally are European and have prior navy and/or merchant marine service experience. The rest of the crew—the dining, kitchen and beverage staff, stewards, and maintenance workers—tends to come from Eastern Europe, Asia, Africa, Latin America, and the Caribbean.

What are the benefits of working on a ship? Topping the list: the opportunity to see the world—and get paid for it. This is especially true with cruise lines that operate nonrepeating, one-way itineraries year-round across the globe. Most likely to have free time in port are employees whose job load lightens when most passengers are off the ship, such as casino and spa staff as well as entertainers. Other benefits of working on a cruise ship are *gratuities* (mostly for food and beverage personnel and stateroom stewards) and the opportunity *to meet interesting passengers* from around the world. Also, most normal day-to-day expenses, such as meals, accommodations, and laundry, are taken care of. The result: It isn't how much you earn but how much you save that will determine how profitable your job will be.

Of course, there's a downside. Working on a cruise isn't a job; it's a lifestyle—one that you must be psychologically equipped for. Most ships (even those headquartered in the United States) are registered in foreign, developing countries and fly "flags of convenience." U.S. labor laws don't apply. Daily working hours are long, often with split shifts (e.g., you work from 6 A.M. to 3 P.M. and then from 8 P.M. to 11 P.M.)—and that's usually six or seven days a week. Salaries are relatively high for officers and senior staff; others are paid well below minimum wage. There's very little job security and few workers' rights. And accommodations are tight and spartan. Officers and senior staff get private cabins, but most other crew members sleep two, three, or four to a room, depending on how high up they are in the ship's job hierarchy.

One exception to the above: Cruise vessels that travel entirely domestic itineraries must observe the work laws of that country. For example, a riverboat that plies the Mississippi River must follow U.S. labor regulations for its staff. Also, expert lecturers don't follow the normal employee pattern. They usually get a free cruise and a regular passenger stateroom in exchange for their services. Salary is rarely involved (except sometimes for celebrity lecturers).

Suppose you do indeed want to work on a cruise ship. How do you get that job? Two paths exist. One is to contact the cruise line itself. Most provide a system for would-be employees to contact them and that, in some cases, lists those positions that are open and what qualifications are needed. These systems are generally Web- or phone-based. A second path is to contact a concessioner that does the hiring for the cruise line. Concessioners tend to handle onboard store, spa, entertainment, and lecturer positions.

To maximize your chances of success, your application should reflect a clear idea of which job area you're interested in and a familiarity with the profile of the cruise line you're applying to. In most cases, you must be at least 21 years old. If you do get a job offer, take it even if it's not precisely what you want. Once aboard, you may be able to break out of your job description after proving your worth. Also, note that you'll be a contracted worker. Such contracts tend to be anywhere from three months to a year (eight to nine months is typical), with the rest of the year off without salary. Afterward, if you've done a good job, you may be offered a new contract.

For more about cruise line employment, see the reference works listed in Appendix C.

Questions for Discussion

1. Briefly describe the responsibilities of each of the following:

   - captain

   - chief purser

   - cruise director

   - executive chef

   - cabin steward

2. Briefly explain how the land-based operations are typically organized.

3. Why do most consumers buy cruises through a travel agent? Why do travel agents like selling cruises to them?

4. Describe four kinds of travel agencies.

Activity

Interview someone you know who has been on a cruise (*not* someone in the travel industry). Ask the person the questions given below. Then, summarize the responses in the spaces given.

Name of the person interviewed:

1. Did you buy your cruise through a travel agent? Why or why not? Had you ever used a travel agent before?

2. In your opinion, who are the three most important cruise line staff members you came in contact with during your cruise? Why did you choose these three?

3. Did you ever entertain the thought of being a travel agent? Of working on a cruise ship (and in what capacity)? Why or why not?

Chapter 6

The Pre-, Post-, and Off-Ship Cruise Experience

Courtesy of Carnival Cruise Lines

After reading this chapter, you'll be able to:

- Categorize various types of pre-cruise and post-cruise options.
- Describe how shore excursions enhance a cruise.
- Explain how a cruise experience is perceived differently according to client types.

A s we've seen, what passengers can experience on a cruise ship are varied and impressive. Indeed, "cruises to nowhere," transoceanic voyages, and repositioning cruises manage to keep guests quite busy.

However, on most cruises, what takes place on *shore* is often crucial to the passenger's vacation. These port experiences can be divided into three categories: *pre-cruise, intermediary port stops,* and *post-cruise.*

Pre-Cruise Packages

Clients will sometimes travel to their cruise embarkation point and go directly to the ship. Often, though, they'll spend a day or more exploring the port. The simplest of pre-cruise experiences is the **air/sea package**. Usually through a travel agent, the passenger will purchase air, the airport-to-dock transfer, and perhaps lodging. The package can be obtained either from the cruise line itself or it can be arranged independently, component by component (e.g., the travel agent will book the flight, transfers, and hotel separately).

What are the advantages—both to the client and the agent—of purchasing a pre- or post-cruise package through the cruise line?

- One phone call or computer transaction can set up the whole package.
- The agent will probably receive a commission on the air portion—not likely if it were booked through the airline.
- Some or all transfers (e.g., airport-to-pier, hotel-to-pier, etc.) may be included in the package price. This could be quite valuable: In some cities, a taxi from the airport to the city or pier costs over $50 one way.
- The cruise line's *air deviation desk personnel* (flight specialists accessed by telephone) and meet-and-greet staff are there to help out if a problem occurs.
- Air and/or lodging rates may be lower via the cruise line or the flight may even be included in the cruise package price. (This latter arrangement, once common, has become increasingly rare.)

There can also be some advantages to arranging the pre-cruise experience directly with non-cruise-line suppliers.

- The selection of airlines and flights may be better.
- The airfares may be lower than those offered by the cruise lines. (This is a case-by-case situation.)

One common misconception: If a passenger misses his or her cruise line–arranged connection to the ship (e.g., a flight is late or canceled), the cruise line will obtain, at no extra cost, a later flight that will connect to the ship's next port of call. This is only sometimes true. The cruise line's personnel will do all that they can with the airline to solve the problem. Ultimately, though, it's the airline's decision. More often than not, no matter how much the cruise line pleads, the airline *will* charge the passenger for the extra flight to the next port of call.

This is why it's so important for a cruise client to take travel insurance (and for a travel agent to offer it). For a relatively reasonable fee, a cruiser can purchase insurance that will reimburse costs because of such things as:

A shore excursion brings a whole new perspective to Amsterdam.
Courtesy of AMAWATERWAYS

- Trip cancellation, delay, or interruption
- Lost or stolen luggage
- Medical expenses for accident or sickness incurred onboard or overseas (including emergency transfer from the ship)

Most travel insurance policies also offer access to a toll-free number. This number puts the client in contact with a multilingual help desk that provides advice, assistance, and even access to physicians in the event of an emergency beyond what the ship's staff can provide.

Both cruise lines and independent insurers offer travel insurance. Since problems may well go beyond an individual's or a cruise line's ability to resolve them without incurring cost, travel insurance is a very wise investment. However, because insurance benefits, conditions, exclusions, and coverage are complicated and change constantly, it's important to clarify your options and make careful comparisons before deciding which provider to buy from.

Cruise Itineraries

As you learned in Chapter 1, two major itinerary types exist: *round-trip* or *circle* (the vessel leaves from and returns to the same port) and *one-way* (the cruise begins at one port and finishes at another).

Round-trip itineraries tend to predominate at mass-market destinations such as the Caribbean. How a one-way itinerary is used, however, differs. Cruise lines that serve mass-market customers and destinations will use a one-way itinerary when logistics dictate that they should. For example, a round-trip Vancouver-Anchorage-Vancouver voyage would be very long and/or require too many days at sea. More manageable is a Vancouver-Anchorage one-way itinerary, followed by an Anchorage-Vancouver voyage carrying a whole new set of passengers.

An increasingly popular pre-cruise option is the wedding package. Thousands of marriages take place aboard ship each year. A common pattern: The ceremony and reception take place on the ship prior to departure—that way, guests can attend. After they disembark, the ship departs, and the couple sail off on their honeymoon.

Some lines—upscale ones, primarily—favor another type of one-way pattern. They will offer, say, a seven-day Lisbon-Morocco-Gibraltar-Barcelona itinerary, followed by another seven-day itinerary that goes from Barcelona to the Balearic Islands, Corsica, and finish at Rome's port. They may then operate a five-day

A visit to a private tropical island. A very popular off-ship experience.
Courtesy of Carnival Cruise Lines

cruise around Italy to Greece. (If you have trouble picturing this, see the maps on pages 115 and 116.)

Why do they do this? First, it permits vacationers to combine voyages, creating their own extended itinerary. (Sometimes, the cruise line offers them a discount on the subsequent cruise.) Also, it might be hard for the cruise lines to fill their ships with repeating itineraries, back-to-back, over a season, like mass-market ships do. Some lines even permit passengers to begin and end their cruises at whichever port they want, creating an even more customized itinerary.

Intermediary Port Stops and Shore Excursions

As you've no doubt concluded, most ships call on several ports as part of their sailing itineraries. When passengers arrive at each intermediate place visited, they have five options:

1. **They may purchase a shore excursion through the cruise line.** The advantages: The quality of the shore excursion provider has been pre-assessed by the cruise line; buying excursions onboard, before arriving at the port, is convenient and easy; the excursion takes into consideration ship meal and departure times; a ship employee usually accompanies the group; if something goes wrong and a delay occurs, the ship will almost certainly wait for the excursion group's return before departing.

2. **They may buy it through a shore excursion company.** Often contracted in advance through a travel agency group, these companies have a network of port-based tour operators whose prices are slightly lower than those of the cruise lines.

3. **They may buy a tour or activity (e.g., a dive package) from vendors who usually await them at or near the dock.** They may be transported via a motorcoach, van, taxi, or even a private car. Private excursions by bus are often a little less expensive, but there are two problems: There's almost no way to pre-assess the quality of the offering. Also, as indicated earlier, if the tour gets back to the ship late, the ship may have already left.

4. **They may simply explore the port and its environs on their own.** They can stroll a picturesque street, do some shopping, and engage in whatever else pleases them. For their reference, the cruise line or travel agent may provide a map of the port. Passengers can even go back to the ship for lunch and then return to the port for the afternoon.

5. **They may elect to stay onboard to relax, get some sun, and feel like they have the ship almost all to themselves (e.g., there's little problem getting a spa appointment or having easy access to health club equipment).** A common reason to stay onboard at a port: The passenger has already had an in-depth visit of the port.

In a few rare cases (very upscale lines or river-based ships), some or all of the shore excursions are included in the cruise price. Most often, though, passengers buy them from the cruise line. This can be done in advance of sailing (through

A ship launches its own water excursions: sailing, waterskiing, and windsurfing.
Courtesy of Windstar Cruises

a mail-in form included with the passenger's cruise documents or, increasingly, booked online) or onboard ship by:

- Filling out a form that's in the stateroom upon check-in and then turning it in at the shore excursion desk (usually near the purser's office)
- Buying it at the shore excursion desk during its open hours (there may be a waiting line, especially on the first day) or from a concierge (for passengers on an all-suite concierge level)
- On some ships, purchasing it interactively via the in-room TV

Passengers find out about the content of each shore excursion through the cruise line's Web site, literature sent in advance of the sailing, in-cabin brochures, video presentations, port talks (usually held the day before arrival at each port), and/or the onboard cruise orientation meeting (which, like the port talks, will be televised into staterooms live and repeated during the day). Shore excursion personnel onboard the ship are also quite happy to counsel passengers individually on which port experiences might be best for them.

Categories of Shore Excursions

Shore excursions come in every size, shape, and theme. They can be divided into three broad categories:

1. **Sightseeing excursions.** A group of people on a motorcoach—is this what sightseeing is all about? Not always. You could take a train from Skagway through the White Pass and Yukon Route. You might take an Atlantis Submarine ride down to view the coral reefs of Barbados or perhaps a seaplane over

New Zealand's fjords and icefields. Even a walking tour of New Orleans's Vieux Carre qualifies.

2. **Sports excursions.** Golf, tennis, sailing, snorkeling—you name the activity, and if it can be done at a particular port, there's probably a shore excursion that will make it possible.

3. **Miscellaneous excursions.** Shore excursions may take you to a faraway beach (e.g., Virgin Gorda's The Baths), to a legendary shopping area (e.g., Beverly Hills's Rodeo Drive), or to a world-class museum (e.g., St. Petersburg's Hermitage).

For more examples of shore excursion options, see Figures 6-1 and 6-2. Veteran cruisers are especially savvy about shore excursions. Here are a few things they—and you—should know:

- Because ships often arrive at a port early in the morning and leave around dinner time, it's often possible to take two shore excursions in one day.

- Shore excursions that include a meal often represent an especially good value.

- Sometimes, hundreds of people sign up for the same shore excursion, and a half-dozen buses will be waiting for them near the dock. The earlier you disembark, the easier it will be to take the first coach to depart and return—leaving you more time later in the day. Also, cruise ships don't always tie up at the dock. Because of the ship's draft and the harbor's depth, a ship may need to stay offshore and transfer passengers to the dock via small boats called tenders. (This is called *tendering.*) Again, if you can take one of the first tenders out, you'll have more time later in the day.

- The larger the ship, the more shore excursion choices are likely to be available. Indeed, some see this as an advantage of a larger vessel.

- Certain cruise lines are very destination-focused. Expect them to offer more ports on an itinerary and more shore excursions (or a few very unique shore excursions) at each port. Other lines put great emphasis on the onboard cruise experience and less on the ports. Some manage to do both.

- Independent concessioners usually operate shore excursions. Cruise lines do all they can to select quality excursion operators—after all, it reflects on their reputation. In some places (especially in Alaska), the cruise line may actually own the local tour operation, assuring even greater quality control.

Post-Cruise Packages

Post-cruise packages are exactly like pre-cruise ones. They're sold the same way. They represent the same possible components, options, and experiences. Some passengers prefer to do a package before their cruise, others after, still others before *and* after. Most people, however, don't schedule any at all. They just fly to the port on the day of departure and fly out the day the ship returns.

One issue that does sometimes come up: If a vacationer wants to expand the trip beyond the cruise but time constraints permit only *one* add-on package (pre- or post-), which should it be? Usually, the pre-cruise package is preferable because

Philipsburg, (Dutch) St. Maarten—Tuesday (8:00 am–6:00 pm)

SHORE EXCURSION		DESCRIPTION	DURATION	DEPARTS	# OF TICKETS
St. Maarten Island Tour		This island's two country existence makes for an interesting sight-seeing tour. All by air-conditioned buses, this tour covers everything from Philipsburg to Marigot. Shopping on the French side included.	3 hrs	1:30 pm	$21 adult ____ $11 child ____
Pinel Island Snorkel Tour		Enjoy beach snorkeling over coral reefs, sunbathe or explore the island. *Some nudity may be observed.*	3 hrs	8:00 am 12:45 pm	$35 each ____
Explorer Cruise & Grand Island Tour		Enjoy the cool breezes, rum punch and live music as you cruise to the French capitol, Marigot. Enjoy one hour of shopping or sight-seeing before you board a bus for a short, guided island tour back to the ship.	4 hrs	8:45 am	$45 adult ____ $25 child ____
'Everyt'ing Cool' Beach Break with Lunch		This is a great value for one of the coolest hangouts on the island! You get one of their famous large frozen drinks, a sandwich, locker rental, full-size floating mat, volleyball and changing facilities PLUS this beach spot has a great **LIVE BAND** considered one of the best on the islands! *Transportation to downtown not included.*		At leisure	$20 each ____
"America's Cup" Sailing Regatta ★		Brag for a lifetime! Thrill to *America's Cup* racing aboard *Stars & Stripes Canada II, True North* and others. Under the guidance of your experienced crew, you will be given the task of operating the yacht in an actual *America's Cup* shortened course! *Minimum age: 12. Can be strenuous based on level of participation. Get $30 off a Massage, Facial or Body Treatment in the Day Spa with this tour. Valid Tuesday only.*	3 hrs	A - 11:45 am B - 1:30 pm	$78 each ____
St. Martin Beach Rendezvous		Celebrate your vacation with our most deluxe beach package! After a 25 minute narrated island drive, Orient Beach is yours to relax and enjoy! Includes 2 drinks, lounge chair and a sit-down lunch at one of the gorgeous French beach restaurants. *Showers available. Some nudity may be observed.*	4½ hrs	9:30 am	$49 adult ____ $36 child ____
Land & Sea Island Tour (*Semi-Submarine*)		A great combination that explores the island, including an hour of free time at the French capital of Marigot, together with an exploration by semi-sub of some of the island's interesting coral reefs.	3½ hrs	12:45 pm	$45 adult ____ $25 child ____
Golden Eagle Island Sailaway ★		What a way to vacation! A pampering crew will whisk you away to the fabulous French island of Tintamar: a true vacationer's dream! Ideal for sunbathing and snorkeling, plus an open bar is included. Snorkel equipment available at no extra charge. Shaded areas available. *Get $30 off a Massage, Facial or Body Treatment in the Day Spa with this tour. Valid Tuesday only.*	4 hrs	8:30 am	$69 adult ____ $40 child ____
Shipwreck Snorkel Adventure		Great if you want a lot of time to snorkel. Here you can enjoy 2½ hours of snorkeling in Shipwreck Cove over tropical reefs teaming with fish. Complimentary rum or fruit punch and water included.	3 hrs	1:00 pm	$42 each ____
Lagoon Kayaking Adventure		Enjoy paddling in kayaks through one of the largest salt water lagoons in the Caribbean followed by a relaxing beach stop. *Bottled water provided. Minimum age: 12.*	3½ hrs	12:15 pm	$69 each ____
St. Martin Mountain Bike Adventure		Explore the beautiful French side in an off-road coastline hugging adventure with 21-speed mountain bikes. Great local guides and a beach stop at Friars Bay. *Wear swimsuit under clothes/closed-toe shoes. Min age: 12.*	3½ hrs	8:00 am	$68 each ____
Butterfly Farm and Marigot		Experience the beautifully landscaped gardens and colorful butterflies as you are guided through the "Butterfly Sphere". Afterwards enjoy one hour of free time in the charming French capitol of Marigot.	3½ hrs	1:15 pm	$34 adult ____ $30 child ____
St. Maarten Scuba Diving *with or without equipment*		In order to assure maximum visibility, the two-tank dive site will be dependent upon sea conditions. *Certified divers only. Minimum age: 12. $89 for all equipment $79 if you only need tanks & weight belt. Guests must have dived within the last two years.*	4 hrs	8:00 am No equipment ⇨	$89 each ____ $79 each ____
Discover Scuba Diving		No certification required. After beach training and written test, you will go on a 25ft one-tank guided dive. *Several dive sites to choose from. Sites are dependent upon sea conditions. Minimum age: 12.*	3½ hrs	1:00 pm	$99 each ____

Castries, St. Lucia—Wednesday (10:00 am–6:00 pm)

SHORE EXCURSION		DESCRIPTION	DURATION	DEPARTS	# OF TICKETS
Island Splendour		This delightful drive encompasses scenic views, banana plantations, vibrant tropical foliage, island art and insight into St. Lucia's historical past. Among the stops is La Toc Battery, a 19th century British fort.	3½ hrs	12:45 pm	$32 adult ____ $22 child ____
North Coast and Beach Tour		This value package allows you to see the city sights and surrounding area, including Pigeon Island Park together with 1½ hours on the golden sands of the exclusive resort area. *Changing rooms available.*	4 hrs	12:15 pm	$35 adult ____ $25 child ____
Land and Sea to Soufrière		Drive to see not only the 2,500ft Pitons near Soufrière, but also the world's only drive-in volcano, the Diamond Botanical Garden & Waterfall, plus enjoy the 75ft catamaran for a scenic sail and swim!	7 hrs	10:10 am	$72 adult ____ $38 child ____
Catamaran Cruise to Morne Coubaril Estate		It's a relaxing and scenic sail to Soufrière in a 60ft catamaran. See the famous Pitons before driving to Sulpher Springs and the plantation of Morne Coubaril. Swimming at Anse Cochon & Creole lunch included.	7 hrs	10:30 am	$72 adult ____ $38 child ____
Forest and Sulphurous Hiking Adventure		Hike through the forests outside Soufrière to a beautiful waterfall, home to an exotic pool of volcano-heated water rich with nutrients. *Creole lunch included. Wear swimsuit under clothes & comfortable shoes.*	7 hrs	10:20 am	$69 adult ____ $35 child ____
Deep Sea Fishing		Fully equipped boats in search of Blue Marlin and other big game fish. Fish are tag & release or, if required, will be kept by the boat and captain. Trolling lines are rotated throughout the tour. *Beverages provided.*	4 hrs	12:45 pm	$130 each ____
Country Saddles Horseback Adventure		A scenic 1¼ hour horseback ride along a river into forests and pastures to cliffs overlooking the Atlantic. Wear long pants and close toed shoes. *Minimum age: 10 (with experience). Maximum weight: 230lbs.*	4 hrs	A- 10:40 am B - 12:40 pm	$69 each ____
St. Lucia Beach Snorkel ★		This exclusive 1½ hour snorkel expedition takes you by boat to a live coral reef near the Pitons teaming with colorful tropical fish. Over 150 fish species have been identified here. *Minimum age: 5. Get $30 off a Massage, Facial or Body Treatment in the Day Spa with this tour. Valid Wednesday only.*	3½ hrs	12:15 pm	$72 each ____
Jungle Bike, Land & Sea Adventure ★		Extreme! Choose a trail and get into the jungle for an awesome 2 hour bike ride. (Snorkeling optional.) *Min. age: 12. Min. height: 5ft. Wear closed-toe shoes. Helmets, lockers & changing rooms provided. Get $30 off a Massage, Facial or Body Treatment in the Day Spa with this tour. Valid Wednesday only.*	4½ hrs	11:45 am	$86 each ____
4x4 Off Road Adventure & Hike		Get into this amazing island by 4×4 vehicle, then hike into the forest and along the rivers and waterfalls of Anse La Raye Valley. *Not for guests with any physical limitations. Wear swimsuit under clothes.*	3½ hrs	10:20 am	$48 each ____
Cap Estate Country Club		*For more information, pick up a Golf Ahoy! information packet at the Explorations! Desk, Deck 4.*	5 hrs	10:00 am	$81 each ____
Sandals St. Lucia Golf		*For more information, pick up a Golf Ahoy! information packet at the Explorations! Desk, Deck 4.* **This is a 9-hole only course. The rate listed is for 9-holes of play only.**	5 hrs	10:00 am	$80 each ____

FIGURE 6-1   Caribbean shore excursions
Source: *Courtesy of Royal Caribbean International*

CRYSTAL SYMPHONY
TOUR ORDER FORM
CIVITAVECCHIA, ITALY TO VENICE, ITALY
AUGUST 20 TO SEPTEMBER 1

ADRIATIC ADVENTURE
CRUISE # 0215

Important Notice:
Many Shore Excursions
are very limited.
Therefore, we suggest
booking early to avoid
disappointment

NAME: _____

STATEROOM: _____

ROOM - MATES REQUIRING SEPARATE CHARGES

YES

Tour Code	SHORE EXCURSIONS	Departure Time	Approximate Duration	Cost Per Person	Tickets Requested
MONTE CARLO, MONACO: ANCHOR ON TUESDAY, AUGUST 22, AT 8:00AM. SAIL ON WEDNESDAY, AUGUST 23, AT 1:00AM.					
MCF-A	Medieval Eze and Monaco ◈	9:00am	4 hrs	$59.00	A
MCF-B	Nice and Eze ◈	8:15am	4 hrs	$56.00	B
MCF-E	Medieval Eze and Wine Tasting in Nice ◈	8:30am	4½ hrs	$89.00	E
MCF-F	Private Cooking Lesson at Le Moulin de Mougins ◈	8:30am	4½ hrs	$140.00	F
MCF-G	Côte d'Azur Helicopter Exploration and Monaco ◈	9:00am	4 hrs	$194.00	G
MCF-H	Visit to Cannes, Grasse and Saint-Paul-de-Vence ◈	8:30am	8½ hrs	$149.00	H
MCF-I	Eze, Nice and Monaco Full-Day Sightseeing ◈	8:45am	9 hrs	$154.00	I
	Afternoon Departures:				
MCF-C	Eze and Cap Ferrat ◈	1:30pm	4 hrs	$56.00	C
MCF-D	Saint-Paul-de -Vence ◈	1:30pm	4 hrs	$54.00	D
MCF-J	The Scenic French Riviera with Less Walking	2:00pm	3½ hrs	$49.00	J
PORTOFINO, ITALY: ANCHOR ON WEDNESDAY, AUGUST 23, FROM 8:00AM TO 5:00PM.					
POR-A	Rapallo and a Scenic Drive to Sestri Levante ◈	8:30am	4 hrs	$56.00	A
POR-B	Cruising the Italian Riviera	9:00am	3 hrs	$59.00	B
SORRENTO, ITALY: ANCHOR ON FRIDAY, AUGUST 25, FROM 8:00AM TO 6:00PM.					
SOR-A	The Excavations of Pompeii ◈	8:30am	5 hrs	$58.00	A
SOR-B	The Amalfi Drive	8:15am	8 hrs	$114.00	B
SOR-C	Pompeii and Herculaneum ◈	8:45am	8 hrs	$119.00	C
SOR-D	Exploring Positano and Ravello ◈	8:00am	8 hrs	$260.00	D
TAORMINA, SICILY, ITALY: ANCHOR ON SATURDAY, AUGUST 26, FROM 8:00AM TO 6:00PM.					
TAO-A	Scenic Taormina ◈	9:00am	4 hrs	$48.00	A
TAO-B	A Drive to Mt. Etna	8:30am	4½ hrs	$48.00	B
TAO-C	Taormina and Mt. Etna ◈	8:30am	8½ hrs	$106.00	C
VALLETTA, MALTA: DOCK ON SUNDAY, AUGUST 27, FROM 8:00AM TO 6:00PM.					
VAL-A	Views of Valletta and Mdina ◈	8:30am	4 hrs	$49.00	A
VAL-B	Malta with Less Walking	9:00am	4 hrs	$45.00	B
VAL-C	In-Depth Malta ◈	8:15am	8 hrs	$104.00	C

**THE DEADLINE FOR BOOKINGS AND CANCELLATIONS OF ALL SHORE EXCURSIONS AND
PRIVATE ARRANGEMENTS ARE LISTED BELOW**

Monte Carlo, France	Sunday	August 20	8:00pm
Portofino, Italy	Monday	August 21	7:00pm
Sorrento, Italy	Wednesday	August 23	7:00pm
Taormina, Italy	Thursday	August 24	7:00pm
Valletta, Malta	Thursday	August 24	7:00pm

FIGURE 6-2   Mediterranean shore excursions
Source: *Courtesy of Crystal Cruises*

Here's an example of a 12-day cruise tour of Canada and Alaska:

Day 1	Sail from Vancouver
Day 2	At sea
Day 3	Ketchikan, Alaska
Day 4	Juneau, Alaska
Day 5	Skagway, Alaska
Day 6	Glacier Bay Cruising, Alaska
Day 7	College Fjord Cruising, Alaska
Day 8	Whittier (Anchorage), Alaska; motorcoach from Whittier to Anchorage. Stop at the Alaska Wildlife Conservation Center and Alaska Native Heritage Center en route. Hotel accommodations in Anchorage.
Day 9	Travel by scenic railcars to Talkeetna. Motorcoach to the Mt. McKinley Princess Lodge for an afternoon of leisure and an overnight stay.
Day 10	Spend the day at leisure. Relax or choose from a variety of optional excursions.
Day 11	Motorcoach from McKinley to the Denali Princess Wilderness Lodge. Enjoy a natural history tour into the park. The evening is free to spend as you choose.
Day 12	Motorcoach to Fairbanks and then take a Sternwheeler Riverboat cruise. Evening at leisure in Fairbanks.
Day 13	Your cruise tour ends in Fairbanks.

Source: *Princess Cruises*

it helps guard against a delayed or canceled flight leading to a missed cruise departure. If a flight after the cruise is delayed or canceled, it simply means that the passenger will get home later, which is usually less troublesome than missing the cruise departure.

We've just described only the simplest of packages. Some are complex, lasting for several days or even *exceeding* the length of the cruise. This sort of package is often called a *cruise tour*.

Port Experiences and Client Types

In Chapter 3, we briefly mentioned that the ship and port experience is very much perceived according to the passenger's likes and dislikes.

For example, families are strongly attracted to cruising because they're value-conscious and time-pressed. Cruises sufficiently solve their needs. Some lines feature special kids' menus. Others offer an "endless soda" option—the child can have as many sodas as he or she wants for one reasonable price. A few lines provide children with their own daily newspaper. Several have a "kids-only" pool. Some cruise lines even go so far as to offer a full children's program, with a wide

Examples of kids' activities:

- "Kids-only" shore excursions

- Ping-pong tournaments

- "Coke-tail" poolside parties

- Nintendo competitions

- "Parents-not-allowed" movies

- Special tours of the ship

- Camp nights, where kids sing around a "campfire," listen to stories, and make s'mores (but don't get to sleep in tents!)

- Puppet workshops

- Beach parties

- Face-painting competitions

- Entertainment and performance programs

- Classes of all kinds: photography, computers, musical instruments, and more

variety of special activities, each divided into several age-appropriate groups and supervised by trained counselors. A few even have staff dressed as cartoon characters onboard. All these features leave time for moms and dads to relax together while still having loads of time to be with their children.

But what about port time? Parents usually select itineraries and ports that satisfy the goals they've set for themselves and their children. Want them to have fun? An itinerary out of Port Canaveral that features a pre- or post-cruise experience in Orlando is an obvious choice. How about children getting in touch with nature? Then, Alaska's ports of call are ideal. Is the child about to study European history? A cruise among the islands of the Mediterranean would be a powerful, real-life motivator to academic success.

Indeed, port experiences can take altogether different shapes depending on the client's profile. Let's say a ship visits Cancun. (It will actually dock at Playa del Carmen, about 40 miles away.) A culture-seeker may devote the entire day to visiting the magnificent Mayan ruins at Chichen Itza. A diver, on the other hand, may spend his or her time exploring the waters off Cozumel. A shopper will head straight for Cancun's hotel zone. A golfer will want to play the Cozumel Country Club course. And someone into fishing may want to deep-sea fish near Cancun or even at Isla Mujeres. Same port. Totally different experiences depending on the client's interests.

One final but important topic: cruise travel for the physically challenged. As a result of the cruise lines' sensitivity to this issue and the nature of the cruise experience itself, many disabled travelers feel that cruising is *the* way to travel. Most modern vessels are fully accessible to the physically challenged, with specially equipped staterooms and maybe even a staff member or two onboard who

One of the more fascinating shore excursions.
Courtesy of Carnival Cruise Lines

specializes in the diverse needs of the physically challenged. Most cruise lines request that a physically challenged person be accompanied by an "able-bodied" companion.

But what of the port experience? Some places, such as Scandinavia, are especially sensitive to providing full accessibility for all people. Others (often underdeveloped countries) may provide a challenge. Or if tendering between port and ship is required, it may be difficult for the physically challenged passenger to get to shore.

How, then, can the physically challenged maximize their enjoyment of a cruise? First, they should ask their travel agent to determine a ship's accessibility. (Both consumer and trade reference resources cover this thoroughly.) The agent will also find out if the line offers or can specially arrange a shore excursion customized to the client's needs and if tendering situations will occur. Finally, many physically challenged travelers book with a cruise tour group made up entirely of physically challenged people, with tour directors who specialize in this market.

Another important point: Some travel agencies and tour operators are especially knowledgeable in arranging travel for the physically challenged. They may know the answers to these and other questions through their extensive experience.

 # Questions for Discussion

1. What are the advantages of booking a pre- or post-cruise package through the cruise line? What are the potential disadvantages?

2. What are the five options that a passenger has when arriving at an intermediate port?

3. List five things a passenger should know about a shore excursion.

 # Activity

Study the two lists of shore excursions given on pages 94–95. If you could pick two from the Caribbean list and one from the Mediterranean list, which would they be and why? Give and explain your answers below.

Caribbean

Shore excursion #1:

Reason:

Shore excursion #2:

Reason:

Mediterranean

Shore excursion #1:

Reason:

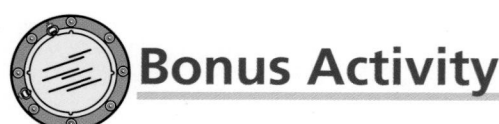

Bonus Activity

In this chapter and others, we've emphasized (and we will again) how a cruise can satisfy a number of different client types. Which type would you be? What would you most want out of a cruise? Here's a quick quiz that will help you find out. The higher your score, the closer you are to that client profile.

For each item, circle the degree to which you agree with the following statements.

5	4	3	2	1
Strongly agree	Agree	Somewhat agree	Agree very little	Disagree

The Adventurous Vacationer

Visiting the world's capitals and seeing all the sites are things I've always wanted to do.	5	4	3	2	1
I like to visit places off the beaten track and see unusual things.	5	4	3	2	1
I've often thought it would be exciting to walk on a glacier, climb a mountain, or explore a volcano.	5	4	3	2	1
Flight-seeing over exotic islands is my kind of fun.	5	4	3	2	1
I enjoy getting close to nature and wildlife.	5	4	3	2	1

Adventurous Vacationer Total Score: _____

The Romantic Vacationer

I like romantic dinners, dancing under the stars, and a show every night.	5	4	3	2	1
I like doing new things with a "special someone."	5	4	3	2	1
I like to make new friends on vacation.	5	4	3	2	1
A breathtaking view, a stroll under a full moon, and a quiet place to talk sound sublime.	5	4	3	2	1
I want our first vacation together to be something special.	5	4	3	2	1

Romantic Vacationer Total Score: _____

The Quick-Getaway Vacationer

I like to take several mini-vacations each year.	5	4	3	2	1
If I have a long weekend coming up, I want to make the most of it.	5	4	3	2	1

I try to sample as much as I can and visit a variety of destinations, even though my vacation time is limited.	5	4	3	2	1
When I take a short vacation, I want to be wined and dined, and I'd like to meet as many new people as possible.	5	4	3	2	1
It's hard for me to get away for long periods of time.	5	4	3	2	1

Quick-Getaway Vacationer Total Score: _____

The Family Vacationer

My spouse and I work and never seem to have enough time to spend with the children.	5	4	3	2	1
Even though we have different interests, our family enjoys vacationing together.	5	4	3	2	1
With a teenager, an eight-year-old, and a toddler, our family needs four vacations in one.	5	4	3	2	1
We need a restaurant that satisfies all our family's tastes—from burgers to continental.	5	4	3	2	1
We're planning a family reunion and are looking for a setting that will please Grandma as well as Johnnie.	5	4	3	2	1

Family Vacationer Total Score: _____

The Affinity/Special-Interest Vacationer

I like to have a focus to my vacation.	5	4	3	2	1
When I'm on vacation, I enjoy meeting people with interests that are similar to mine.	5	4	3	2	1
Learning something new can be as rejuvenating as relaxing by the pool.	5	4	3	2	1
I have a passion for _____ (fill in your special interest) and like to pursue it on vacation.	5	4	3	2	1
Rubbing elbows with a celebrity adds spice to my vacation.	5	4	3	2	1

Affinity Vacationer Total Score: _____

The Single Vacationer

| When traveling alone, I enjoy being introduced to other singles. | 5 | 4 | 3 | 2 | 1 |
| I like meeting other singles in a relaxed and comfortable setting. | 5 | 4 | 3 | 2 | 1 |

I prefer to share expenses with another single, so I need a vacation spot that will arrange this for me.	5	4	3	2	1
I'm a night owl and am looking for a lively crowd.	5	4	3	2	1
My dream vacation is one that offers ready-made bridge, golf, and dinner and dancing partners.	5	4	3	2	1

Single Vacationer Total Score: _____

The Sophisticated Vacationer

When I go on vacation, I demand the very best.	5	4	3	2	1
I've traveled the world on business, and now I'm looking for a special way to revisit my favorite places.	5	4	3	2	1
I usually stay in a suite when I travel.	5	4	3	2	1
World-class cuisine and impeccable service are important to me.	5	4	3	2	1
The more exotic the destination, the more I like it.	5	4	3	2	1

Sophisticated Vacationer Total Score: _____

Chapter **7**

The Geography of Cruising

Courtesy of Seabourn Cruise Line

After reading this chapter, you'll be able to:

- Describe the importance of geography to cruising.
- Define the world's major cruise regions and itinerary patterns.
- Match each region with the kind of traveler who favors it.
- Identify each region's seasonal patterns.

Gil Grosvenor, the chairman of the National Geographic Society, tells of the time when someone sitting next to him on a plane discovered who he was. "Oh, I just *love* geography," she enthused. "That's why I like to travel. One of these days, I'll get around to taking a cruise. Probably to Las Vegas . . ."

That would be quite an achievement, since Las Vegas is about 250 miles inland. The only bodies of water in Vegas are hotel swimming pools.

Las Vegas, though, is one of the few places on Earth where cruises can't travel. Whether by sea or by river, cruise vessels can access thousands of ports. And those places not accessible by ship can be experienced through a pre- or post-cruise package.

Geography plays an essential role in cruising in many ways:

- Cruise clients often decide which voyage to take according to the itinerary, not the ship or the line. (This is especially true of first-time cruisers.)

- Certain places are *best* experienced by ship. To drive or fly from town to town in Alaska, for instance, is difficult, expensive, or, in some cases, impossible. Cruise ships, however, get around Alaska's coastal waters easily.

- Cruises are especially appropriate when you want to visit clusters of islands, such as those of Greece, Indonesia, and the Caribbean. Air connections within these island groups are often awkward and, in the case of the smaller islands, non-existent.

The dramatic Northern Lights, a highlight of many expeditions to the Arctic and Antarctic (but visible on cruises only in late fall or early spring).
Courtesy of Hurtigruten

- Travelers often prefer to visit underdeveloped countries via cruise. The ship is secure, the food familiar, the transportation dependable, and the lodging reliable.

Geography is relevant not only to passengers but also to those in the industry. The ship's staff must have an intimate knowledge of the ports they visit. Land-based personnel must understand how places impact the experience that they market and sell. Travel agents need to be fully familiar with geography, too. Their port knowledge establishes their credibility and professionalism, builds loyalty and trust, and maximizes the probability of client satisfaction.

So, let's explore the world of cruising. To help you along, maps accompany each place described. Study them carefully as you read. Many of the place names you'll encounter will be new to you. Be prepared. And let's make it a bit easier by starting with one of the most familiar places of all: North America.

Cruising North America

More cruises take place in the waters that surround and flow through North America than anywhere else in the world. To simplify things, we can identify five distinct cruise regions in North America: Alaska, the Northeast, the Mississippi River and its tributaries, Mexico's Pacific coast, and the Caribbean. Let's examine each.

Alaska

Few places match the drama of Alaska. Pristine inlets, unpolluted skies, white-blue glaciers, jagged mountains, intimate towns—these are what have made Alaska one of the world's fastest-growing cruise destinations. The cruise season here is limited to around May through early October, when daylight lasts longest and temperatures are most pleasant.

Two cruise itineraries predominate. The first, the Inside Passage route, usually begins in Vancouver, British Columbia, or Seattle, Washington, and threads its way northward among narrow channels, past wooded islands to a turnaround point (usually at or near Skagway). See Figure 7-1. The ship then returns southward to its starting point. The vessel calls at three or four ports along the way. Among the most popular stops:

- **Sitka,** with its traces of Russian influence. (Sitka was once a Russian colonial outpost and capital of Russian America.)
- **Juneau,** Alaska's compact capital, picturesquely nestled at the base of a mountain.
- **Skagway,** a key town in Alaska's gold-rush era.
- **Glacier Bay,** where passengers see chunks of ice cracking off glaciers and thundering into the icy waters.
- **Ketchikan,** a center of Native American culture and the self-proclaimed Salmon Capital of the World.

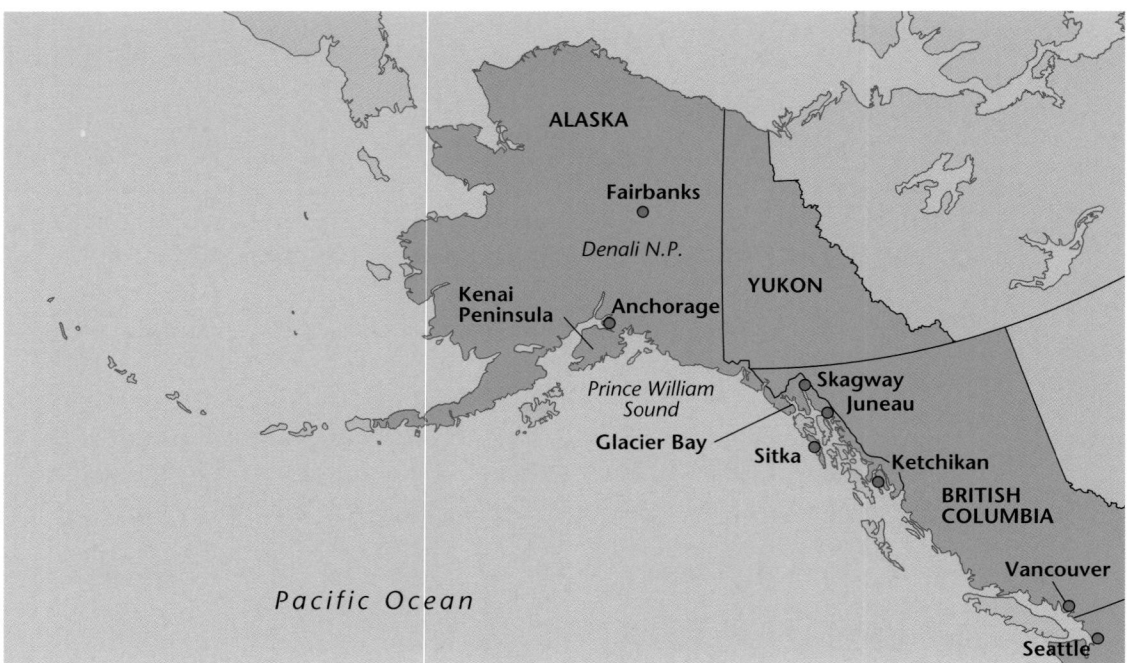

FIGURE 7-1   Map of Alaska

The second common itinerary: a one-way cruise from Vancouver or Seattle to Anchorage (or vice versa). The ship stops at many of the same ports of an Inside Passage cruise and then continues northward to visit Hubbard Glacier, College Fjord, Prince William Sound, and the Kenai Peninsula. From Anchorage, many cruisers extend their vacation experience by taking a 356-mile Anchorage-Fairbanks escorted railroad journey, with a layover stay at Denali National Park. (The park is the home of Mt. McKinley, North America's tallest peak.) Another land-excursion option: Passengers disembark at Skagway for a trip to Canada's Yukon and on to Fairbanks (or the reverse).

What kind of people are drawn to an Alaska cruise? The ecology-minded, for sure, and those who appreciate scenery and a pure outdoors environment. Families with children are more likely to cruise during the summer months, while seniors predominate during the early and late Alaska cruise seasons.

A few smaller cruise lines explore the Pacific Northwest region south of Vancouver, including voyages up the Columbia River.

The Northeast

Passenger ships have plied the Atlantic waters off North America for well over a century. One of the most famous was the Fall River Line, made up of elegant steamers that served as transportation between New England and New York City. Another was the legendary *Bluenose*, a schooner that sailed between Maine and Nova Scotia. And, of course, the great ships of the early twentieth century followed a route from Europe to New York that curved along the Northeast's shores.

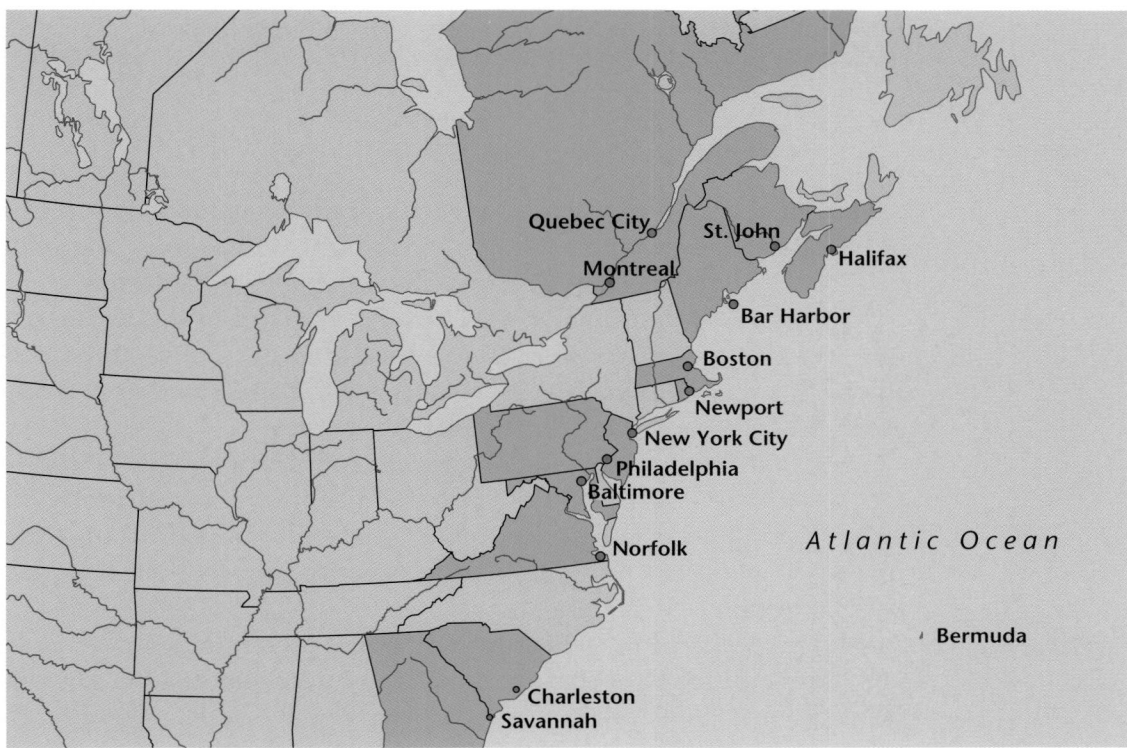

FIGURE 7-2   **Map of the Northeast**

Today, coastal cruising in the Northeast is experiencing a renaissance, with ships sailing between two of North America's great cities: New York City and Montreal. See Figure 7-2. The most common intermediary stops:

- **Newport,** Rhode Island, the site of some of America's greatest mansions.
- **Boston,** Massachusetts, the "cradle of liberty" of the United States.
- **Bar Harbor,** Maine, gateway to Acadia National Park.
- **Saint John,** New Brunswick, and **Halifax**, Nova Scotia, two key cities of the Canadian Maritime Provinces.
- **Quebec City,** Quebec, a little bit of seventeenth-century France right here in North America.

The Northeast cruise season extends from late spring through fall. Fall foliage cruises in October are especially popular. The passengers who are found aboard a Northeast cruise are diverse. History and tradition are what attract them.

Ships occasionally venture into more southerly Atlantic waters, often as part of repositioning cruises from the Northeast to the Caribbean. Among the possible ports visited: Philadelphia, Pennsylvania; Baltimore, Maryland; Norfolk, Virginia; Charleston, South Carolina; and Savannah, Georgia. Boston, Philadelphia, and Baltimore are also increasingly serving as departure ports for cruises.

A very popular cruise itinerary is the East Coast to Bermuda run. Operated from April through October (primarily from New York City or Boston), it provides an intriguing alternative to staying at a Bermuda hotel. (Bermuda limits new hotel construction, so land-based lodging is often at a premium.) Once there, cruise passengers can experience quaint towns and pink-sand beaches.

The Mississippi River and Its Tributaries

A quick quiz: Which of the following cities can you get to from the Mississippi or one of the rivers from which it flows: Pittsburgh, Minneapolis, Nashville, St. Louis, Little Rock, Memphis, New Orleans, Chattanooga, or Charleston?

The answer: All of them. See Figure 7-3. It's amazing how many fascinating places border the great rivers of America. Regular cruise ships rarely sail the Mississippi or its tributaries. The waters are too shallow. But two other kinds of vessels do—riverboats and large passenger barges.

The great riverboats of the nineteenth century were legendary—the stuff of Mark Twain novels. In the early twentieth century, they virtually disappeared. Modern paddle wheelers—every bit as ornate and majestic as the original ones—carry passengers year-round to some of America's most interesting places. They're like time machines to America's past.

Who favors a North American river cruise adventure? Those passengers tend to be older and fairly upscale, with a deep interest in history. They're willing to

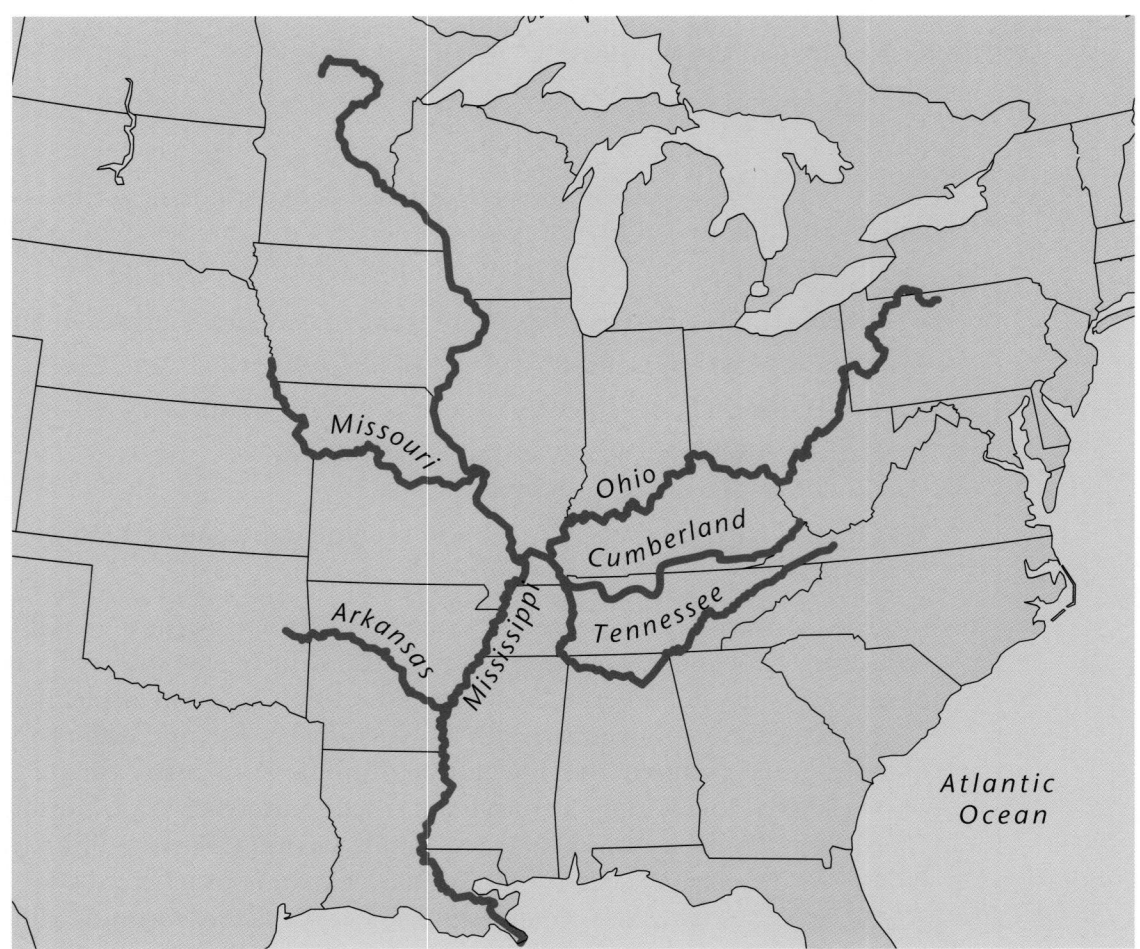

FIGURE 7-3   **Map of the Mississippi River and its tributaries**

forgo a resort-like onboard ship experience for the simple pleasures of visiting a restored plantation home, experiencing a Cajun music festival, exploring a vital city, or simply sitting in a rocking chair on the boat's "front porch," watching America's past and present glide gracefully by.

Mexico's Pacific Coast

Sun, sand, great shopping, sensational food, a fiesta spirit—these and more attract tourists to Mexico. And these very same things appeal to those who wish to take a cruise along Mexico's Pacific coast.

Three itineraries are typical. The first is a three- or four-day round-trip out of Los Angeles or San Diego (often as an extended weekend getaway) to Ensenada, a festive town on the Baja Peninsula. See Figure 7-4. Along the way, ships sometimes stop at Catalina, a charming island only 26 miles off California's coast. This itinerary operates year-round and often serves as a "sampler" for first-time cruisers. Typically, passengers are of all ages and interests.

The second itinerary is longer. It takes passengers one way between Acapulco and Los Angeles or San Diego (in either direction). This "Mexican Riviera" itinerary operates mostly in the winter and features the following ports:

- **Cabo San Lucas,** at the southern tip of Baja. The big attractions here are beautiful coves, snorkeling, and superb deep-sea fishing.

- **Mazatlan,** another fishing paradise that offers jungle tours, shopping, folklore shows, and lively cantinas.

- **Puerto Vallarta,** with pristine beaches, an extensive market, and a dramatic golf course.

- **Acapulco,** Mexico's grand old resort. Numerous night spots, countless restaurants, and the famous cliff divers make Acapulco a dramatic beginning or end to a cruise.

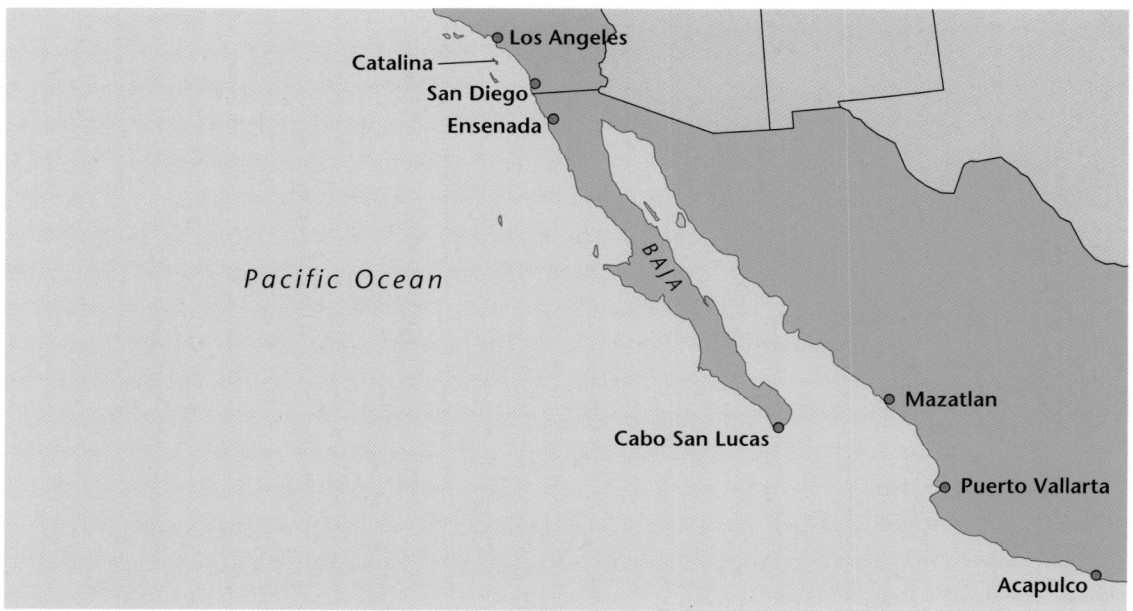

FIGURE 7-4   Map of Mexico's Pacific coast

The third itinerary is a variation of the previous two. The ship sails from Los Angeles or San Diego, visits three ports, and then returns to Los Angeles or San Diego.

Often associated with the Mexican Riviera is a Panama Canal cruise. Beginning in Acapulco, this route takes passengers to the canal, perhaps visiting a Central American port along the way. After passing through the canal, the vessel may call on ports in Colombia, Venezuela, and the Caribbean itself. The itinerary, of course, can operate in reverse, from the Caribbean to Acapulco. Panama Canal cruises generally last from 10 to as many as 24 days. Some shorter itineraries that focus on the Caribbean and Latin America do transit a lock or two of the Panama Canal as a special voyage feature and sometimes call on Colon, Panama.

The Caribbean

It's the number-one cruise destination in the world. And it's also one of the most misunderstood.

Here are three things the layman usually gets wrong. First, Bermuda is *not* in the Caribbean. It's nearly 1,000 miles north of the Caribbean, at about the same latitude as Charleston, South Carolina. See Figure 7-2. Second, the Bahamas aren't in the Caribbean either. They are also in the Atlantic, just east of Florida and north of Cuba. See Figure 7-5. They are, however, often on Caribbean itineraries. More about that later. And third, the Caribbean islands are *not* all alike. There are big ones, small ones, mountainous ones, and flat ones, with just about every culture and nationality represented.

Three basic Caribbean cruise itineraries exist: the Eastern Caribbean, the Southern Caribbean, and the Western Caribbean. For convenience, let's add the Bahamas as a fourth itinerary option. One proviso: What constitutes each region

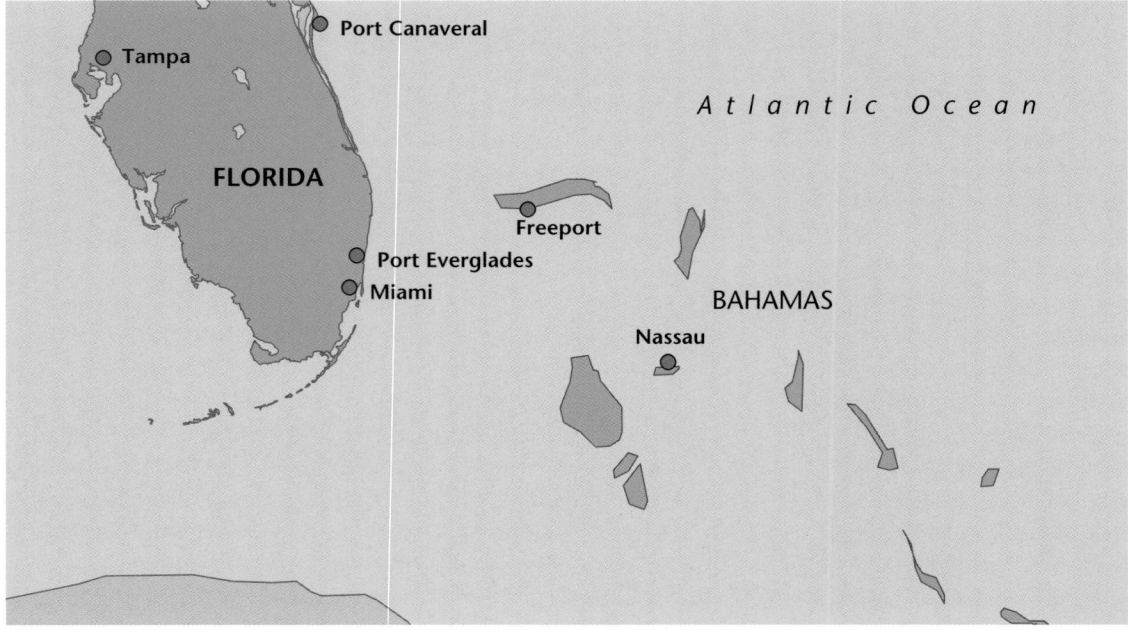

FIGURE 7-5   Map of the Bahamas

is open to debate. Some cruise lines, for example, call on Martinique as part of an Eastern Caribbean sailing. Others include it in their Southern Caribbean program. Still, we need to organize these islands in some fashion. What follows is the *general* pattern. Most of these cruises operate year-round, although fewer ships are positioned here in the summer than in the winter.

The Bahamas   A Bahamas cruise is to the East Coast what an Ensenada/Baja cruise is to the West Coast—a three- to four-day getaway that often provides travelers with their first taste of cruising. Most cruises to the Bahamas depart from Miami or Port Everglades (at Ft. Lauderdale). Others leave from Port Canaveral (east of Orlando) or Tampa. As with an Ensenada cruise, the people onboard are highly diversified. The key Bahamian port is Nassau, with wonderful shopping, historical attractions, and great diving nearby. Four-day itineraries often include Freeport. The Bahamas are also occasionally visited on longer itineraries out of New York City, Baltimore, or Philadelphia.

The Eastern Caribbean   This itinerary (seven days or more) usually begins and ends in Miami, Port Everglades, or San Juan, Puerto Rico, with its historic old city and many lovely beaches. Some cruises depart from Port Canaveral. The ships then sail eastward (see Figure 7-6), calling on a number of the following islands:

- **The U.S. Virgin Islands,** made up of St. Thomas (great scenery and shopping), St. Croix, and St. John (only the smallest ships anchor here).
- **The British Virgin Islands,** much less developed than their U.S. counterparts. On one of these islands (Virgin Gorda) is "The Baths," a unique beachside formation of boulders.

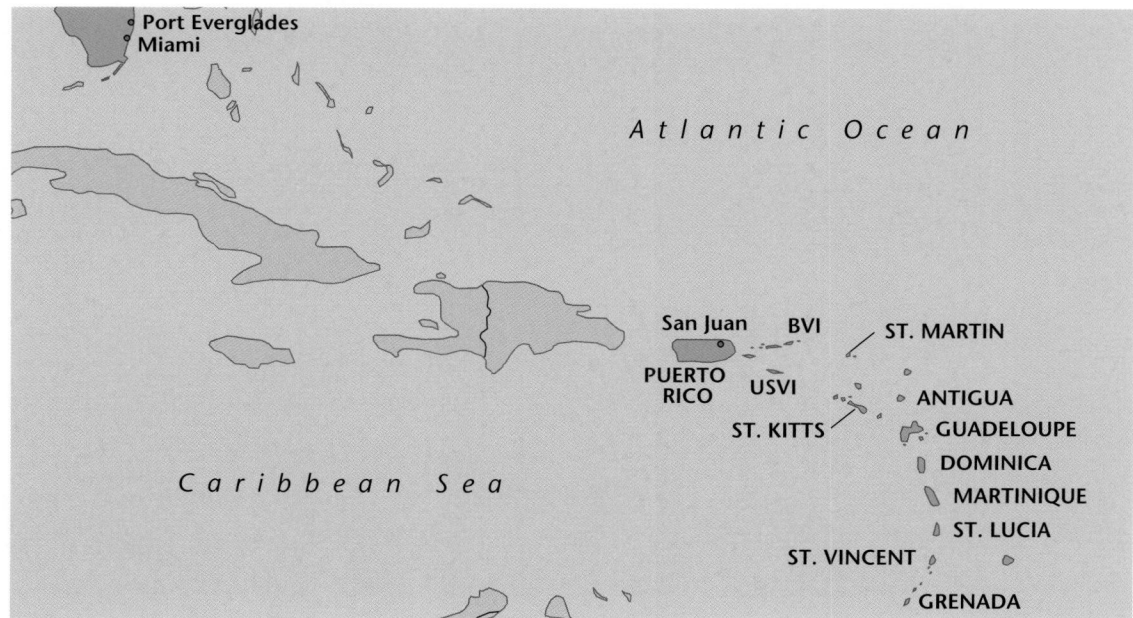

FIGURE 7-6   Map of the Eastern Caribbean

- **St. Martin/St. Maarten,** governed jointly by the French and the Dutch. Ships anchor on the Dutch side (St. Maarten), where most of the shopping can be found. The French portion (St. Martin) is famous for its fine restaurants.

- **Antigua,** a lush tropical island with a unique attraction, "Nelson's Dockyard," where the British Caribbean fleet was headquartered during the eighteenth century.

- **Guadeloupe** and **Martinique**, which share much in common: French culture, volcanoes, deep-green scenery, and plenty of shopping.

- Other Eastern Caribbean islands that some cruise lines call on are **Dominica, St. Lucia, St. Vincent, Grenada**, and **St. Kitts**.

The Southern Caribbean   Less visited than the other Caribbean regions, the Southern Caribbean is a popular choice for those looking for a more exotic, port-intensive itinerary. Cruises generally leave and return from either San Juan, Puerto Rico, or Bridgetown, Barbados. See Figure 7-7. Among the islands visited:

- **The "ABC Islands"** (for the letters that start each of their names): Aruba and Curacao, with their fine beaches, casinos, and picturesque Dutch buildings, and Bonaire, one of the Caribbean's greatest dive destinations.

- **Trinidad,** the home of steel drum bands, calypso music, and the limbo.

- **Barbados,** a busy island with old plantation homes and an underground wonder: "Harrison's Cave".

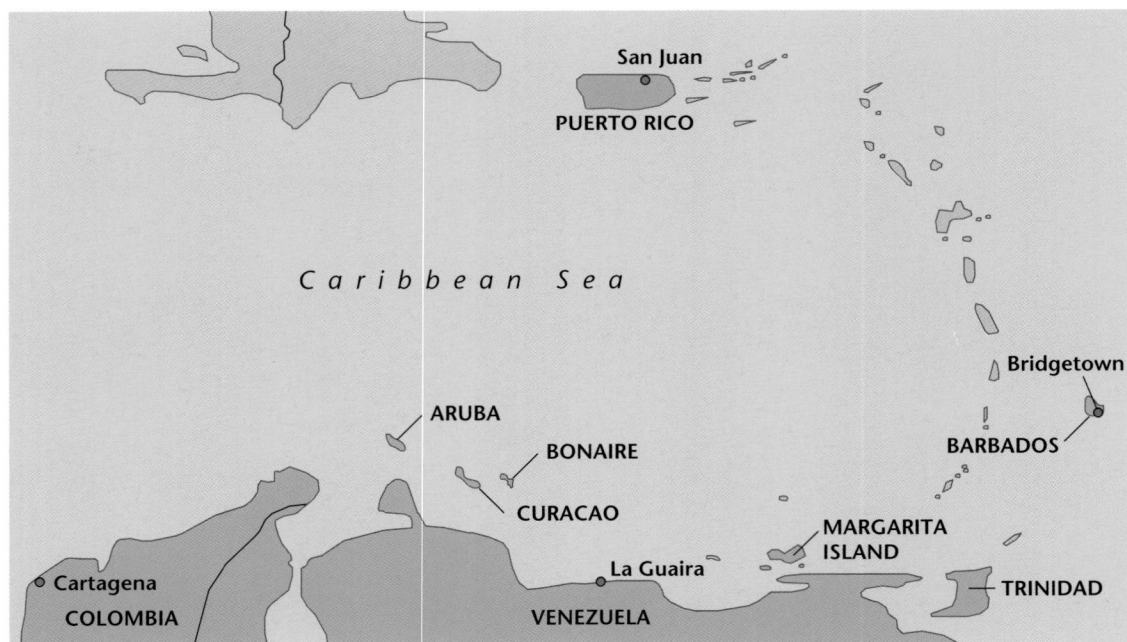

FIGURE 7-7   Map of the Southern Caribbean

Southern Caribbean itineraries sometimes include ports on the South American mainland, such as La Guaira (the port for Caracas, Venezuela) and Cartagena, Colombia. Some also visit Margarita Island, a Venezuelan island just north of that country's coast.

The Western Caribbean   Conveniently accessed from the same Florida ports as Bahamas cruises and occasionally from Houston, Galveston, or New Orleans, the Western Caribbean (sometimes including the Gulf of Mexico's coastal cities) offers a broad spectrum of island and mainland experiences. See Figure 7-8. Here are the most popular:

• **Cancun,** on the Yucatan Peninsula, is one of Mexico's most popular resorts. Cancun has good shopping, great restaurants, and plenty of entertainment. Relatively nearby are several remarkable Mayan ruins. Off Cancun is Cozumel Island, where some ships also dock. Diving and fishing have made Cozumel famous.

• **The Cayman Islands,** another legendary diving spot. Two famous attractions: a turtle farm and "Stingray City," where divers can swim with these ominous-looking yet gentle creatures.

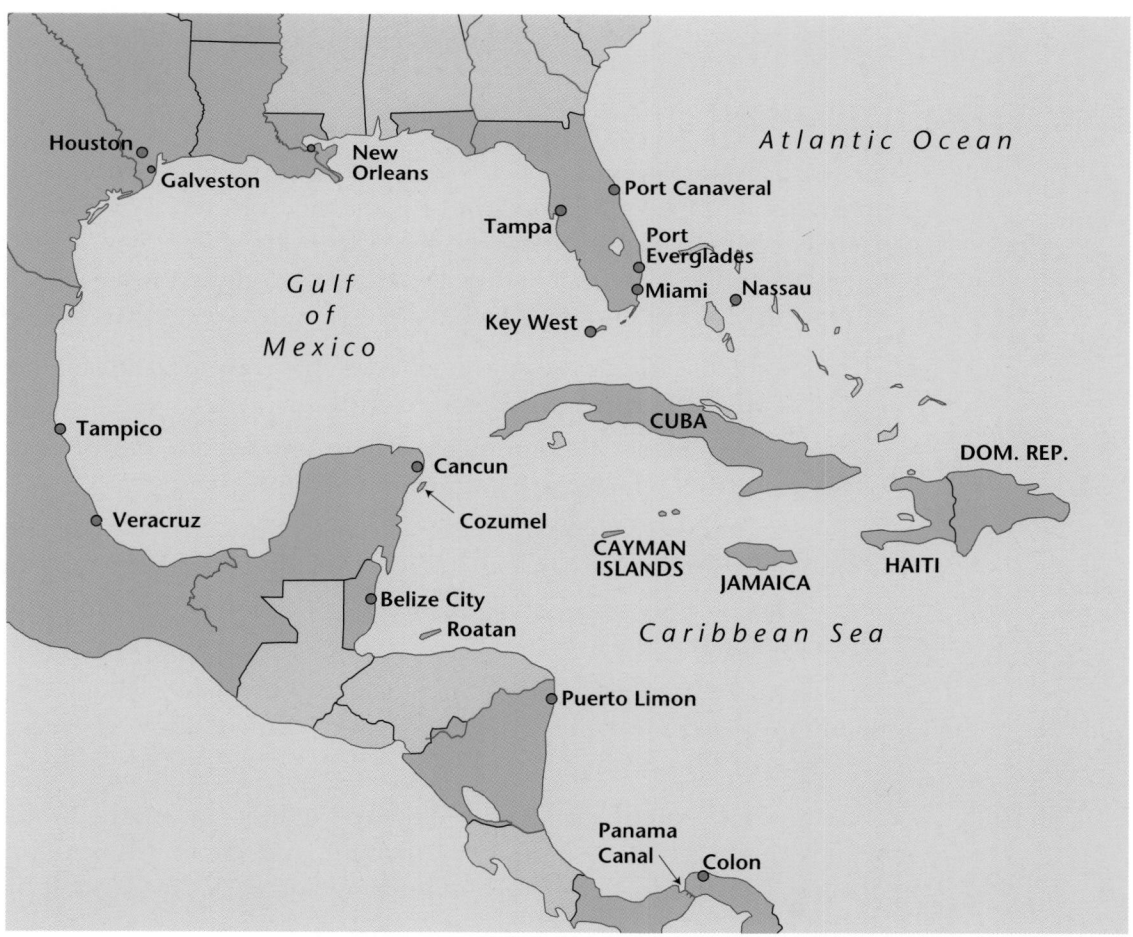

FIGURE 7-8   Map of the Western Caribbean

- **Jamaica,** famous for its reggae music, varied landscape, and numerous attractions. The best-known: "Dunns River Falls," where a river cascades down a series of step-like stones that visitors can climb.

- **Haiti,** on the western side of the large island of Hispaniola. Its blend of French and African cultures is intriguing, and its folk art is widely collected. Unfortunately a major earthquake in 2010 caused great damage in Haiti.

- **The Dominican Republic,** occupying the eastern side of Hispaniola. It boasts historical sites, many golf courses, and shopping venues.

Sometimes included on a Western Caribbean itinerary are such Mexican mainland ports as Tampico and Veracruz, on the Gulf of Mexico, as well as Key West, Florida. The Central American ports of Puerto Limon, Costa Rica, Roatan Island, Honduras, and Belize City, Belize, are also increasingly popular. If the political situation changes, Cuba will probably become a major cruise destination. Remember that many Western Caribbean cruises also stop at Nassau, Bahamas.

The huge variety of options in the Caribbean demonstrates why it's so popular. This diversity also reflects itself in the composition of cruise passengers. Caribbean and Bahamian cruises attract just about every kind and age group of passenger imaginable.

Cruising Europe

After North America, Europe is the world's most popular cruise destination. The combination of history, architecture, cuisine, and elegant living make Europe an especially seductive continent to cruise. Except for a few places, virtually every country in Europe is accessible to seagoing or rivergoing vessels.

Cruising offers many benefits that are especially well-suited to Europe:

- Cruises make visiting the continent efficient. Transfers, border crossings, and the like are inconsequential if you're cruising.

- Language problems are minimized. There's no need to decipher road signs or figure out from which track your train will be departing.

- Cruises guarantee a consistent level of accommodations and dining, something that's somewhat unpredictable with land-based European lodging.

- Considering how expensive gas, tolls, and good European lodging can be, cruises offer a real value.

- Cruises are especially interesting to veteran European visitors, since ships call on many ports off the beaten "land-based" path. Culture seekers and history buffs favor European cruises.

Six itineraries predominate: the Western Mediterranean; the Eastern Mediterranean; Atlantic ports; Ireland, Great Britain, and the North Sea; the Baltic Sea; and river cruises. Most are 7 to 14 days long and take place in late spring, summer, and early fall.

Let's review those six, keeping in mind that—as with the Caribbean—there can be plenty of variations.

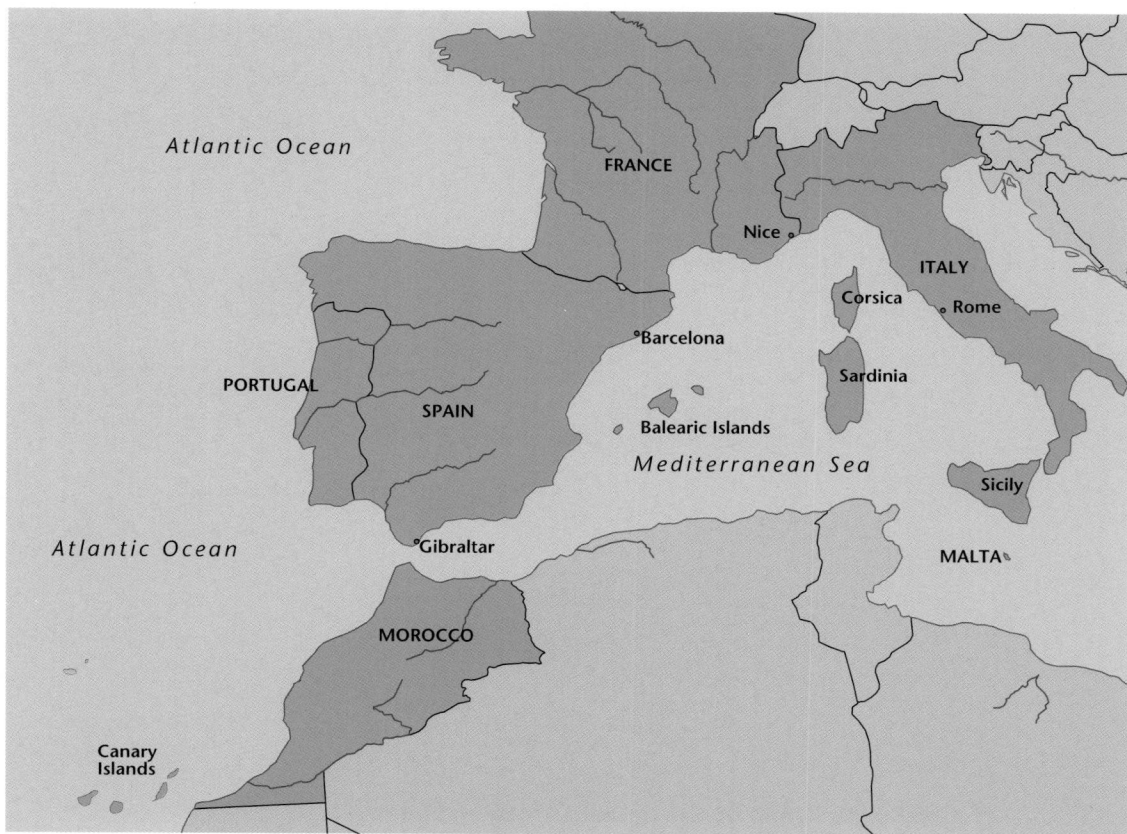

FIGURE 7-9   Map of the Western Mediterranean

The Western Mediterranean

Few regions offer as much culture as the Western Mediterranean. It's known for its sophisticated lifestyle: historic villages, chic boutiques, rich art galleries, fine wines, and refined cuisine. A Western Mediterranean cruise typically calls on ports on the mainlands of Spain, France, and Italy. The Balearic Islands, Gibraltar, and the islands of Corsica, Sardinia, Sicily, and Malta are also popular. See Figure 7-9. Morocco, a North African country south of Spain, is often included on Western Mediterranean cruises. And some ships venture out past the Strait of Gibraltar to the Canary Islands in the Atlantic.

The three most popular ports of embarkation and debarkation in the Western Mediterranean are Barcelona, Spain, Nice (on the French Riviera), and Rome, Italy. Several dozen other ports are popular intermediary stops. (Note: Rome's port is actually the town of Civitavecchia.)

The Eastern Mediterranean

For those who treasure ancient history, few places rival the Eastern Mediterranean. From the key ports of Venice, Athens (Piraeus), and Istanbul, ships sail forth to retrace the paths of Homer, Herodotus, and other greats from antiquity. See Figure 7-10.

FIGURE 7-10 **Map of the Eastern Mediterranean**

Which are the most popular places for ships to visit? Greece, of course, especially its islands of Corfu, Mikonos, Crete, Santorini, and Rhodes; the legendary ancient cities of Turkey (of these, Ephesus is the most famous); and, despite the fact that they're in the Middle East and Africa, not Europe, the ancient nations of Israel and Egypt.

Here are the ports that serve important towns and cities on European/Middle Eastern itineraries:

- Alexandria: Cairo, Egypt
- Cadiz: Seville, Spain
- Civitavecchia: Rome, Italy
- Haifa: Jerusalem, Israel
- Kusadasi: Ephesus, Turkey
- Le Havre: Paris, France
- Leith: Edinburgh, Scotland
- Livorno: Florence, Italy
- Piraeus: Athens, Greece
- Southampton: London, England
- Zeebrugge: Brussels, Belgium

Atlantic Europe

Sometimes, as part of a repositioning cruise (more about that later) and other times as an itinerary in itself, an Atlantic European cruise usually features Portugal, France, and, occasionally, Spain, Ireland, and Great Britain. See Figure 7-11. If it were a long cruise, the itinerary might start at Malaga, on Spain's southern Costa del Sol, journey around to Lisbon, Portugal, continue northward to Bordeaux, France, and finish in London, England. Another variation might commence in Lisbon and finish at Le Havre, Paris's northern port.

Ireland, Great Britain, and the North Sea

Familiarity—that's what makes Europe's northwest regions especially attractive. The culture is familiar and the cities are well-known. But cruising enables even the veteran traveler to experience these places in an altogether different way.

The variations here are many. Some cruises circle Ireland; others go around Great Britain. A common itinerary starts in England and goes on to ports in

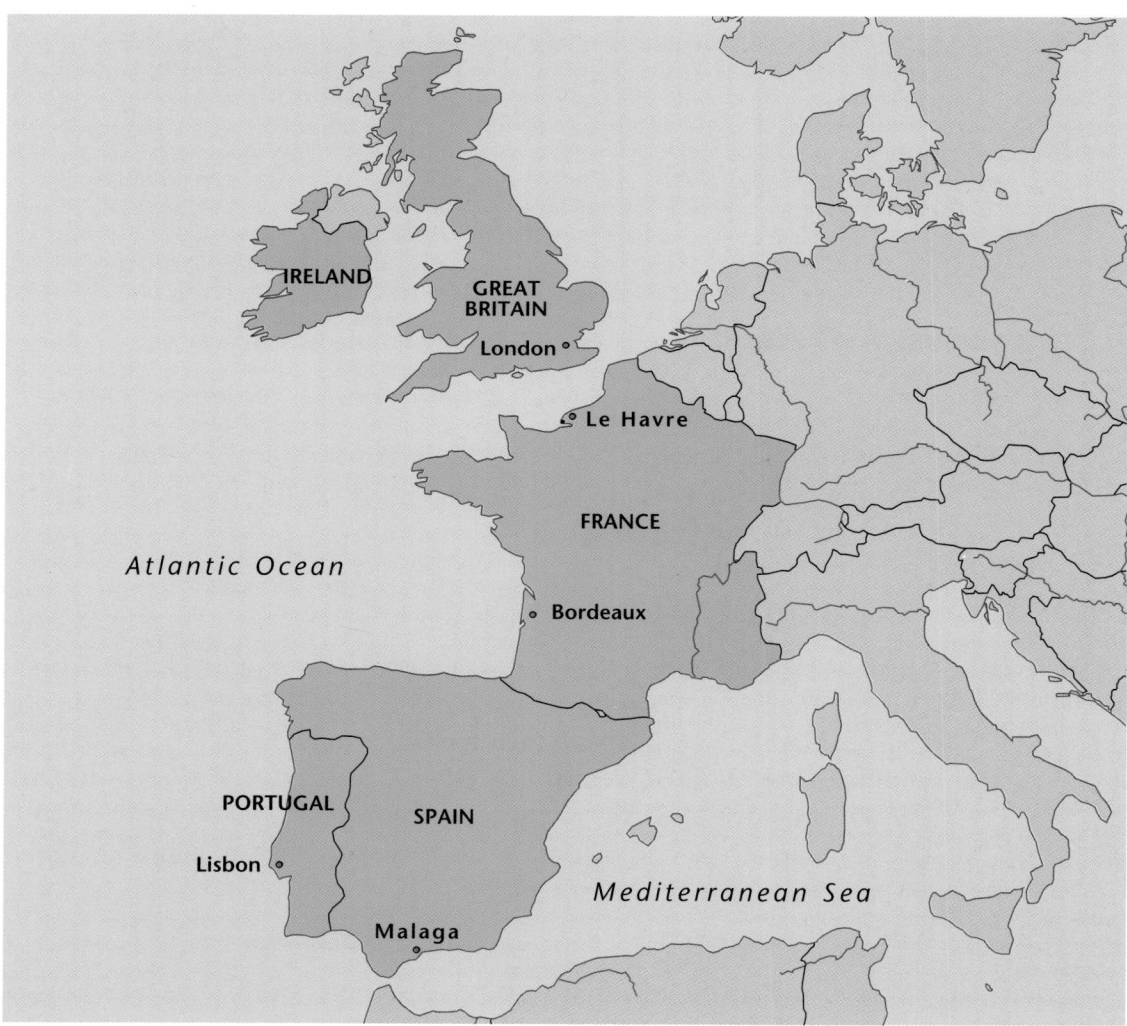

FIGURE 7-11   Map of Atlantic Europe

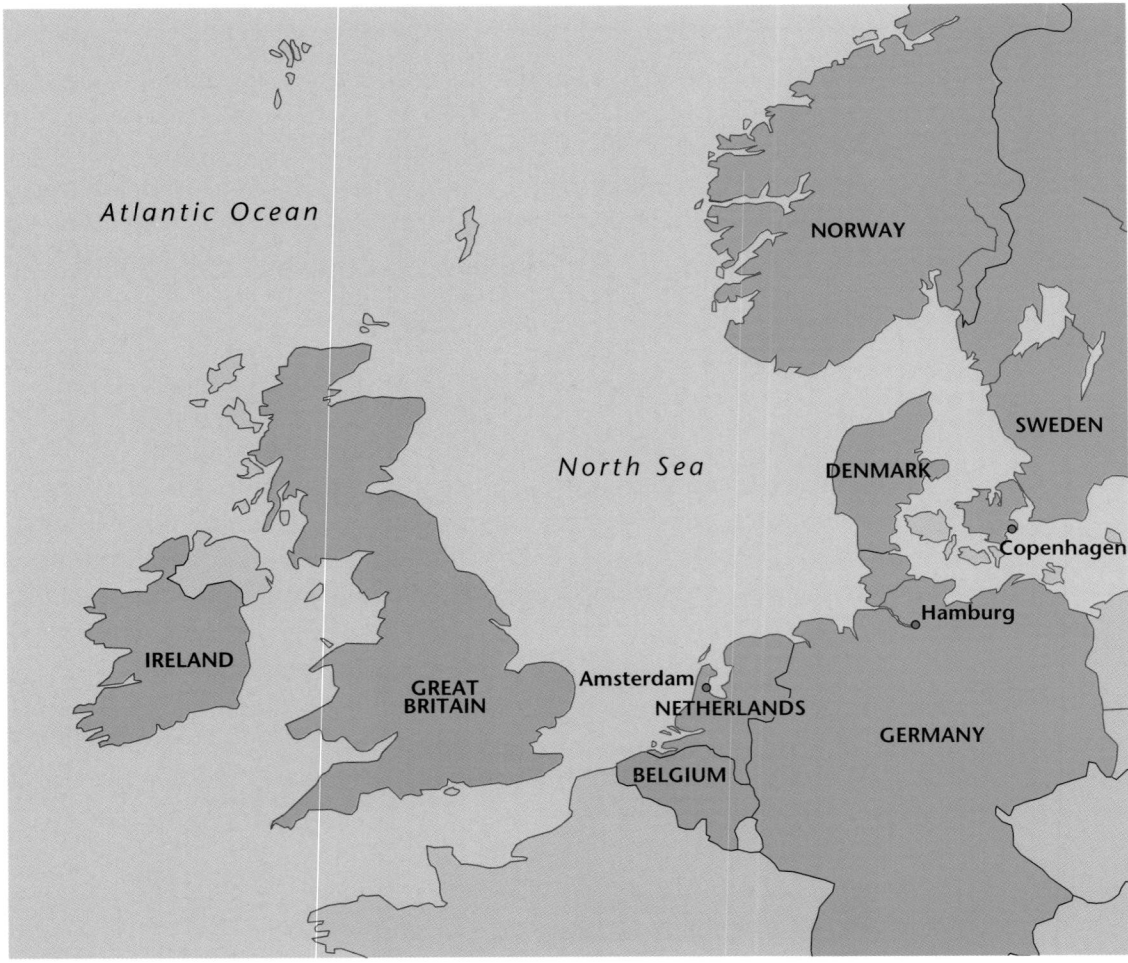

FIGURE 7-12 **Map of Ireland, Great Britain, and the North Sea**

Belgium, the Netherlands (especially Amsterdam), Germany (via Hamburg), Norway and its western fjord coast, and Denmark (the most important port here is Copenhagen). See Figure 7-12.

The Baltic Sea

Increasingly popular, a Baltic cruise takes in many countries that are less commonly visited than other European destinations. Here's one possible itinerary: The ship leaves Hamburg or Copenhagen for Stockholm, Sweden, and ends at the former home of the czars: St. Petersburg, Russia. See Figure 7-13. A more southerly route would take the ship along an uncommon path, past the three Baltic nations of Lithuania, Latvia, and Estonia, with perhaps a stop at Tallinn, Estonia.

River Cruises

Many tourists believe that those destinations in Europe's interior can't be part of a cruise. This is hardly true. Pre- or post-cruise tours, of course, offer limitless possibilities. But so do river cruises.

A passenger enjoys the fjords of Norway.
Courtesy of Hurtigruten

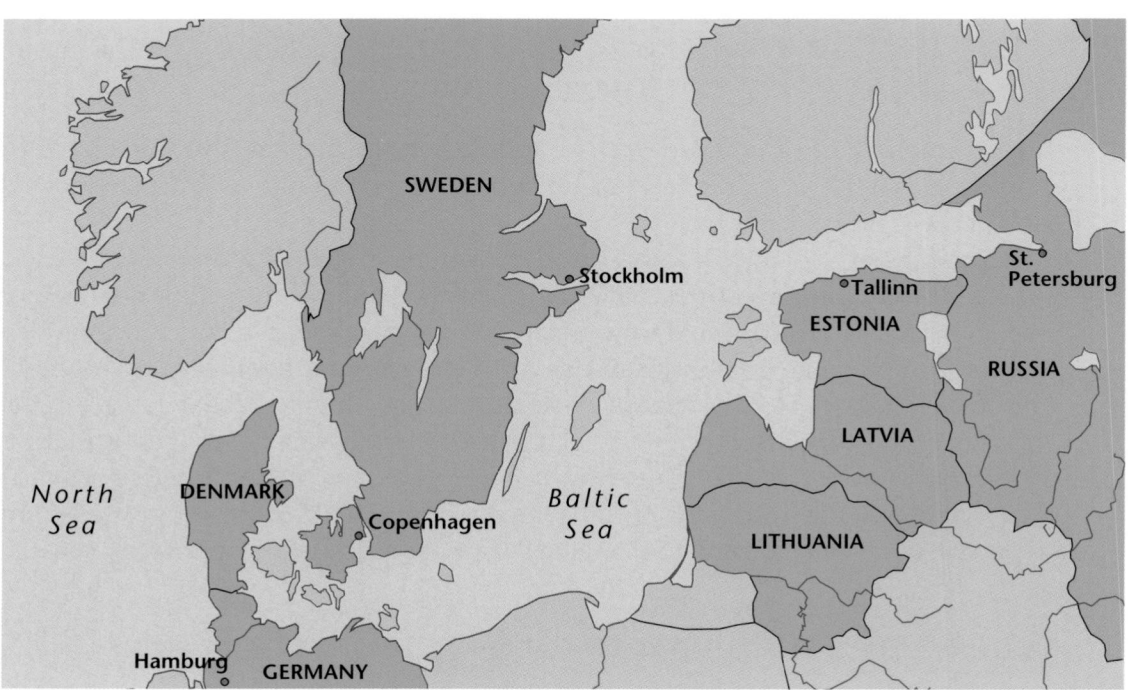

FIGURE 7-13   Map of the Baltic Sea

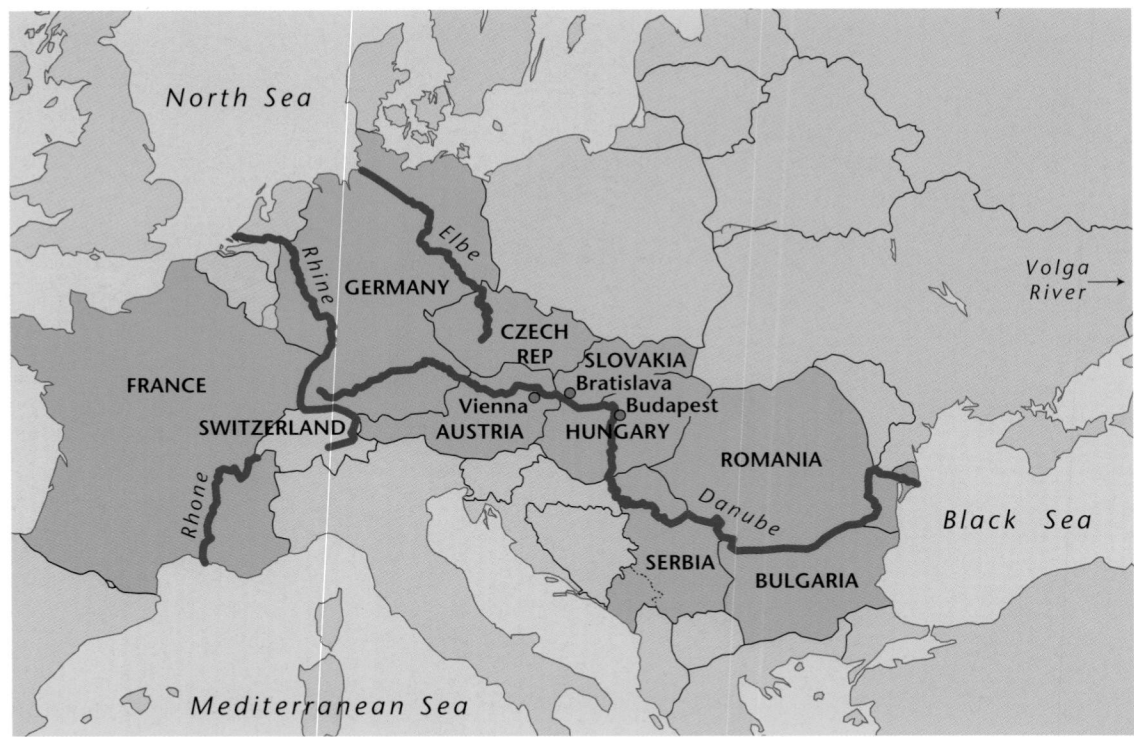

FIGURE 7-14   Map of European rivers

Among the most popular rivers for boat and barge cruises are France's Rhone (and the nation's many canals), Germany's Rhine and Elbe, and Russia's Volga. See Figure 7-14. *The* cruise river, though, is the Danube. Here are three cities that a Danube cruise might visit: Vienna, Austria, Budapest, Hungary, and Bratislava, Slovakia. A glittering trio of cities, don't you think?

Cruising the Rest of the World

North America and Europe dominate today's cruise market. But there's every indication that more "exotic" places are becoming increasingly popular to today's more adventuresome traveler.

Cruising is well-suited to unusual destinations. Air, rail, and roads in Africa, Asia, and South America can be challenging. Border crossings are complex, monetary exchange rates confusing, lodging unpredictable, and safety a concern. A cruise cushions the traveler from much of this, providing a secure, reliable environment from which to explore adventurous destinations. The only thing that can get in the way: terrorism or political unrest, which cruise lines swiftly respond to by altering or, in extreme cases, canceling itineraries and repositioning their cruises elsewhere.

Four regions feature an especially favorable context for off-the-beaten-path cruising: Central and South Americas, the Pacific, Asia, and Africa. Let's look at each.

Central and South America

A land of diverse topography, cultures, and attractions, Central and South Americas offer a wealth of ports to explore. Central America—one of the world's

FIGURE 7-15   Map of Central and South America

prime ecological destinations—is sometimes visited as part of a trans–Panama Canal or Western Caribbean cruise. South America's Atlantic Coast is also quite popular (especially from October to April), with departures typically out of San Juan, Puerto Rico, or Rio de Janeiro, Brazil. Intermediate stops might include Devil's Island (off French Guiana) and such Brazilian cities as Belem, Recife, and Salvador. See Figure 7-15. Some ships journey up the Amazon River—all the way to Manaus.

Occasionally, cruise lines visit South America's Pacific coast or even offer a month-long itinerary around South America. The latter routing would go beyond Rio and visit Montevideo, Uruguay, Buenos Aires, Argentina, the Falkland Islands, through the Strait of Magellan, and on to South America's Pacific coast. Most likely Pacific ports of call are Valparaiso, Chile (Santiago's port), and Callao, Peru (Lima's port), with many other possibilities in between.

Before rounding South America's tip, however, the ship might "detour" to Antarctica, one of the most remote places possible, usually by way of Ushuaia, Argentina, and/or Punta Arenas, Chile. Some cruises visit Antarctica from New Zealand.

Many of South America's grandest attractions are inland but can be visited as part of a shore excursion or a pre- or post-cruise package. Among the possibilities are mighty Iguazu Falls, accessed from Brazil, and Peru's Machu Picchu, reached from Lima via Cuzco. Two other remote destinations are Easter Island and the Galapagos Islands, both far off to the west of South America.

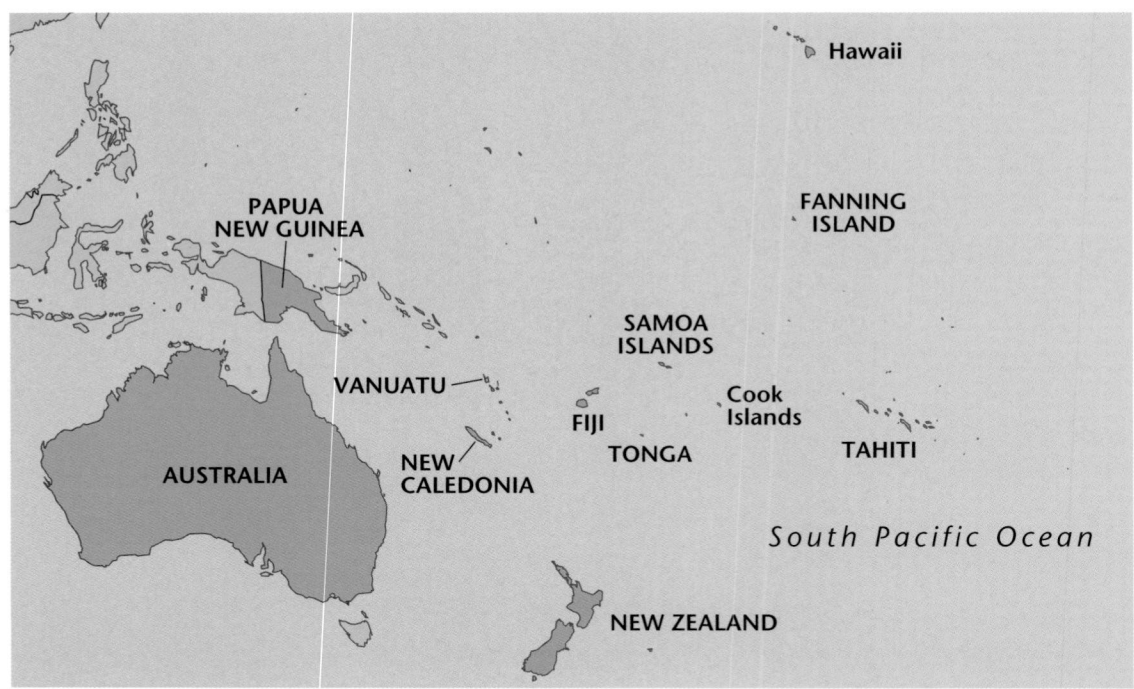

FIGURE 7-16   Map of the Pacific Ocean

The Pacific

The perfect tropical island—of such places dreams are made. That's why the Pacific is a fantasy destination for so many. There are *thousands* of picture-perfect tropical islands sprinkled about the Pacific's 64 million square miles of water. See Figure 7-16.

And what more efficient way to sample them than on a cruise? In the South Pacific, ships primarily sail the islands of Tahiti and Fiji, but Papua New Guinea, New Caledonia, Vanuatu, Samoa, Tonga, and the Cook Islands are also visited. Farther south, cruises around New Zealand and along the eastern coast of Australia are quite popular. Most South Pacific cruises operate November through April, when the Southern Hemisphere's climate is at its best.

In the North Pacific, Hawaii has been a popular cruise destination since the early twentieth century. (Prior to the jet age, ships were the primary way of getting there.) A cruise represents an efficient way of visiting several Hawaiian islands without having to pack and unpack. One cruise line's ship is permanently based there. Repositioning cruises in the spring and fall often stop in Hawaii along the way.

Asia

To summarize all the cruise itineraries that feature Asian ports is next to impossible. A few general patterns exist though. The political climate permitting, several sailings weave through the many islands of Indonesia, Malaysia, the Philippines, and Singapore. See Figure 7-17. A second pattern: Southeast Asia, with Thailand, Vietnam, and Singapore as key countries. India's ports are

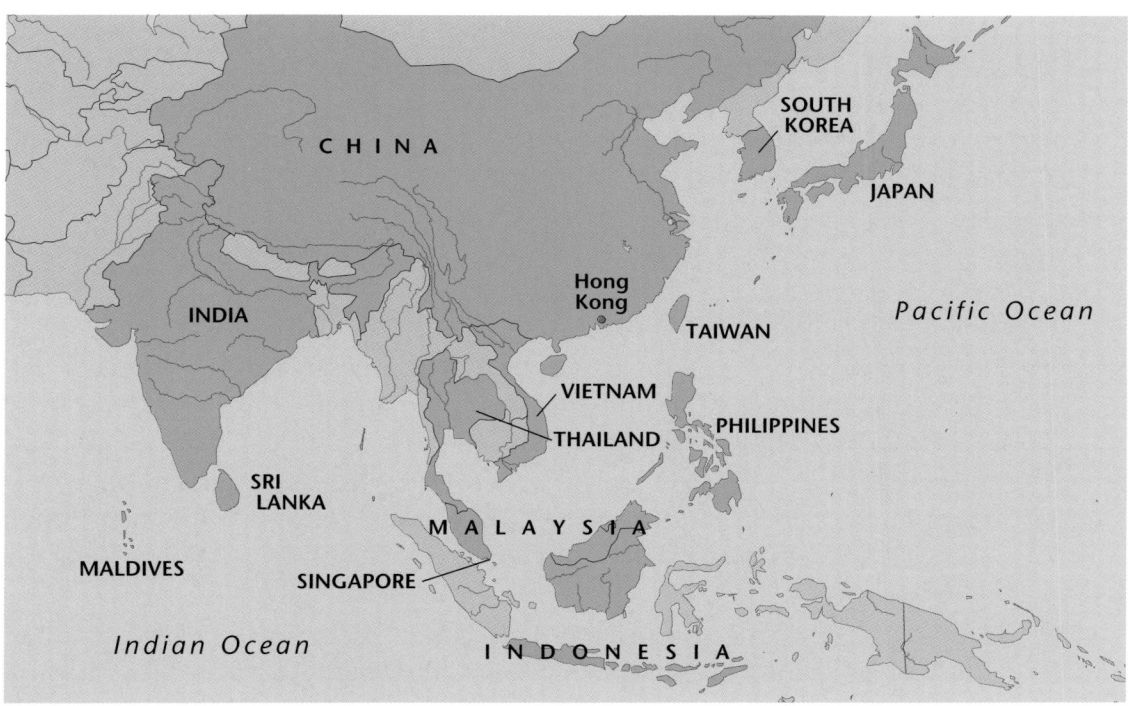

FIGURE 7-17   Map of Asia

A sleek cruise ship shares Hong Kong Harbour with a timeless Chinese vessel.
Courtesy of Seabourn Cruise Line

on a few itineraries, often in conjunction with Sri Lanka and the Maldives. Hong Kong and other major Chinese and Taiwanese ports constitute another typical itinerary. Finally, Japan and South Korea represent a natural geographic combination for cruising. Most cruises that visit Asia take place between October and May, although a few ships remain during the summer months.

Africa

Five major cruise itineraries for Africa predominate:

- The first includes the northwestern African nations of Tunisia and Morocco, sometimes in combination with the Canary and Madeira Islands. See Figure 7-18. These cruises generally take place from May through October.

- The second itinerary lies on and off Africa's east coast. The ports of Mombasa, Kenya, or Dar es Salaam, Tanzania, are usually coupled with such Indian Ocean islands as Zanzibar, Madagascar, the Seychelles, the Comoros, Reunion, and Mauritius.

- The third pattern is a variation of the second. Instead of returning to either Mombasa or Dar es Salaam, the ship sails on to South Africa (or vice versa).

- A fourth itinerary visits Africa's west coast. These last three itineraries typically take place in the Southern Hemisphere's summer, which is November through March.

- Finally, there's one of the most legendary cruise itineraries of all: the Nile River, usually between Egypt's Aswan and Luxor. Nile cruises operate year-round and employ boats specially designed for river cruises; unlike the Amazon, regular cruise ships cannot navigate the Nile.

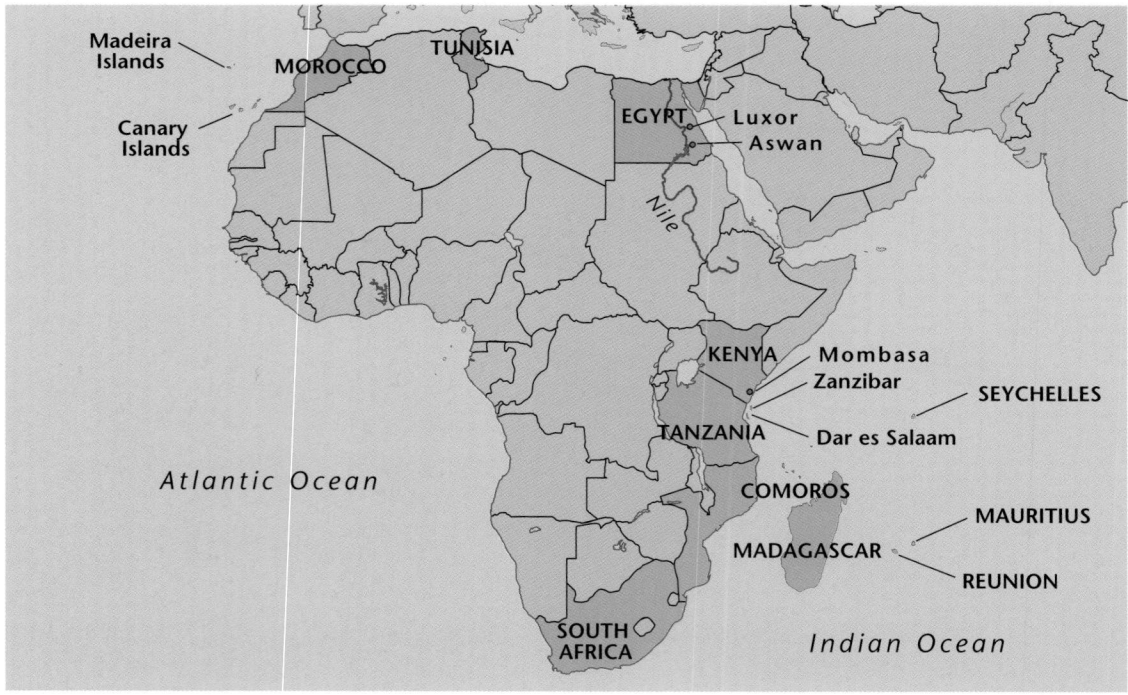

FIGURE 7-18 Map of Africa

Here's a summary of the destination information you've just read:

Region	Starting/Ending	Ports season
Alaska	Vancouver, Seattle, Anchorage	May–October
Northeast	New York City, Montreal	Late spring–fall
North America Rivers	Mississippi River ports	Year-round
Mexico (round-trip)	Los Angeles, San Diego	Year-round
Mexico (one-way)	Los Angeles, San Diego, Acapulco	Winter
Bahamas	Miami, Port Everglades, Port Canaveral, Tampa	Year-round
Bermuda	New York City, other East Coast cities	Late spring–early fall
Caribbean (Eastern)	Miami, Port Everglades, San Juan	Year-round
Caribbean (Southern)	San Juan, Aruba, Barbados	Year-round
Caribbean (Western)	Miami, Port Everglades, Port Canaveral, Tampa, Houston, Galveston, New Orleans	Year-round
Mediterranean (Western)	Barcelona, Nice, Civitavecchia	Late spring–early fall
Mediterranean (Eastern)	Venice, Piraeus, Istanbul	Late spring–early fall
Europe (Atlantic)	Malaga, London, Lisbon, Le Havre	Late spring–early fall
Europe (Ireland, Great Britain, North Sea)	London, Copenhagen	Late spring–early fall
Europe (Baltic Sea)	Hamburg, Copenhagen, St. Petersburg	Late spring–early fall
Europe (Rivers)	Rhone, Rhine, Elbe, Volga, Danube ports	Late spring–early fall
Central and South America	San Juan, Rio de Janeiro, Callao	October–April
Antarctica	Southern South American ports	January–February
Hawaii and Pacific Islands	Various	Year-round
Asia	Various	October–May
Africa (Northwest)	Various	May–October
Africa (East Coast)	Mombasa, Dar es Salaam	November–March
Africa (West Coast)	Various	November–March

Note also that you've just read about the *major* itinerary patterns; many others exist. Some of these lesser-known itineraries may become popular as consumers experience them and become jaded about the more common voyages. Indeed, this has already started in the Caribbean. Mass-market cruise lines have begun to call on islands that most people had never heard of only a decade ago.

Repositioning Cruises

Throughout this text, we've referred to repositioning cruises. But what exactly are they. A *repositioning cruise* is one in which a ship sails from one region to another, usually distant region. The reason for this move: High season is ending at the first location and another high season is about to begin at the second destination. Here's an example: It would make no sense to leave a dozen cruise ships idle in Alaska's winter when they could be deployed in, say, Mexico or the Caribbean, where the winter weather is pleasant.

Here are the most common repositioning cruises in September, October, and November:

- From Europe across the Atlantic to Bermuda, the Bahamas, the Caribbean, the Panama Canal, or even South America.
- From the Mediterranean through the Suez Canal to Africa's east coast and its islands or into Asia.
- From Alaska down the U.S. west coast to Mexico, the Panama Canal, and/or the Caribbean; sometimes, the ship may "sidetrack" to Hawaii along the way.
- From Alaska across the Pacific to Hawaii and on to Asia or the South Pacific.

From March to May, these repositioning cruises are reversed. For instance, a ship stationed in the Caribbean might cross the Atlantic to return to Europe.

Although repositioning cruises typically feature many days at sea (and are quite a value), every attempt is made to call on ports along the way. Sometimes a ship is repositioned with only crew aboard. The idea is to get the ship to its next destination as quickly as possible with no passengers to worry about. More commonly, the sailing is open to passengers, who pay a very reduced fare and who realize that very few ports will be visited along the way. (A ship sailing, say, from Northern Europe to the Caribbean might dock only in the Azores and Bermuda.) So price-sensitive travelers who enjoy days at sea find repositioning cruises quite attractive.

Some Miscellaneous Thoughts

- **Occasionally, cruise lines operate "cruises to nowhere."** Typically, the ship leaves a port, circles out for a few days, then returns—without making intermediate stops. Passengers are kept occupied by the activities that take place on the ship.
- **Allied to this is the concept of the ship *as* a destination.** The vessel is marketed as a floating resort, competing for the consumer's attention and dollars with land-based resorts in Las Vegas, Mexico, Hawaii, and Orlando. The goal is to make the passenger feel that the ship is every bit as interesting a place as the ports visited.
- **Sometimes, a ship's "culture" is strongly affected by its crew's countries of origin.** The ambiance of a vessel with Greek crew members might be exuberant and hearty. Another with a crew from Britain might be more formal and refined.

- **On rare occasions, a port on the itinerary may be substituted or deleted.** Two possible reasons for such a change might be stormy weather conditions or political unrest at the port or region visited.

- **Large cruise lines tend to feature newer and larger ships at mass-market destinations.** Somewhat older and more modestly sized vessels predominate on itineraries to more exotic places, such as Asia, Africa, and South America.

- **Some cruise lines call at their very own privately owned islands.** Most are in the Bahamas or the Caribbean and feature picnics, barbecues, nature trails, organized games, local craft vendors, all manner of watersports, and broad stretches of pristine sand.

- **Meals aboard ship are often themed with appropriate food and waiter "costumes."** One night might have a Caribbean theme; the next, Italian. Oddly, these might have no relationship to where the ship is traveling that night. A Polynesian night can occur in the Greek islands; a Greek night can occur in Polynesia. The cruise lines do try to ensure, through entertainment or food, that the destination and shipboard ambiance, to some extent, match.

- **Some cruise line chefs do believe, however, that food should reflect the region the ship is visiting.** But not in the way you might think. They argue

Cruise Guide for Worldwide Destinations

Cruise Line	Africa (Southern)	Alaska	Amazon River	Antarctica	Australia/New Zealand	Bahamas	Baltics/Russia	Bermuda	Black Sea	British Isles	Canada/New England	Canary Islands/N. Africa	Caribbean	Central America	Chesapeake Bay	Cruises to Nowhere	Europe (Western)	Far East/Orient	Hawaii	India	Ireland	E. Mediterranean/Aegean	SE Mediterranean	W. Mediterranean	Mexico (Pacific Coast)	Mid-Atlantic US Coast	Middle East	Northeast US Coast	Panama Canal	Red Sea/Suez Canal	Scandinavia/North Cape	South America	South Pacific/Tahiti	Southeast Asia	Southeast US Coast	Transatlantic	Transpacific	West Coast US	World
AMAWATERWAYS										■							■							■															
American Cruise Lines											■				■											■		■							■				
Avalon Waterways										■							■																						
Azamara Cruises										■	■		■	■	■		■	■				■	■	■	■		■						■	■		■		■	
Carnival Cruise Lines		■				■		■			■		■	■		■	■		■						■														
Celebrity Cruises		■			■	■		■		■	■	■	■	■			■		■			■	■	■		■			■			■	■	■					
Costa Cruises	■				■	■	■		■	■	■	■	■				■	■		■		■	■	■				■	■	■	■	■		■		■			
Crystal Cruises	■	■		■	■		■	■	■	■	■	■	■				■	■		■		■	■	■				■	■	■	■	■	■	■		■	■		■
Cunard Line	■				■	■	■	■		■	■		■				■	■	■			■	■	■		■		■	■	■	■	■	■	■		■	■		■
Disney Cruise Line						■		■					■				■								■											■			
Holland America Line	■	■	■	■	■	■	■	■	■	■	■	■	■	■			■	■	■			■	■	■		■		■	■	■	■	■	■	■	■	■	■	■	■
Hurtigruten			■	■		■			■	■			■				■															■	■						
MSC Cruises	■					■	■	■	■	■	■		■				■					■	■	■								■	■			■			
Norwegian Cruise Line		■				■	■	■	■	■	■	■	■	■		■	■		■			■	■	■								■	■			■		■	
Oceania Cruises			■		■		■	■	■	■	■		■	■			■	■				■	■	■		■			■	■	■	■	■	■		■	■	■	
Paul Gauguin Cruises					■																												■						
Pearl Seas Cruises										■	■				■											■		■											
Princess Cruises	■	■	■	■	■	■	■	■	■	■	■	■	■				■	■	■	■		■	■	■	■		■	■	■	■	■	■	■	■		■	■	■	■
Regent Seven Seas Cruises	■	■	■	■	■		■	■	■	■	■		■				■	■		■		■	■	■		■			■	■	■	■	■	■		■	■		■
Royal Caribbean International		■			■	■	■	■	■	■	■	■	■	■			■	■	■			■	■	■	■		■		■		■	■	■	■		■	■	■	
Seabourn Cruise Line			■		■		■		■	■		■	■	■			■	■				■	■	■	■		■		■	■	■	■	■	■		■	■		■
SeaDream Yacht Club								■		■	■						■					■	■	■												■			
Silversea Cruises	■	■	■	■	■		■		■	■	■		■				■	■		■		■	■	■		■			■	■	■	■	■	■		■	■	■	■
Uniworld Boutique River Cruise Collection										■							■																						
Windstar Cruises										■	■	■					■					■	■	■					■							■			

FIGURE 7-19   Cruise guide for worldwide destinations
Source: *Courtesy of CLIA*

that cold weather destinations make people want higher-calorie, more bland food, while warm tropical places make passengers want lighter yet spicier cuisine.

- **CLIA publishes a handy grid that cross-references major destination regions with its member lines.** This enables you to find out which cruise lines visit a certain area of the globe. For an example, see Figure 7-19.

 # Questions for Discussion and Activity

This chapter's Questions for Discussion and Activity are combined. They're also different from the ones you've done before. Below is a list of cruise ports. Your assignment: to identify the country or U.S. state for each port. Use any resource at your disposal. (An atlas might be a good start.) A clue: Some—but not all—are mentioned in this chapter.

Port	Country or U.S. State	Port	Country or U.S. State
Auckland		Mombasa	
Bali		Montego Bay	
Bar Harbor		Montevideo	
Barcelona		Mumbai	
Barranquilla		Nassau	
Bergen		New Orleans	
Budapest		Nice	
Buenos Aires		Ocho Rios	
Cairns		Odessa	
Callao		Papeete	
Cape Town		Philipsburg	
Casablanca		Piraeus	
Catalina		Port Everglades	
Charlotte Amalie		Port Kelang	
Civitavecchia		Port of Spain	
Cozumel		Portofino	
Dakar		Pusan	
Ensenada		Recife	

Port	Country or U.S. State	Port	Country or U.S. State
Fort-de-France		Santorini	
Haifa		Seward	
Halifax		Shanghai	
Hamilton		Singapore	
Istanbul		Sitka	
Juneau		Southampton	
Key West		Stockholm	
Kusadasi		Tallinn	
Lahaina		Tunis	
Leith		Valletta	
Mahe		Valparaiso	
Manaus		Vancouver	
Manila		Yokohama	
Marigot		Zanzibar	
Mazatlan		Zeebrugge	

Courtesy of Hurtigruten

Chapter 8

Profiling the Lines

After reading this chapter, you'll be able to:

- Identify the major sources of insight into a cruise product's personality.
- Access the most important industry and consumer research resources.
- Recognize general patterns among cruise products.
- Find information on each cruise line specifically.

Think of your best friend. What words come to mind? What is it about him or her that makes you two get along? You've almost surely thought of some very specific adjectives. Now think of a cruise line that you've heard about or experienced. What words do you think of? What is it about that cruise line that appeals to people? As with your best friend, some very precise adjectives will come to mind.

Like people, cruise lines and even individual ships have specific "personalities." They're even sometimes part of "families" of cruise lines, with several different lines under one corporate umbrella. In this chapter's activities, you'll learn specifics about the cruise lines. But first, here are some general guidelines so you can discover more about each cruise line.

The Cruise Lines Themselves

One of the best sources of information about any cruise line is the cruise line itself. Here's how you can find out more about each:

- **Cruise line promotional pieces,** such as brochures, ads, commercials, videos, and Web sites, are rich sources of information and insight. Some of the most important information, however, requires a little "digging."

  Look at the people portrayed in a cruise line's promotional pieces. Are they mostly families? Older people? Younger couples? In each case, the photo reveals a clue to the cruise line's specialty. Suppose all these kinds of consumers and more are represented. Then, this company is communicating mass-market appeal. It's one that attracts every kind of passenger.

  What the people in these photos are doing is also important. If they're mostly observing wildlife, then this cruise line probably takes an eco-approach to its product and targets a more narrow type of client than does a more mass-market cruise product. Even what the people wear is an important clue to their income and lifestyle.

  Images aren't the only way to understand whom cruise lines target to buy their product. Words, music in a TV commercial, slogans, colors, and even brochure paper texture are all indicators to a cruise line's personality. What might a brochure for a company that targets very upscale consumers, for example, look like? The paper would be thick, connoting high quality; photos would show people who are mature, well-dressed, and wearing expensive jewelry. The prose would be very literate; the more educated people are, the more money they usually make. The food depicted would be beautifully presented and of gourmet quality; studies show that fine food is the most important cruise factor to upscale consumers.

- **Seminars** are another source of critical information. Cruise lines regularly offer live or online seminars where travel agents can learn more about the cruise line's product. A few cruise companies actually give workshops that, in an unbiased manner, analyze each cruise product, including those of their competitors. In essence, the cruise line is saying, "We're so confident in our product that we can tell you what's good about our competitors too." Travel agency chains and consortia also sometimes offer seminars that profile their preferred cruise lines.

- **Ship inspections** (while a ship is in port) and **familiarization cruises** (offered at greatly reduced prices) are powerfully effective ways for travel professionals to experience firsthand the personality of a ship and its parent company.

- **Passengers** who have just returned from a cruise and veteran cruisers are also prime sources of insights into each line's product. One caveat: Their comments may be highly personal and reflect only that individual's opinion.

- **Business development managers** are an important link between the cruise lines and travel agencies. They also represent their companies at consumer trade shows. Deeply informed about the demographics and psychographics of their company, they're often quite happy to provide insights on their cruise products. They may even be willing to share passenger research reports with preferred travel agencies who consistently sell their product.

Trade Publications

Three resources regularly offer in-depth information on cruise lines and ships. Travel agents are their primary customers:

- Throughout this book, we've cited the *CLIA Cruise Manual,* which is CLIA's yearly compendium of important data. This online- and CD-ROM–based publication doesn't really analyze product; it is, after all, a resource vehicle created by the cruise lines. Nonetheless, it provides such valuable content as ship data, deck plans, key telephone numbers, sales policies, ship facilities and services, port descriptions, and grids detailing offerings to client types such as honeymooners, physically challenged travelers, children, and singles.

- *The Official Steamship Guide International* contains sailing itineraries, port maps, ship facts, and specialty cruise products (including freighters, ferries, and barges).

- Most travel agents forget that *The Star Service,* a massive online compendium of hotel reviews, also profiles cruise ships. Thoroughly opinionated, *The Star Service*'s analyses are solid and often entertaining. Each ship is rated according to a 1–5 star system.

Cruise-specific trade magazines and newsletters regularly analyze lines, ships, destinations, and itineraries, as do the industry's more generic publications. For a list of these periodicals, see Appendix C.

Trade Shows

Many travel industry trade shows feature at least a few seminars on cruising. Some conferences are devoted entirely to cruising: CLIA's own *cruise3sixty* is the most popular, with dozens of seminars, a major trade show, ship inspections, and presentations by industry leaders.

A relatively small cruise ship visits some clearly small locals.
Courtesy of Hurtigruten

Consumer Publications

The public's growing enthusiasm for the cruise vacation experience has led to a plethora of consumer publications, many of which profile cruise lines and rate their vessels. Here are the most popular books:

- Berlitz's *Complete Guide to Cruising & Cruise Ships*
- *Cruise Vacations for Dummies*

- *Fodor's Ports of Call series*
- *Frommer's Cruise & Ports of Call series*
- *Stern's Guide to the Cruise Vacation*
- *The Unofficial Guide to Cruises*

These consumer magazines regularly offer cruise-related articles: *Travel and Leisure, National Geographic Traveler, Conde Nast Traveler,* and *Budget Travel. Cruise Travel Magazine* and *Porthole* devote most of their content to cruising.

These and other travel-related consumer publications are also listed in Appendix C.

Video and the Internet

Virtually every cruise line offers at least one video that showcases its product. Some have many more. A one-stop source of cruise line videos is *Vacations on Video.* See Appendix C for more.

As for the Internet, there seem to be as many Web sites devoted to cruise analyses as there are passengers. The problem: How can you be sure the person giving an opinion is truly knowledgeable and reliable? Two of the most popular sites are *Cruise Critic* and *Cruisemates.* Most cruise lines also have Web sites. Each site is usually divided into two sections: one for consumers; the other for travel agents. For a complete list of CLIA member Web site addresses, see Appendix A.

CLIA has its own extremely useful Web site at www.cruising.org. It enables consumers to find CLIA-affiliated agencies and Certified Cruise Counsellors in their geographic area. It also offers answers to typical questions on cruising, information on specific lifestyle needs, data on over 100 worldwide cruise destinations, and current news and features on cruising. Its agent-specific center lists valuable marketing and training resources that are available.

The Internet for Research

So, you've learned how trade publications, trade shows, consumer publications, and CLIA's certification program help travel professionals learn more about the cruise experience, and we also briefly mention the Internet.

But it's now time to greatly expand upon that topic. The reason: The Internet is the most powerful research tool the world has ever known. If you need more information on cruising—or anything for that matter—it's out there somewhere. All you need to do is know how to find it.

The key to a productive—and swift—online research experience rests with the search engine. A search engine uses the keywords you've entered in its search box to find Web sites that contain the information you're looking for. Google and Yahoo! are the most popular.

Here are eight simple time-saving tips to help boost your Internet ability. You may already know some of them, but let's review them anyway. There are some strategies you may not know about:

1. **Use more than one search engine.** No single search engine has information that covers the entire Web. Nor are all results totally up to date. Get into the habit of searching not only Google and Yahoo! but some of the lesser known ones you may come across.

2. **Use a search directory.** Similar to a search engine, a search directory is an index of Web sites, organized by subject. Here are three good ones to get you going: About, Looksmart, and Pandia.

3. **Be specific.** The more specific your search, the more likely you'll find what you're looking for. Enter keywords in the search box that very specifically say what you're looking for rather than using terms that are too general. Try it a few times. You'll see what we mean. For example, on Google, the keywords "Dublin travel" generated more than 31 million Web site links, while "Dublin travel tips" yielded only 963,000—still far more than you need but not so overwhelming and closer to what you're searching for. Finally, enter "Dublin luxury cruise travel tips for the physically challenged." The result: only 21,900 hits. But there's a problem. These words can be totally disconnected at the site. Many of the sites displayed may be useless to you. But there's a way around this, which leads us to. . . .

4. **Use certain characters and words to refine your search.** In some situations, you may want the search engine to find pages that contain all the words you enter. The plus (+) symbol or the word "and" will usually allow you to do this and come up with more targeted results. On the other hand, the minus (–) symbol before a word may help in weeding out unnecessary listings. Also try experimenting with quotation marks (" ") around your keyword phrases and the words "or" and "not" to yield more targeted results. Be aware that these tips aren't foolproof. Success varies from one search engine to another. The keywords you use may also make a difference.

5. **Take advantage of a search engine's search tips and advance search functions.** Look for these valuable help functions near the search box or at the bottom of the screen. (Many people forget they're even there!)

6. **Try linking to a variety of the search engine results.** Go past the first one or two that come up at the top of the page. Companies may have paid to have their sites listed first or the results may be what the search engine *thinks* are the best but aren't. The specific information you're looking for may be further down the list. It may take a number of clicks before you find it. You may even have to go past the first 10 or 20 choices.

7. **Practice. Practice. Practice.** Set aside 10 to 15 minutes each day to practice using search engines and explore different Web sites. Discipline yourself to keep a journal in your word processor or spreadsheet program of each day's activities. The Web site address and a few of its key features are all that's necessary. Bookmark the most helpful by adding them to your Favorites list. Reminder: A bookmark is a hyperlink within a browser that enables Internet users to quickly and easily go to sites they visit frequently.

8. **Evaluate the information.** Just because the information's on the Internet doesn't necessarily mean it's correct or up to date. When using the Internet for research, consider such things as the source and timeliness of the information. Even Wikipedia, the most impressive source of info on the Web, makes mistakes. Because it's user-generated, that's going to happen.

CLIA's Education and Certification Programs

Through CLIA's Cruise Counsellor Certification Program, travel professionals receive comprehensive training in how to maximize cruise sales. Although the program doesn't profile individual cruise lines, the extensive experiential learning it requires inevitably leads to a deeper understanding of products, along with greater client recognition, confidence, and sales success.

This highly rated certification program offers three achievement levels: Accredited Cruise Counsellor (ACC), Master Cruise Counsellor (MCC), and Elite Cruise Counsellor (ECC). Enrollees profit from a rich mixture of learning components: live seminars, videos, Internet-based courses, ship inspections, cruises, and, yes, this book. Nearly 17,000 cruise professionals have achieved certification, and thousands more are completing their requirements.

For more information on the program, contact CLIA.

General Patterns

Each cruise line has its own personality. But distinct patterns also mark certain *categories* of cruise lines. For example, *mass-market, lower-cost cruise products* tend to:

- Appeal to many *different types of consumers*, with an informal atmosphere prevailing.
- Operate *large or very large ships*, offering a wide array of options and activities.
- Concentrate on *popular, mass-market destinations*, such as the Caribbean, Mexico, and Alaska, mostly on round-trip itineraries. Large, lower-cost cruise lines may also have one or two vessels in their fleet that visit more exotic destinations (e.g., Asia, South America, and the South Pacific).
- Offer *plentiful food* and many dining choices.
- Feature *major entertainment shows.*
- Include a little less in the cruise price than more expensive cruise lines do; there are more *small extras to pay for.*
- Provide more *three- to seven-day cruises*, which tend to attract people new to cruising (they want to sample it) and those on a budget, such as young people, families, and some seniors.

It's important to realize that these are *generalizations*. Exceptions do exist. For example, some upscale cruise lines offer very casual experiences. Some budget lines call on exotic ports. And young passengers and families are sometimes found on more expensive cruises.

Midlevel, somewhat more expensive cruise lines (often called "premium" lines) tend to have:

- More *upscale and older travelers*, with a somewhat more formal atmosphere prevailing
- *Midsized to large* vessels
- *Mass-market and a few more exotic destinations* and itineraries, with a mix of both round-trip and one-way itineraries
- *More refined cuisine*, with a main dining room and a few alternative restaurants
- *More modestly scaled entertainment* (although larger vessels in this sector may have entertainment just as grand as that on mass-market ships)
- *More things included in the cruise price* than mass-market ships include (e.g., free espresso, flowers and fruit in each stateroom, bathrobes in the closet)
- More *seven-day cruises and longer*, the kind affordable to their less budget-minded passengers

Very upscale cruise lines refine the experience even more. These tend to:

- Attract *wealthy, experienced, and usually older travelers*, with a more formal atmosphere prevailing
- Operate *smaller ships*, with larger staterooms/suites, mostly or all outside
- Visit *many unusual ports*, along with a few standard ones (especially at the beginning and end of the voyage); mostly one-way itineraries
- Serve *gourmet food*, usually in an open-seating dining format, with one or two alternate dining venues
- Provide *low-key entertainment*; lecturers provide learning and cultural enrichment
- *Almost everything included in the cruise price*, with all sorts of special upscale amenities
- Offer *longer cruises*, which tend to attract very successful professionals (e.g., attorneys and physicians) and older, wealthier, typically retired people
- Feature an *astonishing level of service*, very often with no tipping required

There can also be variations of product level even aboard an individual ship. Nothing like the old "class" system—where first-class passengers never interacted with those in third class—exists today. But guests in suites and on a "concierge" deck on mass-market lines often get a higher level of amenities and services than do those in standard staterooms. There may be a bathrobe for their use while onboard, premium soap and shampoos, free laundry services, and even a separate, exclusive dining room.

Generalized Versus Niche Cruise Lines

Most of us think of cruising as a product so broad that it can satisfy almost every type of traveler. In most cases, this is true. For example, the majority of cruise lines offer special packages for honeymooners. Families with children also find plenty

Cruise Guide for Sports and Fitness

A = All Ships
S = Some Ships
Blank = Not Available

Cruise Line	Cardio Equipment	Free Weights and/or Machines	Personal Trainer	Total Fitness Program	Group Fitness Classes	Yoga/Pilates	Jogging Track	Basketball	Volleyball	Multi-use Sports Court	Paddle Tennis/Ping Pong	Rock Climbing Wall	Bowling Alley	Miniature Golf	Watersports Platform	Snorkel Lessons	Discover SCUBA/Resort Cruise	SCUBA Certification	Golf Programs	Golf Driving or Simulator	Clinics/Lessons	Onboard Golf Pro	Golf Packages
AMAWATERWAYS	S	S																					
American Cruise Lines																			S				S
Avalon Waterways	A	A																					
Azamara Cruises	A	A	A	A	A	A	A																
Carnival Cruise Lines	A	A	A	A	A	A	A	S	S	S	A			A					A	S	A	A	A
Celebrity Cruises	A	A	S	S	S	S	S	S	S	S	A			S			S		S	S	S	S	S
Costa Cruises	A	A	A	A	A	A	S	S	S	S	A			S					S	S	S	S	S
Crystal Cruises	A	A	A	A	A	A	A				A								A	A	S	S	S
Cunard Line	A	A	A	A	A	A	A			S	A								S	A	S	S	S
Disney Cruise Line	A	A	A	A	A	A	A	A			A												S
Holland America Line	A	A	A	A	A	A	A	S	S	S	A										S		
Hurtigruten	S	S					S																
MSC Cruises	A	A	A	A	A	A	A	S	S	S	S			S	S				S	S	S	S	S
Norwegian Cruise Line	A	A	A	A	A	A	A	S	S	S	A	S	S	S		S	S	S	S		S	S	S
Oceania Cruises	A	A	A	A	A	A	A																
Paul Gauguin Cruises	A	A			A	A									A	A	A	A					
Pearl Seas Cruises	A	A			A	A																	
Princess Cruises	A	A	A	A	A	A	A	S	S	S	S			S		S	S	S	S	S	S	S	S
Regent Seven Seas Cruises	A	A	A	A	A	A	A				A									A	S		S
Royal Caribbean International	A	A	A	A	A	A	A	S	S	S	A	A		S		A	A	A	S	S	S	S	
Seabourn Cruise Line	A	A	A	A	A	A	A								A	S							
SeaDream Yacht Club	A	A	A			A									A						A		
Silversea Cruises	A	A	A	A	A	A	A				A								S		S	S	S
Uniworld Boutique River Cruise Collection	S	S			S																		
Windstar Cruises	A	A	A	A	A	A	A								A	S	S	S					

FIGURE 8-1 **Cruise guide for active adults**
Source: *Courtesy of CLIA*

to do on most cruises, as do very active adults. (The *CLIA Cruise Manual* contains grids that display what each member line offers to such specialized clients. For an example, see Figure 8-1.)

On the other hand, some lines target narrow segments of consumers who have something in common. In marketing, these categories of customer types are called **niches**. A niche is defined as a group of people who have a very specialized set of needs and wants. A niche company provides products and services that suit the ways their niche clients buy.

For example, some cruise lines don't simply provide options for the active adult—as generalized cruise lines do—but *stress* them. Adventure is what they're all about. Comfort, pampering, and elegant cuisine may be low on their clients' priority list. There are, however, some niche cruise lines that provide *both* adventure and pampering.

Another specialized market is education. For some lines, learning is at the *core* of the cruise experience. These companies may offer only limited entertainment and no casino. The people who take their cruises care very little about anything but learning. Still other companies appeal to clients who are highly independent and want as unstructured a cruise experience as possible. A plethora of activities onboard ship is precisely what they *don't* want.

Small Ships

As you've learned, the cruise industry isn't just about large ships. There's a whole other segment of the business—a niche one—that's not well-known by the public—except those who have discovered its charms. It's called *small ship cruising*. And it's a segment that's growing at an impressive pace.

Small ships have most of the following eight things in common:

1. They can get into places larger ships can't (e.g., a narrow but dramatic inlet in Alaska), giving guests an up-close experience.

2. They concentrate on destinations, their cultures, and their history. What's outside the ship is more important than what's inside the ship.

3. Entertainment is simple—not the considerable offerings of "regular" cruise ships. There's a strong emphasis on learning experiences, "soft" adventure, and personal enrichment.

4. They provide a strong feeling for the scenery, towns, and cities they visit or pass by—and the waterways and seas they sail.

5. Dining is usually casual, with open seating (you sit where you want, with whom you want). Formal evenings are rare. Informal wear is appropriate.

6. The decor is usually simple and practical. However, a few small ships are luxurious.

7. The basic cruise amenities (TVs, bars, etc.) are available, but multiple dining facilities, casinos, and big showrooms are typical only on the few larger vessels in this category.

8. The most obvious trait: The ships are smaller. If regular cruise ships are floating mega-resorts, small ships are floating "boutique" hotels.

There are three kinds of small ship experiences:

1. **Expedition/adventure cruises.** These cruises focus on unusual, off-the-beaten-path places. Guest lecturers and/or guides help guests appreciate what they're experiencing in a very direct, adventurous, up-close, and intimate way. Most use modest-sized ships, with simple furnishings, a small dining room, perhaps a small entertainment venue, and some deck space. A few larger ships—with 500 to 600 passengers—also fit this expedition/adventure category and provide more of the amenities that we would expect on a larger, more traditional cruise ship.

2. **River cruises.** Rivers were once significant paths for commerce. That's why so many important cities are situated on notable waterways. River cruises provide an efficient, stable way to experience countries and cultures "from the inside." They travel at a leisurely pace, life onboard is very casual, and learning is a high priority. The most important rivers for cruising are the Danube (Europe), the Nile (Egypt), the Rhine (Europe), the Yangtze (China), and the Mississippi (United States). Most river vessels carry fewer than 200 passengers.

3. **Masted sailing ships.** These large sailing ships rely on masts and sails to propel the ship (with auxiliary motors for practical and safety reasons). For many, masted ships fulfill a fantasy: reliving the way all adventurers once traveled by sea. They generally accommodate from 100 to 300 passengers.

The CLIA Member Cruise Lines

To learn about the CLIA member cruise lines, go to CLIA's Web site: www.cruising. org. It'll be the key for one of this chapter's activities.

 # Questions for Discussion

1. Give four ways cruise lines enable you to understand their profile and whom they typically target to buy their cruises.

2. Cite three trade publications of in-depth information on cruise lines and their product.

3. What product patterns generally characterize a lower-cost, mass-market cruise product? A midlevel, premium one? An upscale one?

4. Is it possible for a person to have a "deluxe" experience on a mass-market cruise ship? Explain why.

 Activity 1

Obtain one cruise brochure. Explain how each of the elements listed below is used and what this may say about the clients that the cruise line targets:

Name of cruise line:

Name of brochure:

Colors used on the cover:

Colors used inside the brochure:

Quality of paper:

Quality of the prose inside:

Photo selection:

Overall design:

Activity 2

Go online, choose 10 CLIA member cruise lines (for convenience, you may access them through CLIA's website: www.cruising.org), and then fill out the 10 worksheets that follow.

Worksheet 1:

Name of cruise line:

Itineraries (Circle one):	Global	A few areas	
Ships (Circle one):	Huge	Large	Small
Type of vessel (Circle one):	Conventional	Masted River	
Price level (Circle one):	Luxury	Premium Midrange	Inexpensive

How did you figure out the price level?

Name and explain two things that seem to set this cruise line apart from other cruise lines:

Worksheet 2:

Name of cruise line:

Itineraries (Circle one):	Global	A few areas	
Ships (Circle one):	Huge	Large	Small
Type of vessel (Circle one):	Conventional	Masted River	
Price level (Circle one):	Luxury	Premium Midrange	Inexpensive

How did you figure out the price level?

Name and explain two things that seem to set this cruise line apart from other cruise lines:

Worksheet 3:

Name of cruise line:			
Itineraries (Circle one):	Global	A few areas	
Ships (Circle one):	Huge	Large	Small
Type of vessel (Circle one):	Conventional	Masted River	
Price level (Circle one):	Luxury	Premium Midrange	Inexpensive

How did you figure out the price level?

Name and explain two things that seem to set this cruise line apart from other cruise lines:

Worksheet 4:

Name of cruise line:			
Itineraries (Circle one):	Global	A few areas	
Ships (Circle one):	Huge	Large	Small
Type of vessel (Circle one):	Conventional	Masted River	
Price level (Circle one):	Luxury	Premium Midrange	Inexpensive

How did you figure out the price level?

Name and explain two things that seem to set this cruise line apart from other cruise lines:

Worksheet 5:

Name of cruise line:			
Itineraries (Circle one):	Global	A few areas	
Ships (Circle one):	Huge	Large	Small
Type of vessel (Circle one):	Conventional	Masted River	
Price level (Circle one):	Luxury	Premium Midrange	Inexpensive

How did you figure out the price level?

Name and explain two things that seem to set this cruise line apart from other cruise lines:

Worksheet 6:

Name of cruise line:

Itineraries (Circle one):	Global	A few areas	
Ships (Circle one):	Huge	Large	Small
Type of vessel (Circle one):	Conventional	Masted River	
Price level (Circle one):	Luxury	Premium Midrange	Inexpensive

How did you figure out the price level?

Name and explain two things that seem to set this cruise line apart from other cruise lines:

Worksheet 7:

Name of cruise line:

Itineraries (Circle one):	Global	A few areas	
Ships (Circle one):	Huge	Large	Small
Type of vessel (Circle one):	Conventional	Masted River	
Price level (Circle one):	Luxury	Premium Midrange	Inexpensive

How did you figure out the price level?

Name and explain two things that seem to set this cruise line apart from other cruise lines:

Worksheet 8:

Name of cruise line:

Itineraries (Circle one):	Global	A few areas	
Ships (Circle one):	Huge	Large	Small
Type of vessel (Circle one):	Conventional	Masted River	
Price level (Circle one):	Luxury	Premium Midrange	Inexpensive

How did you figure out the price level?

Name and explain two things that seem to set this cruise line apart from other cruise lines:

Worksheet 9:

Name of cruise line:

Itineraries (Circle one):	Global	A few areas		
Ships (Circle one):	Huge	Large	Small	
Type of vessel (Circle one):	Conventional	Masted	River	
Price level (Circle one):	Luxury	Premium	Midrange	Inexpensive

How did you figure out the price level?

Name and explain two things that seem to set this cruise line apart from other cruise lines:

Worksheet 10:

Name of cruise line:

Itineraries (Circle one):	Global	A few areas		
Ships (Circle one):	Huge	Large	Small	
Type of vessel (Circle one):	Conventional	Masted	River	
Price level (Circle one):	Luxury	Premium	Midrange	Inexpensive

How did you figure out the price level?

Name and explain two things that seem to set this cruise line apart from other cruise lines:

Selling Cruises

After reading this chapter, you'll be able to:

- Analyze six types of experienced cruisers.
- Apply the cruise sales process to the travel counseling process.
- Interpret cruise brochures.
- Propose an effective cruise solution to most clients' needs.
- Overcome barriers to the cruise sale.
- Carry out a cruise reservation.

Who sells cruises? The most obvious response: travel agents. But there's a more subtle answer to that question: People who've been on cruises sell cruises. The number-one reason people buy the cruise vacation experience is word of mouth—someone told them how great it is. Other motivators, in order of importance, are a travel agent's recommendation, an ad, a brochure, and an article.

Who Buys Cruises

Let's take a look at the other side of the equation. Who *buys* cruises? As we indicated in Chapter 2, only about 20% of the North American market has thus far been on a cruise. To help travel agents and its member lines understand people who have already cruised (and probably will again), CLIA decided that it might be useful to identify their demographic and psychographic profiles. They identified six categories of cruise consumers. Here they are (in order of size), with some facts about how they think and buy:

- *Restless Baby Boomers* are in their late 40s and 50s, are thrifty, family-oriented, and a little wary of new things. Because they're still supporting children, they respond positively to the cost-saving value of a cruise. Their lives are complex, so they like the simplifying, all-inclusive nature of cruising. They also perceive cruising as a fun family vacation.

- *Enthusiastic Baby Boomers* are a little younger than our previous category (they're in their 40s). Like older Baby Boomers, they're fun-loving and family-oriented. They're a little more adventurous and gregarious than Restless Baby Boomers. They see cruising as an entertaining way to do many things and meet many people. The romance of cruising very much appeals to them.

- *Consummate Shoppers* are in their late 50s or older, well-traveled, and like the pampering and fine dining available onboard cruise ships. Because they're thrifty, however, they very much want to feel that they're getting the best deal for their dollar. More than most, the ship is as important to them as the destination.

- Even more than Consummate Shoppers, *Luxury Cruisers* value ships that provide fine dining and ever-present pampering. Unlike Consummate Shoppers, though, cost isn't a major issue for them. As long as they perceive value, they're quite willing to pay for the best. In their late 50s, they're cultured, well-educated, experienced, and active.

- *Explorers* are a small but influential segment of the cruise market. They see a cruise as a vehicle for discovering the world. Destinations are far more important to them than the ship itself. They're well-educated and use their sightseeing to learn even more. They're older (late 60s) yet still very active. They plan their cruises far ahead of departure, not so much to get a better deal (they're quite well-off) as to get the vacation that they want.

- *Ship Buffs* are the study's smallest segment and also the oldest (late 60s to mid-70s). The most cruise-savvy of all, they possess an unusual knowledge of ships and itineraries. They love being taken care of, to be comfortable, and to be pampered. They like longer cruises and are very flexible in their cruise choices.

A strong selling point: The best way to experience Alaska is by cruise ship.
Courtesy of Carnival Cruise Lines

The Cruise Sales Process

Understanding who buys cruises is an important step toward effective sales. So too is knowledge of the product. But that's not enough. It's essential for travel agents (and cruise line reservationists) to be familiar with effective sales techniques.

Unfortunately, travel agents sometimes see themselves as service people or order takers rather than salespeople. They think that their job is to respond to client requests rather than to lead their buying behavior. Why? Because, like many people, they have a very negative image of a salesperson: aggressive, exploitative, greedy, and self-serving. Imagine the stereotype of a car salesman. That just about says it all. Agents don't want to be stereotyped as such.

But the sales process need not be manipulative. In fact, today's consumers recognize and reject old-fashioned "hard" sales techniques. They prefer sellers who are sensitive to their needs, who wish to establish ongoing business relationships with them, and who, as a result, don't do things *to* people but *for* and *with* them.

This paradigm suits the selling of travel well. A cruise vacation evokes pleasant emotions. Relaxation, pampering, joy—that's what a cruise is about. The sales process should parallel those feelings. The cruise vacation experience doesn't start when a passenger gets on the ship. It begins in the client's mind, when he or she hears a friend's positive comments about a cruise, when a brochure is skimmed, an ad is seen, or an article is read. And it can really take hold right there in the travel agency, when a wish is about to become reality.

The differences between experiences and commodities

Many consumers seem at ease with buying certain travel products, such as air tickets and car rentals, without the help of travel agents. But they seem reluctant to book a cruise or tour on their own. Why? It has all to do with the difference between commodities and experiences.

Commodities are products that are so simple and similar that price becomes the prime determining factor in the purchase. Air, for instance, is a commodity, since—all things being equal—a flight on Continental isn't much different from one on Delta. Experiences, on the other hand, are products that are complex and different; price is only one factor in the buying equation. Most people feel they need advice before making a purchase.

This difference explains much, including why people seem comfortable using the Internet to book flights but not cruises. Most of the latter are sold through travel agents.

So, let's examine the entire sales process through the eyes of a travel agent. Let's examine what the best travel counselors do.

Opening the Sale

Most people decide if they like someone in *six seconds*.

So concludes a Stanford University study. A salesperson has only a fleeting moment to achieve two things: create a favorable impression and put a client at ease.

Let's assume that the prospect has visited his local travel agency. That's more probable for a cruise purchase, which is a more complicated purchase than, say, an airline ticket. What should you do if you're the travel agent?

- Stand up and greet the client. Your action communicates your eagerness to *take action* for the client.
- Establish eye contact with the client.
- Smile, conveying your pleasure with the opportunity to help.
- Give your name and then obtain the client's name. The exchange of names helps personalize the sale.
- Shake hands. This should be a genuinely warm and open gesture.
- Invite the client to sit down with you. If your office layout permits it, have the client sit to the side of your desk. It's a much more friendly gesture than having a customer sit across from you.

Crew are a key element for client satisfaction.
Courtesy of Windstar Cruises

Opening a phone sale is a greater challenge. You and the client can't see each other. Your voice must convey everything. Here's how:

- **Use the four-part greeting.** "Good morning. *[Your agency's name].* This is *[your name].* How may I help you?" Experts have determined that this four-part greeting is by far the most effective. A few cruise specialist agents even customize its end, dropping the "How may I help you?" in favor of something like the disarmingly friendly "How can I help you with your cruise vacation?" Note also that both of these endings elicit an open-ended response, leading to conversation and clarification.

- **Smile.** Yes, smile. Phone callers can somehow perceive a smile over the phone.

- **Communicate energy and enthusiasm.** The client is excited about the possibility of cruising. You should mirror that fervor with your own.

Qualifying the Client

A standard term in sales jargon, *qualifying* means asking questions to uncover a client's needs. The types of questions you'll ask, though, will depend on why the customer came to you.

Travel agents deal with three general scenarios:

Scenario #1: Clients have only the vaguest idea about what kind of vacation they want. Maybe they only know they want to go someplace "warm" or experience something "different." For such clients, you must ask *many questions* to discover what's right for them. An early question should be: "Have you ever cruised before?" If the answer is yes, you should try to probe the reasons that motivated them to select a cruise. Their answers should enable you to classify your client in one of the CLIA survey categories. Is your customer an Explorer? A Luxury Cruiser? Perhaps a Restless Baby Boomer? Your conclusion will help you steer the sales process in a direction appropriate to the client's needs.

Scenario #2: Clients have a rough idea of what they want. They may be interested in a cruise, but they don't know which itinerary and ship is right for them. Or they may have already selected their destination (let's say the Far East) but don't realize that a cruise might be a great vehicle for experiencing Asia. As with Scenario #1, probe with questions that will profile the client's traveling style. Try to classify them in the appropriate category. The insights you achieve will assist you when it's time to recommend.

Scenario #3: Clients know exactly what they want. They've come to you to save time, get a good price, or verify their own research. And they have a specific cruise in mind. These customers are using your services because they are too busy. Even though they seem to know what they want, you should still ask a few questions. Perhaps there's a cruise product the client knows little or nothing about that would fit his or her needs *better*. Or even a "hidden" need that the customer doesn't realize. Precise questioning will also underscore your commitment to getting to know this client.

What if the client has telephoned with a specific cruise in mind and wants only a price? Telephone shoppers can be trying. You know your chance of getting the sale is low. They'll just keep calling agencies until they get the best price. Just give them a quote. No need to ask questions. Right?

Wrong. Asking questions before quoting a price will set you apart from other agents. In effect, you're not just trying to sell a cruise. You're selling your *agency*—what's unique about it; what benefit there is to doing business with you—showing that you care enough about them and their trip and that you're willing to take the time to explore their needs. You might also offer to try to match the best price quoted once the prospect has finished shopping. If you made a solid, favorable impression, this shopper might just call you back to buy.

Another tactic: Give a reason for the shopper to actually come to your agency. One effective strategy is to offer to loan them a video on the cruise line they're considering. If they borrow one, they'll have to return it. That means *two* visits to your agency. And research shows that a sale is much more likely in person than over the phone.

Here's the flip side to Scenario #3: The client knows what he or she wants, but it's not a cruise. Should you therefore dismiss a cruise as a recommendation option? No! Maybe this client is someone who'll never cruise. Perhaps, though, he or she is indeed a cruise prospect but just doesn't know it. Be alert. If your questions reveal that the client fits the profile of a cruiser and if their mental barriers to buying a cruise prove false, then a cruise may be precisely what satisfies his or her needs.

Qualifying Questions

Two kinds of questions help you determine a client's needs: *closed-ended* and *open-ended*.

Closed-ended questions require simple, factual responses. They're essential to ask in all three scenarios we described above. Here are the classic ones:

- *Who* is going on the trip? (It's essential to get the client's name, phone number, etc., for potential future follow-up.)
- *What* do you have in mind for your trip?
- *When* do you want to go and for how long?
- *Where* do you want to go?
- *How much* do you want to pay? (A better phrasing is "Tell me your price range.")

The answers are generally entered onto a reservation sheet (see Figure 9-1). In addition to filling out this form, you should take notes of everything the client says. It helps keep you alert and conveys how important you consider the client's responses to be.

Taking notes is especially important when asking open-ended questions—the kind that elicit complex and telling responses. Good open-ended questions provide you with important clues to a client's needs. They're especially important to counseling customers with vague ideas of what they want. Even customers who have a rough idea or know exactly what they want should be asked a few open-ended questions. Here are seven classic open-ended questions:

- How do you picture this cruise in your mind?
- Describe your typical vacation.
- What's the best travel experience you've ever had and why? What's the worst?
- Have you been on an escorted tour? At an all-inclusive resort? Did you enjoy it? (An affirmative answer means they may like a cruise too.)
- What do you like to do while on vacation?
- What did you do on your last vacation? Where did you stay? Do you want this vacation to be similar or completely different?
- Have you been on a cruise? What did you most like about it and why? What did you least like and why?

You can also pose "lifestyle" questions. Some of these seem to be closed-ended, but they yield open-ended results:

- Where do you live? (An important clue to a person's lifestyle.)
- What do you do for a living?
- What kind of car do you drive?
- What's your favorite place to eat and why?
- What kinds of hotels do you prefer? (Because a cruise ship is like a floating resort, the answer to this question will give you important clues as to which ship and line to recommend.)
- Do you like to drive while on vacation? (A yes answer may indicate that the customer likes independence on a trip or perhaps is a budget traveler.)

Clubs _____

Organizations _____

CRUISE DATA AND RESERVATION SHEET

Bold face type indicates information essential **before** making a call to the reservation department of a cruise company.

1. **Name of Client** _____ Date: _____

2. Address _____ Zip Code _____

3. Telephone: Home (_____) _____ Business (_____) _____

4. **Total Number of Party** _____ Comprised of: _____Adults _____Children (Age) _____

_____ A or C

_____ A or C

_____ A or C

6. New _____ Repeat _____ Last Traveled _____ Source _____

7. Departure Date _____ Alternate Departure Date: _____ Total Vacation Days: _____

8. Prior Vacations _____ Successful/Unsuccessful

_____ Successful/Unsuccessful

_____ Successful/Unsuccessful

_____ Successful/Unsuccessful

9. Special Interests/Destinations: _____

. . . .

10. Line: _____ **Ship:** _____ **Sailing Date:** _____

11. Alt. Line _____ Alt. Ship: _____ Alt Sailing Date: _____

12. Accommodations: Requested   Offered

    A. **Type, Category, Cabin No.,**

       or Description (Bed Type) _____ _____

    B. **Price (Cruise only)** _____ _____

      AIR ALLOWANCE .... _____ _____

      Air/Sea .... _____ _____

      Air/Sea City .... _____ _____

    D. **Option Date** .... _____ _____

    E. Deposit Amount .... _____ _____

      When Due at Line .... _____ _____

    F. Cancellation Insurance: ❏ Offered ❏ Declined .... _____ _____

    G. Port & Departure Taxes .... _____ _____

    H. Extras (Pre/post cruise package) .... _____ _____

    I. Amount Final Payment from Client .... _____ _____

      When Due at Line .... _____ _____

    J. Form of Payment .... _____ _____

    K. Commission .... _____ _____

    L. Net Due to Line .... _____ _____

13. Citizenship _____ Special Diet/Occasion _____

14. **Dining Room Sitting: 1st** _____ **2nd** _____ **Smoking: Yes** _____ **No** _____

15. **Table For:** _____ **Seated with:** _____

       (number) _____

. . . .

16. **Reservations Made By:** _____ Date: _____   17. Air/Sea Only:

    Booking #: _____   Flight Nos. _____ / _____

    Offered by: _____   Departure Times: _____ / _____

    Accepted by: _____   Arrival Times: _____ / _____

    Gift Order Sent: _____   Seat Assignment: _____ / _____

18. Documents Received: _____   Delivered: _____

FIGURE 9-1   A cruise reservation sheet

Source: *Courtesy of CLIA*

So as not to seem prying, pose your lifestyle questions very carefully. And be alert to what may lie behind each response. For example, a young woman who says she lives in a tony part of town, practices law, drives a BMW, likes to eat gourmet cuisine, stays in Ritz-Carltons, and hates driving while on vacation is probably a strong prospect for a luxury cruise. Don't assume, though, that an attorney who lives a modest, conservative lifestyle wants a budget trip. This very well may be another luxury cruise prospect.

Recommending a Vacation

You've asked plenty of questions. You've collected many clues. You've placed your client in a clear-cut category. And you're pretty sure that a cruise will be the right recommendation. In fact, you have several possibilities in mind.

Before you make your suggestion, however, take a minute to review what your client has told you. This will serve as a reality check for both of you. Then, make a single, best recommendation. (You can and should have one or two alternates in mind.) Show how it solves each need and want that the client expressed. Describe your recommended cruise vacation's features and then its benefits. Paint a picture in the client's mind as to what the cruise will be like—and put the client in that picture. This will make the client mentally rehearse the trip. Buying a cruise will become far more likely. Sell the *value* of a cruise vacation—don't fall into the trap of selling by price. And make your client *feel good* about a cruise—that's precisely what is wanted in the vacation.

Most salespeople fall into the trap of mentioning a product's features but not its benefits. Benefits inject energy and reality into a sale. Here are the differences between each:

Features	Benefits
• Answer the question "What?"	• Answer the question "So what?"
• Represent facts	• Represent the payoff
• Sometimes have the word *you* in them; sometimes not	• Almost always have the word *you* in them
• Are usually impersonal	• Are personal

For example, a ship may be "fast" (a feature), but the real advantages of the ship's speed is that it can stay longer in one port before moving on to the next. Or it will reduce an itinerary's at-sea days. (Both are benefits.) If a stateroom has a veranda, that's a feature. The benefit: Your own private and intimate experience of the itinerary's destinations.

What if your recommendation doesn't "click" with the client? Find out why, clarify any misconceptions, and then, if necessary, go on to your backup recommendation.

Feature: a sleek, dramatic bar; benefit: the opportunity to socialize.
Courtesy of Costa Cruises

The Cruise Brochure

Let's start with the most traditional source of cruise information: the brochure. Cruise brochures aren't simply sources of information. They're also powerful sales tools. They fall into five categories:

- **The All-In-One Brochure.** This kind of brochure encompasses every itinerary and ship that the cruise line has. It may be subdivided according to geographic region or individual vessel. As you can imagine, it's usually a thick document.

- **The Specific Ship Brochure.** This brochure lists only those itineraries that a single ship follows. The vessel is generally unique in or a new addition to the line's fleet.

- **The Specific Region Brochure.** Increasingly common, each brochure explains what the line offers in a distinct geographic region: the Caribbean, Alaska, Mexico, Europe, Asia, etc. Usually, only the larger cruise lines publish these kinds of brochures.

- **The Seasonal Brochure.** Most often employed to ignite sales at a certain time of the year, this brochure might highlight, say, all the winter cruises that the line offers.

- **The Targeted Brochure.** This brochure is highly specialized. It touts a special promotional sailing, such as a reduced-price trip, an around-the-world cruise, a cruise targeted to members of an organization, etc. It may simply be a slightly customized version of a regular brochure.

Although variations do appear, brochures have a rather standardized, predictable, three-part format:

1. *A sales presentation* sets the mood and tone of the promotion piece and presents the broad benefits that this company's cruises offer. This section includes the cover (usually with the brochure's effective dates), a table of contents, photos, promotional text, and perhaps an overview map.

2. *The cruise itineraries section* shows the reader where the cruise line travels. (Some cruise lines call this "the invitation to choice.") Here's where you'll usually find each ship's sailing schedule, individual itinerary maps, promotional and informational text, photos, deck plans, and fares. (Sometimes, fares and deck plans appear in the third section.) If the cruise line offers pre- and post-cruise land options, these will also be listed here.

3. *The back-of-brochure information section* contains descriptions of airfares, transfers, amenities packages (e.g., for a honeymoon), insurance, payment and refund policies, helpful hints, frequently asked questions, and other general information. A common industry saying is "Clients read brochures from the front to the back, but travel agents read them from the back to the front." In other words, a client is initially interested in what a cruise is all about. Travel counselors already know this. They're initially more concerned about information and policies.

One of the cruise line's chief vehicles for information and promotion, the brochure can also serve as a cogent sales tool in the hands of a travel agent. Here's what you should do—and not do—with brochures if you're a travel counselor (assuming you're dealing with the client in person):

- Once you've arrived at your primary cruise recommendation, bring out a sales "file copy" of the brochure. Use its photos to illustrate the benefits of your recommendation. An alternative is to share a new brochure with your client, "personalizing" it with Post-its, highlighting, and underlining. Make the experience depicted as "theirs."

- Just as you shouldn't give more than one initial recommendation, you should share, at first, only one brochure with your client. If your first choice doesn't work, go to your backup one—and a second brochure.

- Above all, don't give your client a stack of brochures to take home, telling him or her to peruse them "to figure out which one you like." A brochure is a device to help you recommend and close the sale. Once you close the sale, *then* give them the brochure for reference. If you can't possibly close the sale, then perhaps it's all right to offer the take-home literature. But remember: If the client is out of sight, you may be out of a sale.

- For the same reason, brochures shouldn't be displayed on racks accessible to a client. A customer may read them while waiting and be led to the wrong product. Or the customer may leave with them if the agency's service is sluggish, never to return.

Web Sites

The Internet has become a significant source of cruise information and a tool for bookings. How can it be used to help sales?

- In a face-to-face sale, you can use your computer monitor in the same way, for the most part, as a brochure.
- If you're on the phone or e-mailing, you can direct your client to key sites, especially through CLIA's Web site.

Note also that electronic, Internet-based cruise brochures (or Web sites that are brochure-like) have several advantages over paper-based ones: They can be instantly updated, easily accessed and sent, and have entertaining features (such as a live video feed from the ship). Some of the same cautions that apply to paper-based brochures are relevant to electronic ones. Sending a client to visit the Web sites of a half-dozen cruise lines but not giving any advice or recommendations (or ever following up) will erode your ability to get a client's business.

Overcoming Barriers

Some clients find it difficult to make decisions. Their minds swirl with concerns. Isn't this too expensive? Won't I feel confined? Or seasick? Or bored?

It's time to overcome their resistance. In Chapter 2, we discussed 15 objections to cruising. Here, we review them, with possible responses. Become thoroughly familiar with them. At one time or another, no matter what segment of the cruise industry you're in, you're sure to encounter these barriers to a sale and will need to know how to respond.

No matter what objection a client gives, you should always reinforce your "counter" by reminding the client of the extremely high satisfaction rate that cruises achieve among consumers. See Figure 9-2.

Objection	Counter
1. Expense	• Cite cost as per diem
	• Compare to a similar land-based vacation
	• Stress inclusiveness and value
	• Recommend a cruise line that mirrors their budget
	• Suggest a repositioning cruise
2. Boredom	• Show a daily activity log
	• Cite their favorite activities
	• Cite testimonials from other clients

FIGURE 9-2   Overcoming barriers

Objection	Counter
	• Recommend an active cruise
	• Mention the people-meeting nature of cruising
3. Old people	• Recommend a cruise with a younger passenger profile
	• Point out brochure photos of younger people
	• Explain this was once true but no longer
	• Cite a testimonial from another client of about the same age as your client
4. Formality	• Recommend an informal cruise product
	• Explain alternate "casual" dining options
	• Look up dress requirements as stated in the brochure's information section
5. Regimentation	• Recommend a flexible cruise product (e.g., upscale cruises, sailing ships, and adventure/education cruises)
	• Cite the "do-it-all-or-nothing-at-all" nature of cruising
	• List flexible features (e.g., multiple dining options)
	• Suggest independent pre- and post-cruise packages
6. Limited port time	• Select itineraries that offer maximum port time
	• Suggest shore excursions as an efficient way to experience a port
	• Offer pre- and post-cruise packages
7. Confinement	• Recommend a ship with a high space ratio
	• Recommend an ocean-view stateroom or one with a veranda
	• Sell up to a larger stateroom or suite
	• Reinforce that ships are really large, floating resorts
8. Forced socializing	• Underscore the do-it-all/nothing-at-all nature of cruising
	• Recommend a product with many dining choices and/or open-seating dining
	• Sell up to a product with all open-seating dining
	• Suggest a stateroom with a veranda
9. Navy experience	• Stress the features inconceivable on a military ship (e.g., entertainment, pampering)
	• Emphasize that this isn't a seagoing military base but a seagoing *resort*

(Continued)

FIGURE 9-2 *(Continued)*

Objection	Counter
10. Too much food	• Cite healthy, "spa" dining options
	• Point out exercise opportunities
11. Ship safety	• Explain how safe today's cruise ships are and how the few problems that have occurred have been rapidly contained
	• Underscore the fact that security is emphasized on today's vessels
12. Terrorism	• Explain how cruise lines take aggressive precautions to avoid such problems
	• Point out that the lines avoid trouble-plagued ports and regions
	• Say that a ship is a highly controlled environment, where unusual situations are quickly noticed
13. Too far	• Underscore that it's worth it
	• Choose a closer embarkation port or one that requires fewer plane changes
	• Remind them that once there, a cruise maximizes their vacation time
14. Motion discomfort/ getting sick	• Explain how ship stabilizers minimize motion
	• Inform them of Sea Bands®
	• Recommend that they discuss this with their physician; pills or Transderm Scop® patches may be prescribed
	• Recommend a river cruise, where motion is rare
	• Book during a time when winds and waves are minimal
	• Cite the aggressive efforts cruise lines are now taking to keep their ships highly sanitized
15. Level of knowledge	• Give more information
	• Help them visualize themselves on the cruise
	• Describe how they'll feel on a cruise
	• Loan them a video about cruising

FIGURE 9-2   *(Continued)*

Adding Value

The pattern is the same in virtually every retail industry: The highest satisfaction is almost always with the most expensive product. The top-of-the-line auto, the dishwasher with all the bells and whistles, the most expensive suit in the store—these are what please customers best.

It's the same with travel products. That's why you should always offer the clients the best product within their budget range. In fact, you should offer them something that costs a little more than their top amount, since clients usually give very conservative figures about what they're willing to spend. This is called *upselling.* Some examples:

- An ocean-view stateroom instead of an inside one
- A stateroom on a higher deck
- A stateroom with a veranda instead of one without
- A suite instead of a standard cabin

You can also offer the client something *in addition* to the cruise itself but related to it. This is called *cross-selling.* Like selling up, it's used all the time in other industries. "How about fries with your hamburger?" "Would you like our extended service warranty?" "Do you want your car waxed after it's washed?"

Some cross-sell opportunities in cruise sales are:

- Travel insurance (this should be an automatic offer, since it protects both the client and the agency from potential hassles and losses)
- An amenities package (e.g., wine in the stateroom upon arrival)
- Pre- and post-cruise packages (tours, lodging, etc.)
- Air to and from the cruise (either purchased from the cruise line or independently)
- Meet-and-greet services, if the air wasn't purchased through the cruise line

A reminder: Upselling and cross-selling not only enhance the profitability of a sale, but they almost always improve the client's cruise vacation experience too.

Getting the Business

What's the most important thing a seller of travel should do? Close the sale. The obvious reason: A salesperson is employed to make a profit for the company. The more subtle reason is to make a customer happy. Few travel products make people happier than a cruise. Remember that high satisfaction rate.

Unfortunately, some clients are indecisive. They're afraid to make a commitment to cruise. Even worse, some *salespeople* are afraid to ask for the business. They fear they'll be rejected. Their efforts, they think, may lead to failure.

There's nothing sadder than a salesperson who does everything right and then falters. He or she greets warmly, qualifies thoroughly, recommends with intelligence, and overcomes resistance with skill. But then, when it's time to close . . .

Perhaps the momentum of the sale will cause the client to close the sale. Out comes the credit card and in goes the booking. No need to ask. Other times, customers give you subtle signals that they're ready to buy. They might do the following:

- Lean toward you
- Ask you a question that shows that they're already imagining themselves on the ship (e.g., What kind of clothes should I wear? What will the weather be like?)

- Become especially excited as they speak
- Nod their head in a small "yes" motion
- Push away some object that sits on your desk and that formed a symbolic barrier between buyer and seller

At such times—or even when the client seems "neutral"—you should deploy at least one of these closing techniques:

- Explain that it would be better to put down a deposit now, since the availability of what the client wants may disappear. (One line's research shows that 95% of people who make the commitment of a deposit actually buy. Without a deposit, that rate drops precipitously to 35%.)
- Just before you ask for the sale, review how your recommendation exactly fulfills your client's vacation needs.
- Point out that an advance deadline is approaching, after which the cruise promotional offer may or will disappear.
- Ask the client why he or she is hesitating. If the concern seems misconceived, explain why.
- Give the client a series of choices as you reach the end of the recommendation stage: "Do you think you'd prefer an ocean-view stateroom or an inside one?" "Do you think the four-day or the seven-day cruise best fits your needs?" The more choices the client makes along the way, the easier it'll be to make the final choice to cruise.
- Sometimes, a simple "So shall I reserve it?" or "So, let's do it!" is all that you'll need to say. Because you carried out the sales process so well, the client will be ready to buy.

Are closing techniques manipulative? No more than helping someone across the street. Unless, of course, crossing the street isn't where they want to or should go. If your client is one of those few for whom cruising is *really* wrong, you'll know long before you get to the close. You'll already have gone off in another sales direction.

The Nuts and Bolts of a Reservation

How does a cruise booking actually unfold? It's quite simple, although at first, it can seem challenging to both a travel agent and a cruise line reservationist.

First, though, you should know a few things about how staterooms sell:

- The first products that sell out are suites, followed by large staterooms (often with verandas).
- The next are the least-expensive ones, especially inside cabins.
- Midship cabins sell first (less walking and less motion perceived).
- Each cabin on a ship is "sold" several times. Someone books a cabin and then has to cancel. Others book a cabin but ask for and get a better one when it becomes available. And cabins are held on an "option" but are eventually "released." (More about options soon.)

Before making the reservation, a travel agent should first complete a cruise reservation form. (See Figure 9-1 for a sample.) This maximizes booking efficiency. He or she should also carefully review the back-of-brochure information section.

The travel agent has three main avenues for booking a cruise: the telephone, the global distribution system (GDS, also sometimes called the CRS, or computer reservation system), or the Internet. More and more, travel agents are booking cruises through the Internet. However, the GDSs in agencies remain a very viable way to book cruises. Because each GDS system has a different set of procedures, we won't go into detail here on how a cruise computer reservation is done. A little agency training, plus following the formats and prompts that appear on the screen, make this a relatively easy thing to learn.

For some, phone transactions remain a popular way to make a reservation. Brochure and reservation sheet in hand, the agent gives the reservationist all the information requested. (He or she should inform the reservationist—at the beginning of the call—if the client is present.) The cruise line reservationist, in turn, confirms all requests if available, recommends alternatives if necessary (the agent should also have these in mind), and discusses the booking choices available. Three are commonly offered:

1. **A confirmed category, stateroom number, and price.** Many first-time cruisers are surprised that this is possible. Hotels don't offer room preselection at all. It's best not to provide exact cabin selection from the brochure to the client, though, until the reservationist or computer gives the inventory available.

2. **A guarantee run-of-the-ship reservation or TBA (to be assigned).** The cruise line confirms the date and price but doesn't give the precise stateroom number. It guarantees a cabin at the category desired or possibly *higher.* Guarantees are offered when the category requested isn't available (but other, higher ones are) and cancellations in the category requested are anticipated. If the cancellations don't materialize, the client gets the higher-category stateroom for the same price. Guarantees aren't a good idea for certain clients who may desire or need a specific location and type of cabin. Examples: the physically challenged, seniors, honeymooners, and people who desire a specific cabin location or bed arrangement.

3. **A guaranteed upgrade.** The specific stateroom isn't assigned, but the client is promised a cabin at a category higher than what he or she paid for.

On a few lines, passengers traveling alone may have a fourth booking choice: the guaranteed share. Although a few cruise lines offer single occupancy staterooms, on most modern cruise ships, a stateroom is designed to hold two or more passengers and prices are basis two. If a cruise line sold such a stateroom to a single passenger at the per-person double occupancy rate, it would potentially lose money—it might have been able to sell that stateroom to two passengers. Therefore, most cruise lines add a single supplement to the fare (anywhere from 10% to 100% of the per-person double occupancy rate). To avoid this supplement, a single passenger may be allowed to book a guaranteed share. The cruise line will try to find another passenger (of the same sex) also traveling alone to share the same stateroom; each passenger would pay the double occupancy rate. Even if the cruise line can't find anyone to share the stateroom, the passenger won't have to pay the supplement.

Once the booking choice is determined and availability is confirmed, the agent has two options:

- **Get a deposit.** Whether refundable or not, a deposit solidifies the customer's commitment. As we explained, if you don't get a deposit, the probability that the sale will occur drops dramatically.

- **Offer an option.** This means that the cruise line will hold the reservation without a deposit (usually for about five days). Options are advisable only for the customer who seems to absolutely need time to think about it or talk it over with a travel partner. The travel agent should give the client a deadline that's ahead of the cruise line option date. That way, if the client is a day or two late in getting back to the agent, the sale won't be lost. Agents who haven't heard from a client usually follow-up with a reminder phone call. If the option won't be exercised (the client decides not to go), the travel agent, out of courtesy, should call the cruise line to cancel. If it will be exercised, then the travel agent should contact the cruise line, in case the deposit arrives after the option date. (The cruise line will extend the option date, just in case.)

But let's assume the client immediately says yes to a wonderful cruise vacation. Here's what happens:

1. The client pays the deposit by credit card, cash, or a check to the agency. If it's by cash or check, the agency deposits the funds and then sends an agency check to the cruise line. (Cruise companies usually don't accept the client's personal check.) Credit card policies differ among cruise lines. The *CLIA Cruise Manual* and the cruise line brochure usually outline credit card practices.

2. The agent informs the client when final payment will be due. (That's explained by the reservationist and in the brochure.) It's best to express it as an *exact* day of the week and due date (e.g., Monday, June 6), not "six weeks prior to departure."

3. The cruise line sends a confirmation of booking and/or invoice to the travel agency.

4. The client makes final payment to the agency, which in turn moves the funds on to the cruise company.

5. The cruise line sends the documents to the agency. (See Chapter 4 for what they include.) As protection against loss, the agent photocopies the essential elements of the documents and then presents the documents to the client, either in person or by mail (preferably registered). If it's a last-minute booking, the documents will be held for the client at the departure pier. Alternatively, the cruise line sends the documents to the client and the agent in electronic form.

6. The client cruises!

Following Up

Is the sale "closed" when it's over? Not if you're a good salesperson. You know that you're creating a loyal client, not just a sale. According to the White House Office of Consumer Affairs, it costs six times more to attract a new customer than to keep a current one.

One of the proven ways of keeping that customer is through follow-up. There are four kinds of follow-up situations:

1. **Follow-up on an unclosed sale.** If clients only want an option or even less than that, remind them before they leave the agency how great their cruise could be. Perhaps loan them a cruise video. Call them within 24 to 48 hours to get their decision. If they say yes, great. If not, gently ask them why. You may be able to clarify things. If they still say no, thank them for the opportunity to have counseled them. You never know. They may someday return—this time with the will to buy from someone who cared.

2. **Follow-up a closed sale.** Send a thank-you note. Leave a bon voyage phone message. If the commission warrants it, arrange for an onboard amenities package for them. Show them that you appreciate their business.

3. **Follow-up when they return.** Send a welcome-back card, perhaps with a satisfaction survey enclosed. Call them to see how they enjoyed their cruise. Have a welcome-back gift delivered to their door.

4. **Follow-up at the same booking time next year.** You know when these clients will think about their next vacation. Why not contact them at the same time the following year? Offer to discuss their next vacation plan. It just might well be a cruise.

Questions for Discussion

1. Give at least three traits for the following buyers of cruises:

   a. Restless Baby Boomers:

   b. Enthusiastic Baby Boomers:

   c. Consummate Shoppers:

   d. Luxury Cruisers:

   e. Explorers:

   f. Ship Buffs:

2. List five things you can do to make a good impression on a client in person and three things if the sale is over the phone.

3. What's the difference between a closed-ended question and an open-ended question? Give at least three examples of each.

4. Explain at least three ways a feature differs from a benefit.

5. Name and describe the five kinds of cruise brochures. What three sections does each kind probably have?

6. Give at least one counter to each of the following objections:

   a. "Cruises are too expensive."

   b. "Cruises are too formal."

   c. "Cruises are too regimented."

   d. "I'll feel confined."

   e. "I'm afraid of seasickness."

7. Give four ways that you could upsell a cruise client and four cross-sells that you could offer.

8. What are the four kinds of possible bookings?

9. Outline the major steps in a phone cruise booking.

10. Cruise professionals often say that a ship sells from "the top down and the bottom up" and "from the middle to the ends." What does this mean?

Activity

Read the agent-client scenario below. Try to identify the things the agent does right—and the many things she does wrong. Write your analysis in the space provided.

AGENT: "Travel, this is Mary."

CLIENT: "Yes, someone gave me your name. I'm interested in taking a vacation. . . ."

A: "OK—where do you need to go?"

C: "I don't know. I was actually looking for some advice. I've got, like, a week and a half off in May, in the spring, and, I don't know, like, maybe Florida."

A: "Well, personally, I'd probably consider a seven-day cruise—a cruise package to the Caribbean. You only have to pack and unpack once. And it includes all your meals and all your entertainment."

C: "Don't you get seasick on a cruise?"

A: "There are a lot of things you can do to combat it. Nowadays, they have these little patches you can put behind your ears, and that cures any kind of motion sickness. I have a friend that used one, and it was great. There are all kinds of things."

C: "Now, aren't cruises expensive? How much are the cruises?"

A: "Generally, for, like a seven-night cruise, with meals and everything included—it starts at about $1,000 or $1,2000 per person."

C: "Well . . . I guess I can afford something like that. What's the advantages of that over, say, going to Florida or something?"

A: "Well, it's the type of thing you can really sit back and relax, and all your meals are included—you can literally eat all day long. They've got lots of activities aboard the ship—and you can get sun at the same time. Uhh, you stop and see different ports—so you do more traveling."

C: "Well, where do the ships go for the most part? Which one would you do?"

A: "I like the Eastern Caribbean, but they have all different destinations. They leave out of Miami, they go down to St. Thomas, St. Martin—different islands in the Caribbean—different itineraries. Uh, there are some very interesting ones. Uh, there are different islands—you may be there for a couple of hours; you may be there all day long, depending on the itinerary. But at least you get out, and get to explore, and get some fresh air. If you want, you can swim in the pool. You know, you have a lot of things to do, and it's all included in one price."

C: "OK, maybe a cruise would be a good idea."

A: "Well, if that's what you want to do, I mean, you know, if that's what you want to do—maybe you want to see Epcot, you want to see Disney World, Universal Studios, I guess a cruise is different from all that—it's a different type of thing. Yeah, definitely, it's probably gonna run you about the same, by the time you get your hotel, your car, your transfers, uh, admissions, your meals, your entertainment—uh, adding all that up, it's pretty costly."

C: "Well, what do you get, like, free on a cruise?"

A: "OK. What would be included in the price would be all your meals—you can eat nonstop all day long—you've got all kinds of entertainment onboard— lounges, discos—or quiet areas—library and movies. Then, at night, you know, they've got different shows—Las Vegas reviews, with singers and dancers, all kinds of different entertainment. Ummm, different contests every night. The only thing that would not be included would be any special services, such as a massage or if you want to get your nails done or your hair done. And your liquor, your drinks. But, generally, the prices of the drinks aren't that expensive. The prices are comparable to what you get on land. They don't really jack up the prices for the drinks."

C: "Well, that sounds good."

A: "Like I said, there's all kinds of entertainment. You can do as much as you want or as little as you want. You want the sun—you want to explore different points in the Caribbean. Umm, it's kind of an all-inclusive type of package."

C: "Well, again, it sounds like a pretty good thing. Let me talk to my wife about it."

A: "OK."

1. What has the agent done right?

2. What has the agent done wrong?

Chapter 10

Cruise Marketing, Groups, and Incentives

Courtesy of Seabourn Cruise Line

After reading this chapter, you'll be able to:

- Analyze and apply a cruise marketing campaign.
- Create a marketing plan.
- Operate a cruise group departure.
- Explain how incentives operate.

Your alarm clock rings. Out of bed and off to the kitchen for some Rice Krispies that you bought yesterday at the grocery store. You watch TV, surfing through the channels until you pause at the Food Channel. There's Emeril Lagasse, showing how to make a great crepe and inviting his viewers to actually join him on a culinary cruise of the French Riviera—a toll-free number is given on the screen. You write it down. You've always wanted to learn how to really cook—to go beyond cereal. And to do it with a famous chef in a legendary region? Sounds good to you.

Before leaving for work, you browse through yesterday's mail. Here's a credit card solicitation. There's an invitation to join a book-of-the-month club. Maybe . . . you put it aside. Oh, and a flyer from your travel agent about a special cruise departure. Sounds interesting.

So, what has just happened? A distribution system has provided your breakfast, your psychographic profile has led you to a niche promotion hosted by a pied piper, several of your hot buttons have been hit, and you're clearly a prospect in several databases. Oh, yes, you've considered purchasing both tangibles and intangibles from companies whose mission statements probably address your needs and whose promotional mix has successfully targeted you.

All this in the first hour of your day.

Yes, marketing—and its language—can be intimidating. But why is it so critical to understand it at all? One reason: Marketing permeates your life. Every day, hundreds of companies direct thousands of marketing efforts and millions of dollars in your direction. Whether you like it or not, marketers are constantly analyzing your behaviors, affecting your ideas, and steering your purchases.

And if you intend to go into the cruise business, you must understand how the cruise industry markets itself. Whether as a travel agent or a cruise line employee, you're part of a formidable marketing engine.

Definition

What is marketing? Many people think it's the same as selling. But it's much more than that. One description: *Marketing* is determining a need and developing products and services to meet those needs. That short sentence encompasses a world of implications.

A solid and effective marketing campaign includes the following elements:

1. Consumer and product research
2. Product/service design
3. Pricing
4. Promotion
5. Distribution
6. Follow-up

When executed properly, marketing yields predictably excellent results. And few industries over recent decades have generated results as spectacular as those of the cruise business.

The Elements of Marketing

Cruising is a near-textbook example of how to achieve marketing success. Let's look at the six steps we gave to you above and how the cruise industry has put each into practice. It'll give you an insight into what good marketing is all about.

1. Research

In marketing, two types of **research** are common: **consumer research** and **product research**. Consumer, or market, research tries to discover who the public is, how they think, and what they like to buy. The many studies we've cited in this book are examples of consumer research: What do people want in a vacation? What barriers exist to buying a cruise? How do consumers compare cruises to other vacation options? The responses to this research serve to guide cruise lines as they develop and refine their offerings.

The sea forms a perfect background for a casual lunch and an enticing photo to promote cruising.
Courtesy of Seabourn Cruise Line

Product research is somewhat different. It focuses on the elements of what is to be sold. Let's say you want to develop a new cruise line. You would want to research the history of cruising, isolating what succeeded and what didn't. You'd certainly find out what other cruise lines have done and perhaps what they haven't—especially if your research indicated that certain consumer needs weren't currently being met.

A company need not carry out its own research. It can plug into the research of others. CLIA studies, for example, are useful not only to its member lines but also to agencies, tour operators, and many other segments of the travel business.

2. Design

Once you've examined the results of your research, you then design a product or service that addresses what you've learned. For example, you might decide that the opportunities in mass-market cruising are few—too many companies are already doing it right. But how about a cruise line that emphasizes learning? Your studies showed that a huge number of Baby Boomers are in their peak earning years and will be increasing their travel as they approach retirement. A significant number of them like to learn things while vacationing. Maybe a cruise line that's a sort of "floating extension school" might work well. You've discovered that several companies are already doing this—and doing well. But it seems that there's room for another such product—the demand, you think, exceeds current and future supply. And perhaps you can give a different "spin" to your cruise line product.

In the cruise business, product design isn't limited to cruise lines. You could, for instance, design a chain of travel agencies that specializes in educational travel products, including tours as well as cruises. Your research could lead you to those communities where learning is highly valued—for example, near major universities or even upscale retirement communities.

3. Pricing

But for how much should you sell your educational cruises? First, you need to budget out what it will cost to operate and sell your product. This is no easy task. That's what cost accountants are for. You'll need to include everything: building or buying the ships, salaries, promotion, overhead, and all the rest. Then, you'd have to project how many cruises you'll expect to sell and in what time period.

Eventually—and it's a long, tricky process—you'll know what it will cost to operate each departure. So, how much should your profit be? That depends almost entirely on what consumers will pay for your cruises and how many of them there will be. Research has told you that people who take educational vacations make quite a bit of money. The people you surveyed also told you what they might be willing to spend on a learning cruise. It was more than you expected. So, perhaps a relatively high cost and profit margin is possible.

Let's be honest though. This marketing step requires plenty of interpretation, assumptions, and guesswork. The superstars of marketing are those who excel at making educated, well-based "guesses."

4. Promotion

No matter how well-researched, designed, and priced your cruise product is, it won't sell unless people know about it. Promotion solves that. It gets the word out.

There are two kinds of promotion: publicity and advertising. **Publicity** is promotion that is nearly or completely cost-free. Some examples: articles in magazines, TV coverage, a free education-oriented Web site, a regular column you write for a newsletter. **Advertising**, on the other hand, is promotion that costs: a listing in the Yellow Pages, a magazine ad, a radio commercial, a poster, a brochure. See Figure 10-1 for the strengths and weaknesses of various types of advertising.

Of course, the cruise lines have entire departments that fashion their promotional campaigns, often using multiple advertising channels. But what about travel agencies? Do they have the resources to do the same?

It's often difficult to decide which direction to go with limited marketing funds. The following is a comparison of strengths and weaknesses that may assist you in making your decision.

Medium	Strengths	Weaknesses
Newspapers	Local market penetration	Usually black and white
	Some targeting available	Size equals the level of impact
	Current message	Affected by ad clutter
	Flexible	Short lifespan
Newspaper Inserts	Low cost	Can't specifically target
	Good for local market	Cheap image
	Coupons possible	Short lifespan
	Measurable results	Read quickly
Magazines	Target opportunities	Ad buy made far in advance
	Distinctive	Limited formats
	Good reproduction quality	Placement is critical
	Involves reader	Targeting is questionable (except for niche magazine)
	Adds prestige	Expensive
	Direct response capability	
	Long message lifespan	
	Trade/consumer option	

(Continued)

FIGURE 10-1 Media comparison
Source: *Holland America Line*

Medium	Strengths	Weaknesses
Radio	Target potential	30–60 seconds is short
	Cost-effective for repeat spots	Short lifespan
	Widespread medium	Not good for visual folks
	Supports other advertising	Segmented audience
	Can be local and promotionally oriented	Very competitive
Television	Powerful reach/awareness	Cost to produce and air
	Prestige	"Clutter" concerns
	Creates credibility	Placement
	Mass market	30–60 seconds is short
	Appeals to many senses	
Cable TV	Powerful reach/awareness	Lower ratings
	Lower cost	Spotty coverage
	Target market	Cost to produce ad
	Limited range	
Billboards	Ability to move consistent ad to multiple billboards	High cost
		Time frame limited
	"Silent" salesperson	Clutter/image consideration
	Dramatic presentation	Message limitations
	Geographic targeting	Mass market, not targeted
Web Sites	Convenient	Impersonal
	Visually interesting	Technology necessary to access
	Can be easily updated	Consumers must find your site
	Huge capacity for information	
	Booking capability	
E-mail	Very low cost	Perhaps perceived as spam
	Instant communication	Easy to ignore, miss, delete
	Easily customized	Technology necessary to receive
	Results easy to track	
	Can be visual and interactive	

FIGURE 10-1   *(Continued)*

Medium	Strengths	Weaknesses
Direct Mail	Most easily targeted	High cost/thousand
	Measurable	Image considerations
	Creates awareness	Possible confusion with junk mail
	Economical compared to other media	Design and testing costs
	Personalized medium	Inaccurate mailing lists
	Offers variety of methods	
	Testable	
	Most bang for your buck	
Telemarketing	Human contact	List purchase expenses
	Quick implementation	Excellent communication skills needed
	Instantaneous feedback	Low results rate (except for existing clients)
	Good for existing customers	Bad image among consumers
	Lead generator	
Brochures	Convey enough information for customer to buy	Can be expensive to produce
	Visual imagery	Need to be read
	Create visibility	
Yellow Pages	Puts you with competition	Possible limited usage
	Huge audience	Not targeted
	List and display opportunities	Not current message
	People are ready to buy	Ad blends in with others
	Convenient	Not especially attractive
	Long lifespan	
Window Displays	Exciting	Requires creativity
	Visual	Location important
	Draws potential clients into agency	Need strong message
	Economic	
	Limited reach	
	Long lifespan	

FIGURE 10-1 *(Continued)*

Certainly, it's a challenge for travel agencies to create solid promotional campaigns. But they don't have to start from scratch. Both the cruise lines and CLIA provide ready-made materials, such as generic PR releases, brochures, radio/TV copy, and collateral material, such as postcards, posters, and mail stuffers (often assembled in a "marketing kit") that agencies can tailor to their own situation. CLIA also provides "how-to" materials that advise agencies about the best ways to promote their cruise products. The chain or consortium that the agency belongs to may also provide promotional materials (including brochures that gather its preferred lines into one promotional piece) and e-mail systems to help get the word out.

It's not enough, though, to have quality promotional materials. For real success, your promotion should target the kinds of people most likely to buy your product. You would probably get more responses for your educational cruise by placing an ad in *Smithsonian* rather than in *Time.* It would cost less too. Conversely, a mass-market cruise line would be better off advertising in *Time.* And e-mail enables you to really target the right people at minimal cost.

To target effectively, you must also keenly understand what appeals to your prospects—and what doesn't. For example, your **prospect** (a marketing term for someone who is a potential buyer of your product) should respond well to a brochure that stresses such hot-button themes as "lifelong learning," "personal development," and "cultural encounters." (A **hot button** is anything that powerfully entices a buyer.) That same brochure would show people visiting famous attractions, attending port lectures, and reading in the ship's library. It would use advertising copy that's intelligent, eloquent, and plentiful. (Educated people like to read.) It might even look more like a well-illustrated guidebook than a brochure.

Your promotional timing must also be correct. Many cruise lines and agencies bring their promotions to their highest levels during "Wave Season"—the period between January through March, when cold weather in much of North America causes consumers to think about tropical getaways and summer vacation.

5. Distribution

How will you get your product out to consumers? With tangible products, the distribution channels are easy to identify. A **tangible product** is one that has physical form, such as a TV set, a toaster, or a tire. You make it, load it on a truck, ship it to a store, and help them sell it.

For **intangibles**—products or services that have no physical form and are more experiential—distribution is less obvious. Some examples: insurance, stocks, and, yes, travel.

How, then, will you "distribute" your cruises? As with most cruise lines, you'll rely most heavily on travel agencies to move your product. It works for them, and you're convinced it'll work for you. Of course, you'll have to identify those agencies or even some specialty tour operators who—because of their client base—are especially motivated to sell educational travel experiences. (How you do that would be a chapter unto itself.) You might also sell some of your cruises via toll-free numbers and the Internet. (There are some people who have never and will never contact an agency or tour company. There has to be a way for you

Small river vessels provide this highly marketable perspective of Europe's charming cities.
Courtesy of AMAWATERWAYS

to reach them.) And you might wish to approach certain educational publications as vehicles for getting your product to those they serve.

At the end of distribution is the sale itself. Sell as many or more cruises than you expected and you have reason to celebrate. Your marketing efforts worked. Sell fewer, and it's perhaps time to reconsider some of your assumptions.

6. Follow-Up

To follow up on all sales—a step once neglected in marketing—has become highly important. Whether sales are doing better, worse, or as expected, it's important to know *why*. That way, you can recommit to what you've done right and re-adjust what you've done wrong. Follow-up helps build loyalty, encourages feedback (both positive and negative, plus the chance to do something about it), and refines knowledge of product and place.

Many mechanisms for follow-up exist: satisfaction surveys (print or electronic), thank-you letters, newsletters, membership in "cruise alumni" clubs, responses to complaints, etc. Remember that follow-up also marks the start of the next marketing cycle. It's an opportunity for you to start your customers thinking about their *next* trip with you.

Marketing Plans

Marketing strategies don't just happen. They're well-thought-out and articulated. The vehicle for those thoughts is usually a marketing plan.

A *marketing plan* is a blueprint for action and a map to success. It explains who you are, what your business is, where you're going, and how you'll get there. Cruise lines certainly have them and many travel agencies do too. Here are the steps that typically constitute a marketing plan:

1. **An executive summary.** On a single page or even in a single paragraph, you summarize what's to follow.

2. **A mission statement.** In a few sentences, you explain your goals: how much net profit you intend to make and why you're in business doing what you're doing.

3. **An analysis of market research.** This summarizes what you've discovered through your studies and to what conclusions they've led you.

4. **An analysis of market attractiveness.** Here, you project the size of your market (how many prospects there are), the potential for market growth, ease of getting to your clients, etc.

5. **An analysis of your product's life cycle.** Like people, products have a "life," usually expressed as four stages:

   - *Introduction,* when the product or service is so new that there are few, if any, competitors. Cruising, as we know it today, was in this stage about 40 years ago.

   - *Growth,* when the public is aware and becoming excited about what you offer. Cruising is probably near the end of this stage and soon to become part of the next stage.

   - *Maturity,* when competition has fully formed, excitement is still high, and profit potential is stable for those who do things best.

   - *Decline,* when demand is dwindling. Still a long, long way off for cruising—assuming decline ever happens.

6. **A SWOT analysis.** This is an acronym for one of the most valuable marketing tools there is. You must determine your:

   - *Strengths:* what you do well
   - *Weaknesses:* what you can't or don't do well
   - *Opportunities:* what can or will benefit you most
   - *Threats:* what could reduce the demand for what you offer

7. **An analysis of your competitors.** What do they do well? What do they do poorly? How can they affect your success? And what must you do to counter their efforts?

8. **An analysis of your customers.** This marshals the demographic (statistical) and psychographic (attitudinal) data about the people to whom you sell. The resulting profile gives a "face" to the type of person who is your best possible customer. It's dependent on something called **database** marketing. A *database* is an organized collection of customer profiles. From this database, you can quickly break down your list into specific, targeted customers (for example, all singles, everyone who makes over $50,000 a year, those of your customers who have only taken a three-day cruise).

9. **An analysis of your cooperators.** Who can *help* you succeed? Among the cooperators that, say, a travel agency might count on are suppliers, vendors,

front-line agents, outside sales agents, clients who refer customers to you, clubs, associations, and other companies (for example, a luggage store) with whom you might have a co-marketing agreement.

10. **An analysis of your products and services.** Here, you examine what you sell now and, based on previous analysis, what you might sell in the future.

11. **Your marketing mix.** This section neatly ties together much of what you've covered in your marketing plan and, more importantly, how they interrelate. They're often referred to as the eight "Ps":

    - *Product:* what you sell
    - *Price:* what it costs the buyer
    - *Profit:* what you plan to make
    - *Place:* from where it's sold. You may be selling from a distinct office and the geographic community it serves. But remember: With the Internet, your "community" can be the whole world
    - *People:* who works for you and how
    - *Politics:* how laws, regulations, and industry practice affect you
    - *Position:* how you're perceived with regard to the rest of the marketplace
    - *Promotion:* how you communicate your message

12. **Your promotional mix.** This final section explains how you intend to persuade the public to buy and where you intend to allocate your promotional resources.

A health-conscious group would expect extensive exercise possibilities.
Courtesy of Costa Cruises

Groups

"Cheaper by the dozen." That's an old saying that expresses an important truth in cruising. But that truth can vary. To travel agents, it means that you save time and make money more efficiently by selling to a group of people rather than to many separate individuals or couples. To a cruise line, it means that you're more or less dealing with only one "client" who occupies many staterooms. And to the consumer, it means that by traveling with other people like yourself, you enjoy your cruise vacation more and almost surely pay less for it.

There are three types of groups: *preformed, speculative,* and *incentive.* Let's examine each.

Preformed Groups

A **preformed group** is one made up of people who belong to a club, association, or other pre-existing organization. These organizations communicate regularly with their members and schedule fairly regular events that the members attend together. Usually, the prospects know each other. Some examples are church groups, professional associations, sports groups, fraternal organizations, alumni societies, labor unions, country clubs, college departments, or even families. Travel agencies and cruise lines love proposing group departures to preformed groups. Because their members know each other and already do things together, preformed groups promise a high probability of success.

For that success to occur, however, three factors must be present:

1. A clear match must exist between the group's profile and the line, ship, destination, and departure date. What would appeal to a church group might be very different from what would attract a country club.

2. The promotion to the group must be well-conceived. In the same way that regular promotions should hit the right hot buttons, so too should a group promotion be tailored to the group's buying style. Brochures, flyers, correspondence, ads, presentations at meetings, and cruise nights should all reinforce the group's identity and the product's suitability.

A cruise night is a special event where the travel agency and/or the cruise line previews the proposed group cruise for the organization's members. It can be part of the group's regularly scheduled meeting. Ideally, though, it should be an event unto itself.

To maximize its attraction, you should give your cruise night a clever name and theme. The room where you'll be staging it is important too. Can you decorate it? Which audiovisuals should you use and will they work well in this environment? Is there enough room for registration, display, and bookings tables?

Another key question: How much will this cost and who pays? Hopefully, the cruise line will be supportive here. Remember that a cruise night may cost more than you think. Among the possible costs: AV equipment rental, invitations, postage, and refreshments.

Staffing—both to organize and to operate the event—is also crucial. Someone has to coordinate things with the line's business development manager, order support materials, order and install equipment, refreshments and decorations, and perhaps call all invitees who have RSVP'd—usually a day or two before the event.

And what of the cruise night itself? Think of it as an entertainment event. It should be energetic, lively, informative, and convincing. Have your brochures ready. Invite any of your other clients who have cruised before to share their enthusiasm with the group. Above all, provide the opportunity for attendees to place their deposits then and there. If you do the job right, there will be no better time to convert their enthusiasm into cash.

For those who don't sign up, send follow-up literature as a reminder or even place phone calls.

3. A pied piper should anchor the cruise promotion. A **pied piper** is a member of the organization you're targeting who is especially respected and admired by its members. The pied piper may or may not be one of the group's official officers. He or she is someone with strong leadership skills. The group fiercely respects this person's ideas and suggestions. A pied piper leads. The group *wants* to follow.

Pied pipers may assist you in mailings, cruise nights, obtaining e-mail addresses, and planning some or all of the group cruise event. They may even serve as your tour conductor—in exchange for a free cruise.

Speculative Groups

The second kind of group is a **speculative** or **promotional group**. To create such a departure, you must attract a group of individuals who probably do not know each other—at least not until they take the cruise. All they have in common is the desire to buy a certain, special cruise. For example, a travel agency might block space on a specific cruise departure, obtain a special price, and then promote that cruise in its newsletter, through a flyer, or even in a newspaper ad.

Speculative groups are more challenging to sell than preformed ones. They require more time, money, and promotion. One way to facilitate the process: Narrow your focus to people who have some psychographic trait in common (e.g., a love of cultural exploration). Such a speculative group is sometimes called an **affinity group**. Another way: Find a pied piper who is well-known to the public, such as a radio or TV personality. It's also vital to tap into a cruise line's advice and resources to help guarantee the trip's success.

Note that the line between a speculative and a preformed group is sometimes blurred. For example, suppose you marketed an adventure cruise to all the members of a large health club. It's *sort of* a preformed group—they all belong to the same club—but only a few of them know each other. In some ways, therefore, they're a *speculative* group—an affinity one with at least two things in common: where they work out and a commitment to health.

Here's what a cruise line can provide an agency to support a group departure:

- A video for a cruise night

- A speech by a business development manager at the cruise night

- Free *shells* (a shell is a slick color brochure with empty space for the agency to print its message) and other promotional material or "collateral," often assembled in a group marketing kit

- Promotional dollars (for a mailing, to stage the cruise night, to create flyers, etc.)

- Onboard amenities (e.g., reception cocktail party) at low or no cost

- Onboard service assistance (larger ships often have a group coordinator onboard)

Or imagine that you're promoting a special cruise for the alumni of a university. In the loosest sense of the word, they're a preformed group. But they're much closer to being a speculative group. They almost surely don't know one another, and there could be tens of thousands of them to whom to make the offer.

Creating and Marketing a Group Cruise Departure

Selling a cruise to a group may be easier than selling to individuals, but it's still a complex process. Here are the 15 steps you might follow to create, market, and operate your own group departure:

1. **Select your group.** If it's a preformed group departure, you're targeting a group that will probably like the idea of a group departure but which hasn't yet done one. If it's speculative, then it might be selecting a niche that's been underserved in your area, such as adventure travelers.

2. **Research by qualifying the group.** Just as you qualify individual clients to determine what they desire, so too must you probe a group's needs and wants. This is especially true for preformed groups. Among the things you must determine: previous travel, if any; membership size; organization and leadership; special interests; what they read; how they communicate; and how frequently they meet. Ideally, this should be done nine months to a year in advance.

3. **Project what percentage of the "audience" will book.** For speculative groups, this is a real challenge. If you do a direct mailing to all your clients and if your promotional piece is perfectly conceived, then you may get a 1% response rate. If the mailing is targeted (e.g., an adventure cruise to a mailing list of adventure-seekers), that percentage might be higher. If it's to the general public, it'll be much less than 1%. Often, it's a matter of trial and error. But that's why it's called *speculative*.

   Your projection may be somewhat easier with a preformed group. Participation in past travel or other events will provide a valuable clue to future behavior. Don't forget that for each person who responds, there will probably be another going. A club member, in effect, "sells" the cruise to their companion for you. Also, remember that no matter how many people say they're going, you don't have a booking until you have a deposit.

4. **Determine the purpose of their trip.** Why will they travel? How will they benefit from a cruise? Answer these questions, and you'll know better which hot buttons to push when you promote to them.

5. **Establish the flexibility of their time.** The more flexible they are, the more leverage you'll have for prices, times, and deadlines as you negotiate with your cruise supplier.

6. **Determine their value range.** What would be an acceptable price for this cruise? The price they're willing to pay will determine which cruise you'll ultimately propose to them. If you're doing a speculative group, you'll need to do some demographic research or rely on your experience. For a preformed group, the organization's leadership will be the best source for insights.

7. **Determine the itinerary, destination, and cruise line recommendation.** This will flow naturally from the value range, your knowledge of the business, and input from the district sales representative.

8. **Contact and negotiate with the cruise line.** Just as with an individual, you should have a number one choice and a backup just in case. You should probably set things up through your sales representative, although some choose to go directly to the line's group desk. For what's typically negotiable, see the box on page 184.

   The cruise line will ask how many cabins you wish to reserve (i.e., blocked space). Each cruise has different criteria for how many persons constitute a group. Most require between 10 and 16 passengers (five to eight cabins). Some require less; a few require more.

9. **Review the contract.** The line will send you a detailed, written confirmation of what you have agreed upon, plus plenty of fine-printed terms and conditions. (For an example, see Figure 10-2.) Read it all—and carefully. Contact the line on anything that's unclear. Don't be prepared to sign until you're sure of every detail. The contract or the correspondence that accompanies it should also stipulate the contact person at the cruise line.

10. **If doing a preformed group, present your recommendation to the group's leadership.** You should outline it first in a brief written proposal. Then, schedule an in-person meeting with them. Clarify all issues up front, including how the TC ticket will be used. This all should be done six to nine months before departure.

    If you receive the group's commitment, inform the cruise line. Send in the signed contract. At this stage, the cruise line may request a first deposit (usually nonrefundable) and ask which dinner seating your group will prefer.

11. **Plan your promotion.** Select and design your promotional materials and media. Schedule a cruise night. Make sure you know exactly what to say to the group to build maximum enthusiasm. Make sure the "who, what, when, where, why, how much, and how long" questions are all covered. Most important: Your promotional materials should clearly state deposit and final payment policies. The dates that clients should pay you should precede by

Here's what's generally open to negotiation with a cruise line:

- **Cruise price.** Typically 20–40% off the brochure rate, although this very much varies depending on the cruise line. Season, itinerary, group size, performance record on previous trips, and many other factors strongly affect what group rate will be offered. Most often quoted as a noncommissionable "net" rate.

- **Free tour conductor berth(s).** Usually, the tour conductor, however, must pay port charges and taxes. For every 15 full-fare adult passengers, the majority of cruise lines give one free cruise (that's one berth in a cabin). Several cruise lines require 16; others require fewer (especially for longer or more expensive cruises). The tour conductor (or TC) berth can go to the tour conductor, the pied piper, or even to a client.

- **Airfare, if obtained from the cruise line.** "Deviations" from the usual patterns to and from the port (e.g., on days that aren't the ones when passengers typically arrive and depart) will often lead to extra charges.

- Free airfare for the tour conductor(s) if air is booked through the cruise line

- Transfers

- Onboard functions

- Special onboard amenities

- Insurance

- Pre- or post-cruise packages (e.g., tours, hotel stays, etc.)

- Shore excursions

- Promotional support

- Deposit and final payment dates

Depending on the cruise line, any one or all of the items listed above may be very negotiable, not very negotiable, or not at all negotiable. You'll quickly find out which ones are and which ones aren't.

about two weeks the dates when you must pay the cruise line. Your deposit—determined by cruise line policy—is typically about 10% to 20% of the cruise price, nonrefundable in the event of client cancellation.

12. **Establish your "fulfillment center."** Who will answer inquiries, send out materials, and track bookings? Determine your staffing needs and responsibilities before the first bit of promotion occurs. Responding to client queries and requests is called *fulfillment*.

13. **Plot your timeline.** Here's a rough guideline:

    - 5–8 months prior to departure: Operate your promotional campaign, including a second wave of promotion, if necessary.
    - 4–7 months prior: Review results and deposits received. Send additional deposits to cruise line, if required.
    - 3 months prior Review current space. Make a go/no-go decision. Release majority of unsold space. Invoice clients for final payments.

A Signature of Excellence

Group Administration
300 Elliott Ave West
Seattle, WA 98119

Phone: (888)425-9477
Email: groups@hollandamerica.com

GROUP TERMS & CONDITIONS

BASIC REQUIREMENTS

SIZE AND COMPOSITION The minimum requirement for a group space allocation (" allocation ") is fifteen full fare guests traveling together on the same cruise or tour. For groups of 25 staterooms or more, a Large Group Request form is required. Please contact Group Administration to obtain required forms. Group participants are to be drawn from a specific and defined social, professional, commercial or similar affinity group of individuals or booked through targeted promotional efforts. Allocation pricing <u>may not</u> be advertised in newspapers, on radio, on television, on the Internet or through similar mass circulation mediums.

WHOLESALING This allocation may not be wholesaled to other travel agencies nor may it be consolidated with allocations granted to other agencies without prior approval from HAL senior management. Violations will result in immediate cancellation of all group allocations.

STATEROOM ALLOCATION Stateroom space for an allocation is held on a category guarantee basis and is subject to recall as provided below. The allotment shown on the confirmation represents the total allocation HAL is holding on AGENCY's behalf and cannot be increased except with prior approval from Group Administration. Certain stateroom categories are ineligible for group discounts. Allocation is based on double occupancy. Triples and quads are capacity controlled and subject to availability. Staterooms booked outside of the given allotted categories will trade space from similar categories held in allocation.

DISCOUNTS Group discounts do not apply to pre or post-cruise packages, home city air, cancellation protection plans or other HAL optional programs.

POLICIES HAL reserves the right to supplement or modify, from time to time, its generally applicable procedural policies that are provided for in these Group Terms & Conditions or are otherwise established by HAL (e.g., cancellation policies, name change policies, change charges, tax estimates, all as specified in the HAL brochure). AGENCY agrees to adhere to the procedural policies of HAL as such may be in effect from time to time.

CRUISES REMOVED FROM PUBLIC SALE HAL reserves the right to unilaterally withdraw any sailing from public sale, with or without prior notice (e.g., if HAL elects to charter the vessel). In that event, HAL will provide you with reasonable alternatives and will otherwise work with you to address issues caused by the withdrawal. If HAL and you are unable to agree on an alternative sailing, HAL will refund all amounts received by HAL under this Agreement in which event neither you nor HAL will have further rights or obligations under this Agreement.

ERRONEOUS PRICING NOTICE HAL reserves the right not to honor any published rates that it determines were erroneous due to printing, electronic, or clerical error.

PROMOTION AND UPFRONT DEPOSIT REQUIREMENTS

GENERAL REQUIREMENTS HAL assumes that AGENCY has requested group allocation for the purpose of promotion and sale in a timely manner. In return for commitment of allocation from HAL, AGENCY agrees to actively promote and publicize the group program through promotional efforts approved by HAL. Promotions must adhere to "Contents of Promotion," below; violations of these restrictions may result in cancellation of the allocation. HAL reserves the right to recall unsold group allotments at any time. "Unsold allotment" is defined as group allotted staterooms that have not been sold to specific guests and deposited according to HAL policy.

CONTENTS OF PROMOTION All promotions of HAL products by AGENCY must be conducted in the name of AGENCY and must include information identifying AGENCY (including name, address and telephone number). HAL reserves the right to require AGENCY to cease any promotional activity involving HAL products which HAL, in its sole discretion, determines may impair or damage the reputation of HAL. Promotions should only refer to prices that are inclusive of non-discountable amounts. Use of HAL trademarks and trade names requires the prior approval of HAL.

UPFRONT DEPOSITS For allocations of more than 16 staterooms, HAL requires a $50 per stateroom upfront deposit for allocations in excess of 16 staterooms. **This upfront deposit is due within 30 days of initial confirmation; and is in addition to guest deposit requirements described below. Failure to remit upfront deposit will result in the release of group allocation.**

REVIEW SCHEDULE

150 AND 120 DAYS REVIEWS If no staterooms are sold, HAL will automatically recall 100% of the allocation. If staterooms are sold, HAL will automatically recall 50% of the unsold allocation. <u>AGENCY will not receive a phone call notification when this recall occurs.</u> All new bookings made thereafter will be subject to availability and rates at time of booking.

90 DAYS REVIEW All unsold allocations will be automatically recalled at this time. <u>AGENCY will not receive a phone call notification when this recall occurs.</u> All new bookings made thereafter will be subject to availability and rates at time of booking.

BOOKING PROCEDURES

GROUP ADVANTAGE PROGRAM (GAP) Points may be awarded at HAL's discretion. Amenities must be selected when group is initially set up. Changes to selected amenities may be made prior to the group being finalized 90 days prior to sailing. Some promotions may not be combined with the GAP program. Please direct questions regarding applicability to Group Administration.

BOOKING NAMES/GUEST DEPOSITS AGENCY should book names and send guest deposits to HAL as soon as they are received from the client. Guest deposit requirements are set forth in the applicable HAL brochure. Cancellation Protection Plans are available for purchase by clients. Please refer to the HAL brochure for details.

NAME CHANGES Requests for name changes or substitutions shall be considered cancellations.

CANCELLATIONS Failure to remit any deposit or payment when due shall result in a canceled booking and shall be subject to the cancellation fees set forth in the applicable HAL brochure. Staterooms for canceled bookings shall be released from the allocation unless otherwise agreed by HAL. In the event of a canceled booking, HAL reserves the right to allocate amounts received on that booking to offset amounts owed for other bookings in the same allocation, in which event AGENCY shall refund the canceled booking from its own monies.

DINING / ONBOARD REQUESTS Dining requests are confirmed on a first come, first served basis. AGENCY should contact Ship Services at (800)541-1576 to discuss available options for groups requesting to dine together. AGENCY should contact Onboard Event Services at (877) 885-4259 to arrange any on board activities or meeting requirements. All requests for onboard assistance with group activities are reviewed for confirmation on a first come, first serve basis.

ACCOUNTING At least two weeks prior to the final payment due date, HAL will prepare a guest list and finance summary for AGENCY. Questions regarding the finalization of AGENCY'S group should be directed to the Group Administration representative at (888)425-9477, no later than 7 days prior to the final payment due date. If AGENCY still disputes the finalization statement, AGENCY is required to forward the full final payment to HAL, together with a statement of amounts subject to dispute. HAL shall review such statement and return disputed amounts owed, if any, within thirty days of receipt. Travel documents will not be released until full payment is received by HAL. Please note that credit or charge cards issued to AGENCY (corporate cards) or AGENCY employees may not be used for bookings made by clients. Requests to charge guest credit cards for non-HAL products will be accepted up to a maximum of $250 per person and are subject to a separate indemnification agreement. Requests for overcharges in excess of $250 per person, if approved by HAL, will be assessed a minimum $35 per person service charge and will require a separate indemnification agreement.

HOME CITY AIR While HAL will endeavor to accommodate group guests originating from the same air city on the same airline; group guests from the same air city will not necessarily be accommodated on the same air flight.

GROUP TOUR ESCORTS

Groups will be credited with an average cruise fare (excluding home city air, non discountable amounts, taxes and optional packages) for every 15 double or single occupancy paid guests booked within a group. The earned tour escort credit will be applied to every 16th guest. Different earned tour conductor ratios may apply to various HAL products as referenced on the group confirmation. Third and fourth paid guests sharing a cabin with two full fare paid guests do not count toward the tour conductor credit. Earned tour conductor credits may be affected by late cancellations within the group. If the number of double or single occupancy paid guests falls below the required minimum, the tour conductor credit will be removed. The tour conductor credit is in lieu of free cruise or tour travel.

Rev 08/26/08

FIGURE 10-2 Contract

Source: *Courtesy of Holland America Line*

- 2 months prior: Send final payment, along with passenger list, to cruise line.
- 1–2 months prior: Send special service requests (e.g., vegetarian meals, medical needs, etc.).
- 1 month prior: Reconfirm special service requests. Finalize meeting space, private receptions, and AV requirements, if needed. Receive documents from cruise lines, check for accuracy.
- 1 month to 2 weeks prior: Distribute documents, either by mail (preferably registered) or in person at a pre-cruise meeting.

14. **Operate the group cruise departure.** This easily could constitute an entire chapter. For more details, consult Appendix C.

15. **Stage a post-cruise party.** It's a great time to exchange photos and also to promote next year's cruise!

Incentives

Earlier, we said that there were *three* kinds of groups. The third is a very specialized kind called an **incentive group**.

The incentive business is a unique segment of the travel industry. (It also spans other industries.) A **travel incentive** is a program to motivate people to perform better through the potential award of an exceptional travel experience.

Here's how it works: Let's say you approach a large chain of car dealerships in your state. You propose that every salesperson who sells 40 cars or more in a given year will be awarded a free seven-day cruise in the Caribbean. (Their average is 25 per salesperson per year.) All the awardees will be on the same cruise departure, each with an ocean-view superior stateroom, and will enjoy special onboard and shoreside events. They'll be pampered as never before, have fun, and be treated as VIPs. They can even bring along a guest.

What's the catch? There's none. The cost of the cruise will be paid from part of the increased sales and profits that result from the incentive offer. If sales don't increase, the trip won't happen. But it will. Incentives have an astonishing power to work.

What's amazing is that with incentive groups, everyone wins:

- The client company makes more money with minimal risk. Morale is improved and goodwill is created.
- The employees get travel and prestige.
- The cruise line fills prime cabins.
- The incentive company or travel agency makes a handsome profit.

Incentives and group departures constitute a complex, unique, and highly lucrative business. CLIA offers courses, both live and online, on incentives and group travel as well as two videos on groups.

A Final Note

Never thought there was so much to the cruise business, did you? Neither did I when I took my first cruise two decades ago. Since then, I've taken dozens. And each time, my respect, delight, and love for the cruise vacation experience grows.

If you've never cruised, then a remarkable adventure awaits you. And if you've already taken a cruise vacation, I hope that your next one brings you even richer insights into this significant, exciting, and wondrous segment of the travel industry.

 # Questions for Discussion

1. Define each of the following:

   • marketing

   • hot button

   • distribution

   • mission statement

   • SWOT analysis

   • database

   • fulfillment

   • incentive

2. What are the six steps of marketing?

3. What's the difference between product research and consumer research? Between advertising and publicity? Between a tangible product and an intangible product? Between a preformed group and a speculative group?

4. Give the 12 steps to a marketing plan.

5. Name at least six things a cruise line can provide an agency to support a group departure.

6. Give 10 items that are potentially negotiable with a cruise line.

7. How do each of the following "win" on an incentive cruise—the client company, its employees, the cruise line, the travel agency, or incentive company?

 # Activity

Are there groups in your community who might be prime prospects for a group cruise?

Using every means at your disposal, identify three specific groups in your community to whom you think you could sell a group cruise. Explain why you think they would respond favorably to a cruise and what kind of cruise (or even specific cruise) you would pitch to them.

Group #1: _____

- What kind of cruise?

- Why?

Group #2: _____

- What kind of cruise?

- Why?

Group #3: _____

- What kind of cruise?

- Why?

Key Addresses:
CLIA Member Cruise Lines

Please note that the member cruise lines of the CLIA are subject to change. Visit CLIA's Web site, www. cruising.org, for the latest list. Internet resources are of a time-sensitive nature and URL sites and addresses may often be modified or deleted.

Amawaterways
21625 Prairie St.
Chatsworth, CA 91311
(818) 428-6198
www.amawaterways.com

American Cruise Lines
741 Boston Post Rd., Ste. 200
Guilford, CT 06437
(203) 453-6800
www.americancruiselines.com

Avalon Waterways
5301 S. Federal Cir.
Littleton, CO 80123
(303) 703-7000
www.avalonwaterways.com

Azamara Club Cruises
1050 Caribbean Way
Miami, FL 33132
(305) 539-6000
www.azamaracruises.com

Carnival Cruise Lines
3655 N.W. 87th Ave.
Miami, FL 33178
(305) 599-2600
www.carnival.com

Celebrity Cruises
1050 Caribbean Way
Miami, FL 33132
(305) 539-6000
www.celebritycruises.com

Costa Cruises
200 South Park Rd., Ste. 200
Hollywood, FL 33021
(954) 266-5600
www.costacruises.com

Crystal Cruises
2049 Century Park East, Ste. 1400
Los Angeles, CA 90067
(310) 785-9300
www.crystalcruises.com

Cunard Line
24303 Town Center Dr., Ste. 200
Valencia, CA 91355
(661) 753-1000
www.cunard.com

Disney Cruise Line
P.O. Box 10210
Lake Buena Vista, FL 32830
(407) 566-3500
www.disneycruise.com

Holland America Line
300 Elliott Ave. W.
Seattle, WA 98119
(206) 281-3535
www.hollandamerica.com

Hurtigruten
5100 N.W. 33rd Ave., Ste. 256
Fort Lauderdale, FL 33309
(800) 323-7436
www.hurtigruten.us

MSC Cruises
6750 N. Andrews Ave., Ste. 100
Fort Lauderdale, FL 33309
(954) 772-6262
www.msccruisesusa.com

Norwegian Cruise Line
7665 Corporate Center Dr.
Miami, FL 33126-1201
(305) 436-4000
www.ncl.com

Oceania Cruises
8300 N.W. 33rd St., Ste. 308
Miami, FL 33122
(305) 514-2300
www.OceaniaCruises.com

Paul Gauguin Cruises
1000 Corporate Dr., Ste. 500
Fort Lauderdale, FL 33334
(617) 878-6207
www.pgcruises.com

Pearl Seas Cruises
741 Boston Post Rd., Ste. 250
Guilford, CT 06437
(203) 458-5280
www.pearlseascruises.com

Princess Cruises
24844 Ave. Rockefeller
Santa Clarita, CA 91355
(661) 753-0000
www.princess.com

Regent Seven Seas Cruises
1000 Corporate Dr., Ste. 500
Fort Lauderdale, FL 33334
(954) 776-6123
www.rssc.com

Royal Caribbean International
1050 Caribbean Way
Miami, FL 33132
(305) 539-6000
www.royalcaribbean.com

Seabourn Cruise Line
6100 Blue Lagoon Dr., Ste 400
Miami, FL 33126
(305) 463-3000
www.seabourn.com

SeaDream Yacht Club
601 Brickell Key Dr., Ste. 1050
Miami, FL 33131
(305) 631-6100
www.seadream.com

Silversea Cruises
110 E. Broward Blvd.
Fort Lauderdale, FL 33301
(954) 522-4477
www.silversea.com

Uniworld Boutique River Cruise Collection
17323 Ventura Blvd.
Los Angeles, CA 91316
(800) 733-7820
www.uniworld.com

Windstar Cruises
2101 4th Ave., Ste. 210
Seattle, WA 98121
(206) 292-9606
www.windstarcruises.com

Key Addresses: Associations

American Society of Travel Agents (ASTA)
1101 King St., Ste. 200
Alexandria, VA 22314
(703) 739-2782
www.asta.org

**Association of Canadian Travel
Agencies (ACTA)**
2560 Matheson Blvd.
Mississauga, ON L4W 4Y9
Canada
(905) 282-9294
www.acta.ca

**Canadian Institute of Travel
Counsellors (CITC)**
505 Consumers Rd., Ste 406
Toronto, ON M2J 4V8
Canada
(416) 484-4450
www.citc.ca

**Cruise Lines International
Association (CLIA)**
910 S.E. 17th St., Ste. 400
Fort Lauderdale, FL 33316
(754) 224-2200
www.cruising.org

**National Association of Career
Travel Agents (NACTA)**
1101 King St., Ste. 200
Alexandria, VA 22314
(703) 739-6826
www.nacta.com

**National Association Cruise Oriented
Agencies (NACOA)**
7378 W. Atlantic Blvd., #115
Margate, FL 33063
(305) 663-5626
www.nacoaonline.com

National Tour Association (NTA)
546 E. Main St.
Lexington, KY 40508
(859) 226-4444
www.ntaonline.com

Niche Cruise Marketing Alliance
12920 N.E. 32nd Pl.
Bellvue, WA 98005
(425) 867-0399
www.nichecruise.com

Outside Sales Support Network (OSSN)
22410 68th Ave. East
Bradenton, FL 34211
(941) 322-9700
www.ossn.com

The Travel Institute (formerly ICTA)
148 Linden St., Ste. 305
Wellesley, MA 02482
(781) 237-0280
www.thetravelinstitute.com

United States Tour Operators Association (USTOA)
275 Madison Ave., Ste. 2014
New York, NY 10016
(212) 599-6599
www.ustoa.com

Bibliography

1. Books and Pamphlets

Alaska by Cruise Ship. By Anne Vipond. Published by Ocean Cruise Guides Ltd., P.O. Box 2041, Port Roberts, WA 98281; (604) 948-0594; fax: (604) 948-2779; e-mail: info@oceancruiseguides.com. The complete guide to the Alaska cruise experience. Includes over 70 maps and over 300 photos.

Caribbean by Cruise Ship. By Anne Vipond. Published by Ocean Cruise Guides Ltd., P.O. Box 2041, Port Roberts, WA 98281; (604) 948-0594; fax: (604) 948-2779; e-mail: info@oceancruiseguides.com. The complete guide to the Caribbean cruise experience. Over 80 maps and 300 photos.

Caribbean Ports of Call—Eastern and Southern. The Globe Pequot Press, P.O. Box 480, Guilford, CT 06437; (888) 249-7586. Profiles, tours, sports, shopping, history, and more on the islands from Puerto Rico to the Panama Canal. Available at www.globe-pequot.com.

Caribbean Ports of Call—Northern and Northeastern Region. The Globe Pequot Press, P.O. Box 480, Guilford, CT 06437; (888) 249-7586. Profiles, tours, sports, shopping, history, and more on the islands from the Bahamas to the Virgin Islands. Available at www.globe-pequot.com.

Caribbean Ports of Call—Western Region. The Globe Pequot Press, P.O. Box 480, Guilford, CT 06437; (888) 249-7586. Profiles, tours, sports, shopping, history, and more on the islands from the Bahamas to Columbia. Available at www.globe-pequot.com.

CLIA's Cruise Manual. Published by Cruise Lines International Association, 910 S.E. 17th St., Fort Lauderdale, FL 33316; (754) 224-2200; CD-ROM, $59.95 ($29.95 for CLIA affiliates). The manual is published mainly for the travel agency community as a reference source on CLIA's Member Cruise Lines. This annually updated, clearly organized, comprehensive volume reflects suggestions made by travel agents. In-depth information on cruise ships and their companies includes new and improved data on: dining aboard CLIA vessels, suggestions for onboard tipping and gratuities, summary of credit card policies of individual member lines, and lots more.

The Complete Cruise Handbook. By Anne Vipond. Published by Ocean Cruise Guides Ltd, P.O. Box 2041, Port Roberts, WA 98281; (604) 948-0594; fax: (604) 948-2779; e-mail: info@oceancruiseguides.com. A comprehensive introduction to cruising for first-timers. How to pick the cruise and ship that's right for you.

Cruise Business Review. Cruise Media, Ltd., Claughton Island Association, 9 Woods Way, Redding, CT 06896. International magazine focusing on the cruise business.

Cruise Industry News Annual. Published yearly by Cruise Industry News, 441 Lexington Ave., Ste. 809, New York, NY 10017; (212) 986-1025; 400 pages, $695. This annual provides an objective overview and forecasts of the worldwide cruise industry, including supply and demand scenarios, and an analysis of each market segment and sailing region. The book also provides expert discussions of relevant subjects and issues as well as analysis of the earnings reports of the leading cruise lines. In addition, the *Cruise Industry News Annual* profiles all cruise lines around the world and their ships, cruise ports, and shipyards. It also features directory listings of the entire cruise lines, ports, shipyards, and supply and service companies. Published since 1988, the *Cruise Industry News Annual* is mainly subscribed to by industry executives, financial analysts, port and tourism officials, and others on a decision-making level.

Cruise Reports. Cruise Reports, 25 Washington St., Morristown, NJ 07960; (973) 605-2442; cr@gti.net; www.cruisereports.com. Monthly newsletter features reviews of ships with ratings based on independent surveys of passengers. News and comments about cruises and cruising.

Cruise Vacations with Kids. By Candyce H. Stapen. Prima Publishing, 400 Hahn Rd., Westminster, MD 21157; (800) 726-0600. Includes tips on choosing the

right family cruise, the advantages of cruising, and getting the most for your money. 400 pages. Available in bookstores and at www.pearsonhighered.com.

Cruises: Selecting, Selling, and Booking. By Juls Zvoncheck. Both a training manual and guide to major cruise lines, it includes useful appendices. Available on Amazon.com.

Cruising: Q&A. Published by Cruise Lines International Association, 910 S.E. 17th St., Fort Lauderdale, FL 33316; (754) 224-2200; pocket size, 25 pages, free. Pamphlet answering most frequently asked questions about cruise vacations, with charts showing worldwide cruise destinations, ship line services for children, singles, active adults, honeymooners, shipboard shopping, and shipboard cuisine. Obtained by sending a self-addressed stamped envelope (75 cents postage) to CLIA.

Dictionary of the Cruise Industry. By Gioria Israel and Laurence Miller. Seatrade Cruise Academy, Seatrade Communications Ltd., Seatrade House, 42 North Station Rd., Colchester, C01 1RD, United Kingdom, +44 1206 545121 or www.seatrade-global.com; $25 or €30. Comprehensive dictionary of nautical and business terminology of the cruise industry.

The Essential Little Cruise Book. By Jim West. Cruise Concepts, 117 West St. Paul St., Springville, IL 61362; (888) 867-8600; available at local bookstores or Amazon.com. This compact collection of cruise wisdom has everything you need to know for a perfect vacation at sea. Jim West has logged many nautical miles as a cruise director and doles out the answers to cruise questions with wit and style. How can you get the best cabin in your price range? The best table in the dining room? The best service from the crew? It's like having your own personal cruise consultant. *The Essential Little Cruise Book* will help you make the most of your time at sea.

Mediterranean by Cruise Ship. By Anne Vipond. Published by Ocean Cruise Guides Ltd., P.O. Box 2041, Port Roberts, WA 98281; (604) 948-0594; fax: (604) 948-2779; e-mail: info@oceancruiseguides.com. The complete guide to all Mediterranean cruises. Over 100 maps and over 400 photos.

Seatrade Cruise Review. Seatrade Organization, Seatrade House, 42 North Station Rd., Colchester, C01 1RB, United Kingdom, +44 1206 545121 or www.seatrade-global.com. Quarterly magazine reporting on the business of cruising worldwide.

The Total Traveler by Ship. Northstar Travel Media LLC, 500 Plaza Dr., Secaucus, NJ 07094; (201) 902-2000. Directory of ships, cruise lines, and ports of call.

2. Periodicals/Consumer

Agent's Cruise Monthly. Published by World Ocean & Cruise Liner Society, P.O. Box 92, Stamford, CT 06904; (203) 329-2787. Annual subscription $30.

Cruise Industry News Quarterly Magazine. Published four times a year by Cruise Industry News, 441 Lexington Ave., Ste. 1209, New York, NY 10017; (212) 986-1025; $75 per year. The magazine's editorial focus covers all aspects of cruise operations: shipbuilding, new ships, cruise companies, ship reviews, onboard services, food and beverage, and ports and destinations. Published since 1991, its worldwide readership includes cruise line executives, shipboard officers and crew, shipyards, ports, service and supply companies, and travel agents.

Cruise Travel. 990 Grover St., Evanston, IL 60201; (847) 491-6440; www.cruisetravelmag.com. Subscription price $23.94. Color magazine with feature articles about ships and cruising; six issues per year.

International Cruise Market Monitor. Prepared and published by G.P. Wild (International) Limited, 15 Gander Hill, Haywards Heath, West Sussex, RH16 1QU, United Kingdom, +44 (0) 1444 413931. An authoritative quarterly publication covering the economic, marketing, and operational aspects of the cruise industry worldwide. Sectorial capacity growth, corporate activities, and supply and demand are examined critically, with a view to providing an independent, analytical, and objective appraisal of the industry, together with a guide to its future development. $650 for all four quarterly issues.

Lloyd's Annual Cruise Review. Prepared by Management and Marketing Consultants G.P. Wild (International) Limited and published by Lloyd's of London Press. Subscriptions Dept., Lloyd's of London Press, Sheepen Pl., Colchester, Essex, CO3 3LP, England; +011 44 1206 772277. An authoritative study, published annually, covering the economic, marketing, and operational aspects of the cruise industry worldwide. Sectorial capacity growth, corporate activities, and supply and demand are examined critically, with a view to providing an independent, analytical, and objective appraisal of the industry, together with a guide to its financial data and fleet details for future development.

Maritime Services Directory. Published by Simmons-Boardman Publications Corporation, 1809 Capitol Ave., Omaha, NE 68102; (800) 895-4389; fax: (402) 346-3670; $119.95 + $9.50 shipping and handling. Extensive listings of maritime vendors, services, associations, and port authorities.

Ocean and Cruise News. Published by World Ocean & Cruise Liner Society, P.O. Box 4850, Stamford, CT 06907; (203) 329-2787. Single issue price $2.50 or $30 per year. Newsletter published 12 times per year. Profiles of "ship of the month" and other features. www.wocls.org.

Official Steamship Guide International. 298 Village St. #145, London, TN 37774; (865) 458-9703. Quarterly publication; four issues at $105. Catalog of cruise ship departures listed by major cruising areas and date. Includes prices and itineraries. www.officialsteamshipguide.com.

Porthole Cruise Magazine. Published by Bill Panoff, PPI Group, 4517 N.W. 31 Ave., Fort Lauderdale, FL 33309; (800) 776-7678. One-year subscription (six issues) for $19.95. Two-year subscription (12 issues) at $29.95. Devoted to the cruise industry and is the number-one source of cruise information for the travel savvy cruise consumer. This publication provides in depth cruise ship feature reports, product evaluations, and general cruise industry news.

3. Other Sources

Lloyd's Cruise International. 1 Singer St., London, EC2A 4LQ, England; +44 (0) 171 250 1500. Covers important aspects of the cruise industry, including marketing, passenger services and related equipment, port developments, business developments, regulatory issues, and market trends.

Porthole Insider. Published by Bill Panoff. PPI Group, 4517 N.W. 31 Ave., Fort Lauderdale, FL 33309; (800) 776-7678. A publication exploring industry issues, includes state of the industry reports on marketing and financial information and integrates information on all aspects of the cruise industry from an operations standpoint. Directed toward cruise line executives and other industry decision-makers.

Vacations on Video. 7662 East Gray Rd., Ste. 101, Scottsdale, AZ 85260; (480) 483-1551. Source for purchase of travel videos with list that includes 300 videos from 35 major cruise lines as well as other travel suppliers. Contact Vacations on Video for further pricing information.

Port Descriptions by Country

Ports. They're what tie an itinerary together, what counterbalance those activity-filled days at sea. In fact, in surveys, those who buy cruises usually rank the ports visited as the first or second most important factor in their decision to cruise. In Chapter 7, you learned about the world's most important ports. That chapter always challenges readers. Our school systems do such a mediocre job of teaching geography that many people today confuse Austria with Australia or Auckland with Oakland. But even geographic geniuses don't know every port, where each is and what each offers. This is why we have included the pages that follow. They list and describe just about every port that cruise ships visit today. We hope you find this research tool a valuable feature. Remember, someday you might not just read about these ports. You'll see them

Antarctica
Argentina
Australia
The Bahamas
Bahrain
Belgium
Belize
Bermuda
Borneo
Brazil
British Virgin Islands
British West Indies
Bulgaria
Cambodia
Canada
Cayman Islands
Chile
China
Colombia
Costa Rica
Croatia
Denmark
Dominican Republic
Egypt
Ecuador
Estonia
Fiji
Finland
France
French Guiana
French Polynesia

French West Indies
Germany
Ghana
Gibraltar
Greece
Guatemala
Honduras
Iceland
India
Indian Ocean Islands
Indonesia
Ireland
Israel
Italy
Jamaica
Japan
Jordan
Kenya
Kiribati
Korea
Latvia
Libya
Madagascar
Malaysia
Malta
Mexico
Monaco
Morocco
Myanmar
The Netherlands
Netherlands Antilles

New Zealand
Norway
Panama
Papua New Guinea
Peru
Philippines
Poland
Portugal
Puerto Rico
Russia
Samoa
Senegal
Singapore
South Africa
Spain
Sweden
Taiwan
Thailand
Tunisia
Turkey
Ukraine
United Arab Emirates
United Kingdom
United States
U.S. Virgin Islands
Uruguay
Venezuela
Vietnam
Yemen
Yugoslavia

ANTARCTICA

Antarctic Peninsula
A giant finger pointing toward Cape Horn, this peninsula is the destination of most Antarctic cruises. It is rich in scenic beauty, wildlife, and in the history of Antarctic exploration. There are numerous opportunities for scenic cruising and to go ashore by inflatable expedition boats.

Half Moon Island
One of the most pleasant landings in Antarctica, Half Moon Island has a sizable rookery of chinstrap penguins as well as nesting Antarctic terns and kelp gulls. Whales are quite often seen patrolling the shores, and this small island offers stunning views of surrounding mountains.

Neumayer Channel/Port Lockroy
The soaring cliffs of Neumayer Channel form the entrance-way to Port Lockroy, one of Antarctica's most exciting harbors ringed by towering mountains. It is here that Winston Churchill established a secret British station during World War II to protect interests in the Southern Ocean. Although now abandoned, you will find the recently restored base plus a large gentoo rookery and vestiges of past whaling activities.

Paradise Harbor
This protected harbor lives up to its name. Ringed by hanging ice cliffs and dotted with floating bergs reflecting every color of the spectrum, it has a heavenly aura about it. At the sometimes occupied Chilean station, there are sizable colonies of gentoo and chinstrap penguins.

ARGENTINA

Buenos Aires
Possibly Latin America's most sophisticated city, Buenos Aires has often been referred to as the "Paris of South America." It offers a dazzling array of stores downtown, broad tree-lined boulevards in adjoining neighborhoods, and the historic Casa Rosado of Evita fame. Tour the Teatro Colón, one of the world's greatest opera houses, and visit Evita Peron's tomb. If time permits, enjoy a performance of the Tango in the many venues where this is available.

Cape Horn
The southernmost point of the Americas is a gray rugged rock, enduring in a notoriously weather-beaten spot. With luck, your ship can cruise close by this rocky promontory, which has marked the passage from the Atlantic to the Pacific Ocean for centuries. Time and weather permitting, vessels equipped with landing craft can take you ashore where you can climb to the top of the Cape.

Puerto Madryn
Situated snugly in a well-protected bay of the Golfo Nuevo, Puerto Madryn is the natural gateway to the starkly beautiful plains of Patagonia. This vast area covers one third of the country but is occupied by less than four percent of the population. Patagonia characteristically encompasses three different regions: a vast and windy, treeless plateau; the Atlantic coast; and the southern part with its national parks, awesome mountain ranges, glaciers and fjords.

Ushuaia
The world's southernmost city, Ushuaia overlooks Beagle Channel, named after the ship that took Charles Darwin to the bottom of the world. Founded just over one hundred years ago, this rustic town is situated amidst incredible snowcapped mountains, dramatic waterfalls, massive glaciers, and a forest known for its red foliage. Tierra del Fuego, the "Land of Fire," is 12 miles west of Ushuaia. It is known for its glacial landscape and national park, a bird-watcher's paradise.

AUSTRALIA

Adelaide
Adelaide is a quiet, conservative town but embracing South Australia's liberal traditions. It is a city of old wealth, with a free and laid-back lifestyle. Home to more than one million inhabitants, it has a large European population, with Italians making up the largest non-Anglo cultural group.

Brisbane
Nestled between the Gold Coast to the south and the Sunshine Coast to the north, laid-back Brisbane makes the most of its magnificent beaches, offering an ideal blend of Aussie ease and urban energy. Wander in the lush Botanical Gardens, shop in the Queen Street Mall, or enjoy the countless cafes and restaurants along the banks of the Brisbane River.

Broome
Tiny Broome sits in the windswept "Far Corner" of Western Australia, on the scenic arid shores of the Indian Ocean. It became famous early in the

century for its pearls and mother of pearl, both among Australia's finest. Pearls are still important here, but tourist attractions are currently its greatest wealth. These include the dramatic pearl fishermen's cemetery and superb 10-mile-long Cable Beach.

Burnie
This city is the gateway to scenic Tasmania and Australia's fifth-largest port, boasting a deep, natural harbor. Within its interior lie the rain forest and Cradle Mountain National Park, a World Heritage Site. The gentle rolling hills that grace this area include rich farmlands and pastures that produce some of the finest Merino wool in the world. Northern Tasmania is also rich in picturesque villages and historic houses, some dating from the Georgian colonial era.

Cairns
One of Australia's hottest vacation destinations, Cairns serves as a gateway to three of Australia's great natural wonders: the Great Barrier Reef, where a spectrum of colorful marine life thrives; 16 miles of superb beaches north of the city that form the famed Marlin Coast; and the immense Daintree National Park in North Queensland.

Cid Harbor
Cid Harbor is an access point for the Great Barrier Reef, the most massive structure on earth created by living organisms. Formed over 10,000 years by tiny, limestone-secreting coral polyps, the Great Barrier Reef is actually a vast coral complex composed of more than 2,000 individual reefs and 71 coral islands.

Darwin
Named after evolutionist Charles Darwin, this tropical city on the north end of Australia serves as a gateway to the Australian Outback and its aboriginal community, the world's oldest culture. From here, you can visit Kakadu National Park, a World Heritage Site renowned not only for its Australian wildlife but Aboriginal rock art. Darwin itself is a former frontier town with a rough-and-tumble past. Its growth was achieved back in 1871 with the discovery of gold at Pine Creek. A number of historic buildings from that era remain.

Fremantle (Perth)
The port of Fremantle is a quaint colonial town of terraced houses and a bay that was a haven for America's Cup yachts. The city is also the gateway to Perth, the capital of Western Australia. Situated some 15 miles upriver from Fremantle on the banks of the Swan River, Perth is a growing, bustling city where soaring high rises coexist with sandstone buildings from the colonial era. The population in and around Perth makes up some eight percent of Western Australia's population. And it's here that life moves at a slower pace, from the wonders of the bush to the wineries of the Swan Valley.

Great Barrier Reef (see also Cairns, Cid Harbour, Cooktown and Townsville)
The Great Barrier Reef is 1,250 miles long and covers 80,000 square miles – the largest structure on earth built by living organisms. Ever since Captain Cook ran aground on the reef back in 1770, people have been enjoying its incredible beauty. Over 600 pristine islands stud the reef, each with its brilliant corals and spectacular sea creatures.

Hobart, Tasmania
Australia's second-oldest city is notable for its Georgian buildings, picturesque harbor, and fine galleries and gardens. Nearby are the ghostly ruins of Port Arthur, the infamous penal colony, and its Isle of the Dead cemetery. You can also visit one of the perfectly preserved colonial villages nearby.

Melbourne
Australia's "Garden City" rejoices in its greenery, from the Fitzroy Gardens to the magnificent Royal Botanical Gardens. Hiding behind the skyscrapers along the Yarra River are the graceful 19th-century mansions of the city's Gold Rush years. Since Australia is an ethnic melting pot, hosting immigrants from throughout the world, it is not surprising that local cuisine offers 60 different international genres. However, it is the city's English personality, enhanced by its many gardens that will stay with you long after you leave.

Sydney
Sydney possesses one of the most beautiful and famous harbors in the world. The harbor goes on seemingly forever, with residential areas perched on bluffs overlooking the various waterways. The city is Australia's oldest settlement, its largest and most thriving city and a cultural melting pot. It curves around idyllic Port Jackson, where sandstone cliffs and bright islands complement the Opera House and Harbour Bridge. It is fun to explore cobbled colonial streets of the historic Rocks quarter.

Townsville

Townsville is the heart of North Queensland, a focal point attracting many people to its beautiful climate and relaxed lifestyle. This is also a gateway to the Great Barrier Reef, a magnificent undersea wonderland composed of more than 2,000 individual reefs and 71 coral islands.

Whitsunday Islands

The 74 islands that comprise the Whitsunday archipelago are scattered on both sides of the Whitsunday Passage, rising out of the sea as the tips of underwater mountains. Many feature a hilly terrain and fringes of coral reefs around them. All but five of the Whitsundays are predominantly or totally national park territory. A few of the islands are inhabited or developed as tourist resorts.

THE BAHAMAS

Eleuthera

Famous for its rosy-pink beaches, sickle-shaped Eleuthera is long and lean. Although new resorts have sprung up, the island's little towns of Spanish Wells and Rock Sound still retain their charm. Natural attractions like Boiling Hole and Glass Window are fun to visit. You can also browse the Straw Market in Governor's Harbour or play a round of golf.

Grand Bahama Island (Freeport)

Grand Bahama offers visitors a wealth of attractions. You can try your luck at one of two casinos, enjoy a day of shopping at the 10-acre International Bazaar or nearby Port Lucaya, visit the lush Garden of the Groves, go deep-sea fishing or discover life beneath the sea on a snorkeling or scuba diving excursion. Here you also have the opportunity to swim with dolphins at the Underwater Explorer's Society, which is accredited by the Alliance of Marine Mammal Parks and Aquariums.

New Providence Island (Nassau, Paradise Island)

New Providence Island is one of the over 700 coral-based islands that comprise The Bahamas. However, its capital, Nassau, is perhaps best known to cruise vacationers. Only about 100 miles from Miami, Nassau is a city known for its architecture of Victorian mansions, cathedrals and 18th-century forts. Nassau also offers its visitors several casinos, a variety of white-sand beaches, and excellent shopping opportunities along Bay Street and at the city's famous Straw Market.

BAHRAIN

Al Manamah

Al Manamah is the capital city of Bahrain and is situated on the Persian Gulf in the northern region of Bahrain Island. It is Bahrain's largest city with approximately one-third of Bahrain's population.

BELGIUM

Antwerp

The chief city of Belgium's Flemish region, Antwerp was renowned for centuries as a center of the diamond trade. More recently, it has become a major cultural center for the continent. Its Royal Museum contains magnificent works by Rubens, Van Dyck, and other old masters.

Oostende (Brugge, Ghent)

Oostende serves as a gateway to the perfectly preserved town of Brugge, where you can enjoy a boat ride on picturesque canals and shop for delicate Belgian lace. Nearby, the medieval city of Ghent, Belgium's most populous city in the Middle Ages, is home to the Van Eyck brothers' famous painting "The Adoration of the Mystic Lamb" and other attractions.

Zeebrugge (Ghent, Brugge)

A trading center on the English Channel for centuries, Zeebrugge is an access port for Ghent and Brugge – a jewel of a town beribboned with picturesque canals and a truly charming medieval beauty. In this region, museums proudly display the glories of the old Flemish masters from Van Dyck to Rubens. Summertime is delightful. You can see when window boxes with colorful flowers and the graceful arcs of windmills.

BELIZE

Belize City

A mixture of old and new, Belize City offers a glance into history amid the bustling growth of a country. Formally known as British Honduras, this area offers some of the best diving and water sports in the Western Hemisphere. There are an array of historic attractions – St. John's Cathedral, the Swing Bridge, Government House Museum and the colorful fruit market. This is also a gateway to historic Mayan ruins.

BERMUDA

Hamilton
The neatly maintained vintage shops of Front Street are at your doorstep when you dock in Hamilton. British influences have blended comfortably with casual island style. Explore the town, including the Royal Yacht Club, the Cathedral with its memorials, and the Historical Museum. Take a drive around the island to the Botanical Gardens and to St. George's, the old capital with its 18th-century town hall and cobblestone lanes.

St. George
On the East End of Bermuda lies St. George. This postcard-come-to-life features cobblestone streets with names like Petticoat Lane and Featherbed Alley. Glorious beaches and historic King's Square on the waterfront are favorite attractions as well. The town contains branches of most of the major stores in Hamilton.

West End (King's Wharf)
West End, Bermuda's third port of call, offers a complex built around the remarkable Royal Naval Dockyard. A shipyard that was the British Royal Navy's headquarters until March 1995, has been beautifully restored to offer shopping, restaurants, art galleries, craft markets and eight wonderful museums. For water-lovers, there is also a snorkel park and an extensive watersports facility.

BORNEO

Brunei
Wedged between two Malaysian states on the island of Borneo, Brunei is as exotic and unexplored as its name implies. Despite the fact that oil has made Brunei the richest sultanate in the world, the friendly water-villagers of its capital Bandar Seri Begawan, maintain their traditional values, living in stilted houses on the river. Only the TV antennae, the huge golden-domed mosque and the sultan's opulent 1,000-room palace reveal the vast wealth that this tiny jungle nation enjoys.

Kuching
Kuching escaped bombing in World War II and has retained much of its old charm. It is by far the largest city in the state of Sarawak. Kuching is divided by the Sarawak River. The south is a commercial and residential area dominated by Chinese while the north shore is predominantly Malay, characterized by old kampong houses lining the river. The recently renovated riverfront area provides a pleasant area for strolling, dining and boat rides.

Sandakan (Sepilok)
Surrounded by thick, mountainous jungles where wild orchids grow, this Malaysian coastal trading town serves as a loading port for the rich tropical hardwoods found in the interior of Borneo. About 15 miles from Sandakan, Sepilok is the home of the famous orangutan sanctuary, one of the few places in the world where you can see these animals in their natural setting.

BRAZIL

Belem
A gateway to the Amazon, the 371-year-old city of Our Lady of Bethlehem (now shortened to Belem) bears all the gifts of a tropical jungle. Vendors in dug-out canoes bring exotic fish, fruit, Amazonian handicrafts and religious artifacts to Ver-O-Peso, Brazil's largest outdoor market. The 18th-century Baroque Merces Church is one of Belem's most beautiful landmarks.

Boca da Valeria
Located between Santarém and Manaus, Boca de Valeria is the entrance to the Valeria Channel (boca meaning mouth). The channel leads to Lake Valeria, which marks the border between the Brazilian states of Amazonas and Pará. Frequently while ships are at anchor, a colorful picture unfolds as canoes with the local population come out to greet visitors.

Buzios
Up until the 1960's, few outside the confines of this charming fishing village on Brazil's "Costa del Sol" even knew of its existence. That all changed when a young starlet named Brigitte Bardot found Buzios' white-sand beaches and tepid clear waters too good to keep to herself. While retaining its pre-sixties' charm, Buzios has evolved into a respectable fashion destination. Shopping along the Rua des Pedros is a highlight.

Curua Una River
Venturing from the main stream of the Amazon into this black water tributary, you'll view the impressive plant and bird life thriving along its shores. Here too, meet the Caboclos, a people of mixed Indian, European and African ancestry living in the heart of the Amazon Basin.

Ilha Grande

This destination offers the opportunity to enjoy beautiful hiking trails, kayaking, snorkeling, diving to spectacular sites or simply relaxing on its gorgeous beaches. The island is one of 365 of the Angra dos Reis archipelago in the state of Rio de Janeiro. Since this is an ecologically preserved area, most activities are nature-centered.

Itaji

Itaji only really started to develop during the mid-19th century when surrounding areas began to receive European immigrants who generated business for the port. Towards the close of that century, the town itself received a considerable influx of Italian, German and Polish immigrants, whose descendants now make up the bulk of the population. Neat countryside farms and the distinct European architecture seen in towns such as Blumenau and Joinville never fail to amaze visitors to this southern part of Brazil.

Manaus

A cultural outpost in the heart of the Amazon rainforest, Manaus was famous for the extravagant lifestyle and architecture of the 19th century rubber barons who made their fortunes here. The city's renovated Opera House stands as an opulent testament to their vast wealth. This is also a convenient starting point for trips into the neighboring rain forest.

Natal

Deemed the "Sun Capital," Natal has much more to offer than its spectacular sand dunes that tumble down to the sea. Founded on Christmas Day (Natal in Portuguese) in 1599, the city has preserved a number of edifices dating to colonial days. Three King's Fortress and the recently restored Metropolitan Cathedral both date back to the turn of the 16th Century. The landmark Albert Maranhão Theater dates back to 1898.

Parati

Parati, about 180 miles south of Rio de Janeiro, has remained fundamentally unaltered since it was inhabited in 1660. It was a staging post for 18th-century trade in Brazilian gold from the State of Minas Gerais to Portugal. Raids and pirate attacks necessitated establishing a new route and a decline in Parati's fortunes resulted. Since the town is off the beaten track, it remained quietly hidden away. Today, Parati has been declared a national historic monument by UNESCO as one of the most important examples of colonial architecture.

Paranagua

Founded in 1585, this is an important coffee shipping port located about 200 miles south of Santos. Attractions include the fort of Nossa Senhora dos Prazeres built in 1767 on a neighboring island.

Parintins

This is an isolated island town in the middle of the Amazon River that is steeped in Indian culture. Its stadium has become the focus of the Boi-Bumba Festival, an annual event similar to carnival.

Recife

Known as the "Venice of Brazil," Recife is built on islands and connected by bridges. The lovely city is graced with churches from its Portuguese colonial past. These are ornamented with frescoes and bright tiles. Browse the teeming market, spend the day at popular Boa Viagem Beach, or visit the beautiful suburb of Olinda, a perfectly intact 16th century town.

Rio de Janeiro

Undoubtedly the highlight of everyone's South American experience, glittering Rio is a city that enchants mind, body and soul. Radiant beaches, like Ipanema and Copacabana, stretch like bejeweled arcs around the city's perimeter. The monumental 120-foot statue of Christ the Redeemer towers over Rio atop Corcovado Mountain. Take a cable car up Sugarloaf Mountain for stunning panoramic views. Founded in the early 16th century, Rio was once the capital of Brazil. It remains the nation's cultural and spiritual center, a dazzling amalgam of Latin and African cultures, with more than five million inhabitants.

Rio Grande do Sul

This lovely old Portuguese city offers its visitors gracious squares and beautiful churches. Attractions include the Museum of Sacred Art and the fascinating Oceanographic Museum. Excursions to the vast pampas (ranches) beyond the town offer the opportunity to visit the land of the gauchos.

Salvador da Bahia

A dynamic collage of diverse religious and cultural groups, colorful open-air markets, tropical flowers, majestic colonial buildings, golden-sand beaches and bubbling sensuality come together in Salvador in the State of Bahia. Visit the lovely Sao Francisco Chapel. Sample Afro-Brazilian cuisine, including such mouth-watering specialties as "ensopada" (seafood poached in fresh coconut milk) and "vatapa" (spicy fresh shrimp).

Santarem

This colorful town along the Amazon River has a Town Hall Museum with displays of pottery made by the local Tupai Indians, a Municipal Market and the Casa da Farinha – an old manioc flour factory where demonstrations can be seen on how to extract latex from rubber trees. Take a stroll along the river front with its craft of all kinds connecting Santarem with neighboring island settlements. Nearby lakes and lush forests that are home to numerous species of birds.

Santos (Sao Paulo)

Santos achieved fame as a coffee-processing and shipping port at the turn of the 20th century. While it has lost much of its prosperity, the buildings and grounds that housed this thriving industry are still to be seen. This port is also a starting point for tours to Sao Paulo, largest city on the continent and Brazil's most modern. Its museums are among the finest in South America and its surrounding coastline is graced with many lovely beaches.

BRITISH VIRGIN ISLANDS

Tortola (Road Town)

Tortola, the tiny island that starts the long crescent of the Lesser Antilles, is a fragment of Britain complete with right-hand drive automobiles, elaborate teas and soft-spoken graciousness to visitors. Wander through genteel, laid-back Road Town, then select one of the marvelous beaches and enjoy the most un-British eternal sunshine. Tortola is also home to the Virgin Islands Folk Museum, where visitors can learn about the islands' rich history.

Virgin Gorda

Two outstanding sights highlight this port of call. First is "The Baths" – unique in all the Caribbean, this natural wonder consists of giant boulders that form labyrinthine caves and clear, saltwater pools illuminated by the rays of the sun. Second is Gorda Sound, a protected anchorage known the world over by seasoned yachtsmen.

BRITISH WEST INDIES

Antigua (St. John's)

With a beach for each day of the year, Antigua is a water-lover's delight. It is recommended that you visit English Harbour, a superb restoration of the 18th-century dockyard where Admiral Lord Nelson once ruled the British fleet. This is one of the finest historical attractions in the Caribbean. Be sure that you also visit Drake's Seat. In an all-day port call, you'll have time to do both this and enjoy a nearby beach.

Barbados (Bridgetown)

Barbados is set far away from most other Caribbean islands, nearly 1,000 miles east of the Netherlands Antilles chain. The Bajan British accent is very distinctive, reflecting both Great Britain and the lovely island they live on. Barbados has lovely parish churches, great manor houses and a proper Trafalgar Square. The capital, Bridgetown, is a mix of bustling activity and quaint surroundings. Visitors enjoy fine dining, miles of exquisite beaches, scuba diving, seaborne excursions and folkloric festivals.

Dominica (Roseau)

Roseau is the capital and largest city in Dominica. However, it is it important to get beyond the city to the rainforests, waterfalls, and caves that are the island's attractions. There are excellent opportunities for hiking and the abundant marine life make it a superb area for diving and snorkeling. Common to this area are the stingray, snapper, barracuda, parrotfish, and dolphin. Equally as common are charming stilt houses and the sound of reggae and calypso music.

Grand Turk Island, Turks and Caicos Islands

Home to the Turks and Caicos' capital, Cockburn Town, Grand Turk attracts visitors from around the globe for its pristine diving and excellent beaches. There are also seasonal whale watching, snorkeling and historical attractions which round out this Caribbean island. Landlubbers will want to visit the National Museum where you can view story of the Molasses Reef Wreck, the oldest European shipwreck (1505) discovered in the Western Hemisphere.

Grenada (St. George's)

Called the "Spice Island" for its abundance of cinnamon and nutmeg, the spices are still sold at the waterfront market. Grenada is spicy in many other ways. St. George's has historic buildings in brick and mellow stone, and one of the loveliest harbors in the Caribbean. The coastline is full of secluded coves, while the mountainous interior is rich in rainforests and frothy rivers.

St. Vincent and The Grenadines (St. Vincent, Mayreau, Bequia)
The hundred islands of the Grenadines are definitely off the beaten path in the Caribbean. However, the lush beauty, rugged coastline and rushing waterfalls attract many visitors to the volcanic island of St. Vincent. The island's distinct West Indian flair combines with British customs and Gallic culture, mostly seen through the music, sports, cuisine and cultivation of its people. Mayreau, tossed like a tiny emerald among the Grenadines, is an idyllic spot where there are no cars, just one tiny village and one resort, hidden away in the palms.

St. Kitts (Basseterre)
This fertile isle is a land of rain forests, tropical flowers, and abundant sugar cane. After a stroll around the charming colonial streets and shops of the capital, Basseterre, tour the island or visit Brimstone Hill Fort, an impressive construction that is one of the wonders of the Caribbean.

St. Lucia (Castries, Soufriere)
The first thing cruise guests will notice when sailing into St. Lucia's Bay are the majestic Pitons, two 2,000-foot mountains that rise from the sea in dramatic, breathtaking fashion. Thriving coral reefs provide ample snorkeling and diving opportunities while the mountainous rain forest preserves offer superb hiking and bird watching. This is also the location of the world's only drive-in volcanic crater. With its hot, bubbling holes of sulfuric waters, the Soufriere area has the most dramatic scenery on the island.

Tobago (Scarborough, Spanish Town)
Tobago is a classic West Indian haven, the subdued sister of nearby Trinidad. When the plantation lifestyle collapsed with the world sugar market in 1888, land was sold to slaves, and over time Africans here have held on to their cultural richness. West African music, folklore and beliefs – including Obeah, the island's magic – still thrive, as do several hundred species of tropical birds, living in virgin rain forests and along Tobago's deserted beaches.

Trinidad (Port of Spain)
Steel drums and calypso were born here. Nature lovers will delight in the Asa Wright Nature Center and the Caroni Bird Sanctuary, two of the Caribbean's best-known conservation centers. Port of Spain, the island's capital city, is home to art galleries, restaurants and the National Museum where visitors can discover the country's diverse people and culture.

BULGARIA

Nesebur
Founded by Thracians and colonized by Greek settlers from Megara in the 6th century, Nesebur is one of the oldest and most picturesque towns in the Balkans. Nesebur's rich cultural heritage can be seen in numerous Byzantine churches, beautiful old houses or Roman ruins. The town sits on a small peninsula connected to the mainland by a narrow isthmus. Scattered through town are several medieval churches.

BURMA, see MYANMAR

CAMBODIA

Sihanoukville
By 1960, what had begun as a housing project for workers evolved into Sihanoukville, a town named in honor of King Norodom Sihanouk. In the years to come, Sihanoukville experienced commercial success due to its new port. It also became a transit point for anti-American forces during the Vietnam War. Then in 1975, after the Khmer Rouge regime captured the American container ship Mayaguez, the United States attacked several strategic points in and around the city in retaliation. Despite its war-torn past, Sihanoukville has re-emerged as Cambodia's second-most important city after Phnom Penh. Rebuilt with Soviet aid, Sihanoukville is rich in cultural diversity, home to unspoiled beaches and a certain charm that is just now being discovered.

CANADA

Charlottetown, Prince Edward Island
French explorer Jacques Cartier described it as "the fairest land 'tis possible to see!" With its 500 miles of smooth, sandy beaches, vast stretches of verdant woodland and peaceful rolling pastures, Prince Edward Island is indeed one of the fairest spots to be found. It was here that Canada's founding fathers envisioned the Dominion of Canada.

Halifax, Nova Scotia
You can walk on hillside streets to the Citadel, a star-shaped fort built in 1749, where the traditional Noon Gun recalls the British garrison. There are also restored wharves of Historic Properties, now filled with shops, and the Halifax Public Gardens,

the oldest formal Victorian gardens in North America. A highlight is a visit to the rustic fishing village of Peggy's Cove, a postcard-perfect Nova Scotian fishing village with lobster pots, fishing boats, and a shining Atlantic seascape just offshore.

Lunenburg, Nova Scotia
This charming port may well be "the prettiest town in Canada" as some claim. A UNESCO World Heritage Site, it also opens the way to other picturesque South Shore villages like Mahone Bay, and to whale-watching excursions on the nearby bays.

Montreal, Quebec
Founded by fur trappers, Montreal is now the largest French-speaking city outside France. Cosmopolitan and lively, it is a center for cinema, high fashion and finance. Here the finest shops are underground, around the modern subway. You can visit Mont-Royal for a view, or venture into the Laurentian Mountains for stunning wilderness scenery.

Quebec City, Quebec
The only walled city in North America and a UNESCO World Heritage Site, Quebec City has a distinct French flavor and is blessed with a spectacular location on a cliff overlooking the St. Lawrence River. Quebec City is an explorer's delight with cobblestone streets, 17th- and 18th-century buildings, an immense star-shaped fortress and a funicular that you can ride between the upper and lower towns. The Petit Champlain quarter, the oldest part, has the Place des Armes and Plains of Abraham, all with a genteel, European character.

Saguenay Fjord
The largest fjord in eastern North America, this majestic fjord was created during the last Ice Age when glaciers deepened an ancient river bed. In some places the cliffs tower 1,500 feet above the river and you'll delight in watching for cavorting whales at the junction of the Saguenay and St. Lawrence rivers.

Saint John, New Brunswick
Canada's oldest incorporated city, Saint John sits at the juncture of the Saint John River and the Bay of Fundy. Here, visitors may witness the worldrenowned phenomenon of the reversing falls, created by the Bay of Fundy's 28 1/2-foot tide swell rising above the level of the Saint John River at high tide. Saint John is also home to

Canada's oldest museum and Market Square with its charming shops and restaurants. Saint John has the quaint atmosphere of a small American city in the 1950's.

Saint-Pierre/Miquelon, France (in Gulf of St. Lawrence)
These are the only French possessions remaining in North America which once was a critically important and large French possession. These are small fishing villages, interesting to walk through and soak up the atmosphere.

St. John's, Newfoundland
North America's oldest European-settled city is also home to the easternmost point of the continent: Cape Spear. A good vantage point for viewing the city is Signal Hill, where Marconi received the first transatlantic wireless message. You can also hike the dramatic coast, or try your hand at sea-kayaking.

Sydney, Nova Scotia
Nova Scotia's second-largest city, Sydney is located on Cape Breton Island. While the tradition is definitely Scottish, one of the highlights of a visit to Sydney is the restored French fortress at Louisbourg – where shopkeepers and inhabitants dress, live and produce goods in the tradition of the 18th-century. At Sydney, you'll also find some of Eastern Canada's most beautiful parks and trails. The Alexander Graham Bell Museum is worth a visit, too.

Vancouver, British Columbia
In Vancouver, you're never out of sight of mountains or of the sea. It is a prosperous city adorned with flowers lining the streets and lush greenery. Museums offer fine collections of the dramatic northwest native arts. Vancouver's Chinatown is the second-largest in the world. The waterfront Gastown district recalls the city's colorful past as a premier Pacific port since the days of the Clipper ships. The very large and pleasant Stanley Park offers a cool respite from city shopping and sightseeing.

Victoria, British Columbia
Prim and proper, neat and clean, friendly little Victoria island is like a breath of fresh air. Its British heritage is apparent in the double-decker buses, the Royal British Columbia Museum and in the elaborate tea at the Empress Hotel. Go out to the renowned Butchart Gardens, where sunken floral beds reflect international themes.

CAYMAN ISLANDS

Grand Cayman (Georgetown)

Grand Cayman is the biggest of the three Cayman Islands, which also include Cayman Brac and Little Cayman. The Caymans fully deserve their reputation as a paradise for divers: unclouded waters and a colorful variety of marine life are protected by the government. Several shipwrecks add to the underwater attractions. Seven Mile Beach, located on Grand Cayman's western shore, is the island's main tourist development. Golf lovers will find a beautiful golf course nearby, while sun worshippers relish some of the whitest sand in the Caribbean.

CHILE

Arica

This seaside oasis among golden sand dunes is a rapidly developing oceanside resort. Just 30 miles from the border with Peru and linked to Bolivia by land and air, the city is endowed with a unique and exciting international atmosphere. Arica lies at the mouth of the Azapa Valley, a green oasis in the middle of the Atacama Desert that produces many tropical fruits and vegetables, including olives famous for their size and flavor.

Puerto Chacabuco

This small but busy port lies at the east end of a narrow fjord. Located eight miles across a large suspension bridge from Puerto Aisen, Puerto Chacabuco was the site of Chile's first road (actually a trail) in 1903. In the 1930's, the trail was expanded to reach as far as Coihaique. The road twists around cliffs and through dramatic landscape, finally reaching the Rio Simpson National Reserve. Stretching along the Simpson River, the reserve is squeezed in between sheer cliffs and graced by numerous waterfalls.

Puerto Montt

Located on the northern tip of the vast Reloncavi Bay, Puerto Montt is the gateway to the Chilean Lake District. Crowding the harbor are vessels that ply the route between Cape Horn and Puerto Montt, finding shelter here from the storms of the Pacific. The first German colonists arrived in 1852; their descendants have remained a small but influential percentage of the 130,000 inhabitants. The town, which spreads along a narrow seaboard and climbs the slopes that enclose Puerto Montt,

offers scant attractions for the visitor apart from shingle-roofed houses around a flowered central square.

Punta Arenas

Located on the western side of the Strait of Magellan, Punta Arenas is the capital of Chile's Magallanes province and is the bustling center of one of the world's largest sheep-farming areas. Its free-port facilities have promoted local commerce and encouraged immigration from central Chile. The best and largest port for thousands of miles, it provides a base for South Atlantic fishing boats and Antarctic research vessels. The city center features impressive mansions dating from the late 19th and early 20th centuries.

Valparaiso (Santiago)

The port city for Santiago, Valparaiso is a charming city in its own right. Steep hills rise to make the surroundings an amphitheater, with wharves and business buildings at the base and residential neighborhoods above. Santiago, Chile's capital, is a two-hour drive away. With over five million people and many born in Europe, the city offers restaurants of every ethnic background, museums, parks, gardens, and Spanish Colonial buildings alongside of modern high-rise structures. Alternatively, visitors can head north five miles along the coast to Viña del Mar, a fashionable and attractive seaside resort that is home to the summer palace of Chile's presidents.

CHINA

Canton, see Guangshou

Guangshou (Canton)

Canton, now known as Guangshou, has been a foreign trading port for over 2,000 years and a center for revolutionary activities for which it gained recognition as the "Birthplace of Modern China." It was here that Sun Yatsen and Mao Zedong began reshaping their nation over 60 years ago. You can visit Sun Yatsen's impressive Memorial Hall, the famous Flower Pagoda, and Shamian Island, an enclave of aging but still grand British and French colonial buildings. Or, visit the Canton Zoo, home of Canton's most famous residents, the giant pandas.

Hong Kong

Situated at the Eastern tip of China, Hong Kong is one of the world's truly great cities. This former

British colony reverted to Chinese control in 1997, yet the culture-rich atmosphere remains. As the financial capital of the Far East and the premier gateway to China and Southeast Asia, Hong Kong offers one of the world's truly great travel experiences. Within the little more than 400 square miles of Hong Kong, Kowloon and the New Territories, visitors will find everything from hiking, horse racing and sailing to internationally renowned art galleries. Some of the best hotels, dining, and shopping in the world are found in this dazzling metropolis. At the same time, it offers a delightful realm of natural wonders and serene rural villages.

Shanghai

From the Opium Wars to junks and barges, images of Shanghai flood the senses. The real Shanghai is a teeming metropolis of 11 million, bustling with energy, towering skyscrapers and Art Deco buildings, honking traffic and shopping crowds. But once you enter China's largest city, you'll find Eastern ways abound: Tai Chi along the Bund, the serenity of exquisite ponds and gardens, and an endless flotilla of sampans edging along the Huangpu River. Explore Shanghai old and new: the busy bazaars and alleyways of the Old Town, Yu Garden, the Wuxingting Tea House, Long Hua Temple and other landmarks.

Tianjin (Beijing)

Tianjin serves as the gateway to Beijing, the ancient capital of China. Known as Peking under British rule, the city is a veritable treasure-trove of historic wonders, including the Great Wall and the Forbidden City, where you enter the world of The Last Emperor, a complex of incredible historic significance and physical grandeur. Just outside the walls of the Imperial Palace lies the largest plaza on earth, Tiananmen Square, home to Mao's Monument and his Mausoleum.

COLOMBIA

Cartagena

Cartagena is a Spanish colonial city on the country's north Caribbean Coast. The old city, almost completely surrounded by lagoons, bays, and the Caribbean Sea, is still girded by its 17th-century fortifications. Once these guarded the gold and treasures of the New World, bound for Spain; now they shelter ornate churches and convents, the dramatic Palace of the Inquisition, and other historic gems.

COSTA RICA

Caldera

Tiny Caldera is situated between the volcanic beaches of Golfo de Nicoya and some of the country's highest mountain peaks. It often serves as a starting point for those touring the country's interior including the capital, San José.

Drake Bay/Bahia Paraiso

Named after Sir Francis Drake who anchored here in 1579, Drake Bay offers some of Costa Rica's most stunning scenery: Fiery Pacific sunsets, crystalline waters, and the blue wedge of Cano Island floating offshore. Nearby is Corcovado National Park. Terrain in Corcovado varies from soft sandy beaches to dense forests of spectacularly tall trees, eight ecological habitats in all. The park also is home to incredible wildlife. Jaguars, ocelots, and tapirs roam its forests, and flocks of scarlet macaws and monkeys cavort overhead.

Puerto Limon

Puerto Limon, once an important banana port, is the capital of Costa Rica's Limon Province on the Caribbean coast. The town offers few sights, but serves mainly as a gateway to Costa Rica's rugged wilderness. Costa Rica's capital, San José, is about a 2-hour drive from Puerto Limon.

Puntarenas

This major port on the Gulf of Nicoya is a convenient departure point for trips into Costa Rica's interior, renowned for its unspoiled nature and beautiful scenery, including waterfalls, the Cloud Forest, the Corobici River and Manuel Antonio National Park. Volcanic beaches along the coast give way to verdant jungle and coffee plantations further inland.

Quepos

This former banana-exporting town can serve as a basecamp for a day of exploring the rainforest. Enjoy walking along forest trails that lead to waterfalls. Horseback riding is also popular. Nearby is Manuel Antonio National Park with its lovely beaches, easy trails, and animal life.

CROATIA

Dubrovnik

This Jewel of the Dalmatian coast, girded in ninth-century walls that rise in sheer fashion from the water's edge, is one of the best-preserved medieval towns in Europe. Within the ancient fortifications is a labyrinth of narrow alleyways and a striking Renaissance boulevard called the "Stradun." This makes for one of the most colorful and atmospheric ports of call in the Mediterranean.

Hvar

This is the longest of the Croatian islands, and a well-known tourist destination due to its mild climate. Noted for its lush vegetation, quaint towns and fertile vineyards. A particularly rich cultural and monumental heritage complements Hvar's natural and unique beauty. Often called the Lavender Island, the name refers to the aromatic, purple plant that grows in abundance on the island's stony slopes.

Split

An ancient city on the Adriatic coast, Split achieved fame when the Roman emperor Diocletian had his retirement palace built here from 295 to 305 A.D. After his death the great stone palace continued to be used as a retreat by Roman rulers. The old town is built around the harbor on the south side of a high peninsula, sheltered from the open sea by many islands. The high coastal mountains set against the blue Adriatic provide a striking backdrop.

DENMARK

Copenhagen

Copenhagen, the capital of Denmark, is an elegant city, rich in history and tradition. One of the city's most celebrated sights is Tivoli, a unique combination of picture-perfect gardens, lakes and more than a hundred thousand colored lights. Take a stroll down Langelinie Promenade to see the heart of Copenhagen. It runs along the water from the port, skirting the 300-year-old, moated citadel near the celebrated statue of Hans Christian Andersen's Little Mermaid. The surrounding park is home to the Gefion Fountain, Copenhagen's most spectacular fountain.

Nuuk, Greenland

Nuuk, capital of Greenland, is one of the largest cities in the Arctic region. Some of the oldest traces of life, carbon-based organisms presumed to be algae 3.8 billion years old, were found near Nuuk. The first known human presence was the Saqqaq culture, dating from 2200 B.C. to 1000 B.C. Subsequent inhabitants include the Dorset culture; the Norse, led by Erik the Red; and the Thule culture, Inuit forefathers of the present-day Greenlanders.

Finally, in the 16th century, Dutch, Basque and Scottish whalers began to travel to Greenland.

Prins Christian Sound, Greenland

While Greenland is the largest island in the world with more than 1,348,872 square miles, fewer than 60,000 call it home. A massive ice cap over two million years old covers more than 85 percent of the island, sculpting a landscape of intricate fjords and blinding snowfields punctuated by dramatic rock formations. Located on the southern most tip of Greenland, Prins Christian Sund is a 55-mile-long channel a mile wide with mountains rising up 6,000 feet above sea level.

Qagotoq, Greenland

This is one of several ports of call that provide access to Greenland. See entries for Nuuk and Prins Christian Sound, above, for more information on this, the largest island in the world.

Thorshavn, Faroes

More than 600 miles from Denmark's west coast lie the Faroes, a triangle of 18 windswept islands, 17 of them inhabited. Only 47,241 people and some 70,000 sheep roam these remote lands. Sheer cliffs and waterfalls carve Streymoy, the largest of the islands, where Torshavn is one of the world's smallest capitals with about 12,470 inhabitants, plus another 4,000 living in the suburbs of Argir and Hoyvik. Visitors find interesting museums, churches, monuments and all the amenities of a modern town as well as a thriving harbor.

DOMINICAN REPUBLIC

La Romana

Although this destination is a relatively new one for tourists from Europe and the United States, La Romana has been attracting visitors for many centuries. The island's earliest settlers, the Taino Indians, are thought by historians to have been a friendly, peace-loving race who farmed the land and lived quietly and simply in harmony both with nature and their fellow men. The destination is home to the 7,000-acre Casa de Campo resort.

EGYPT

Alexandria (Cairo)

Alexander the Great traveled to Egypt after conquering Greece and selected a small fishing village in the Mediterranean for his new capital, Alexandria. It's now Egypt's second largest city, and a juxtaposition of modern influences and ancient culture. Its lighthouse, the world's first, was one of the Seven Wonders of the Ancient World. Alexandria is also the departure point for excursions to Cairo and the Pyramids of Giza.

Port Said (Cairo)

Port Said was founded in 1859 when excavation work for the Suez Canal began. Upon completion of the canal in 1869, the city continued to develop until the bombing attacks in 1956 during the Suez crisis. Port Said suffered additional damage in 1967 and 1973 during the wars with Israel. Today most of the structures have been rebuilt. Port Said is also a gateway to Cairo and the great pyramids.

Safaga (Luxor, Karnak)

From Safaga most travelers head inland to discover the magnificent antiquities of Luxor and Karnak. Site of the ancient metropolis of Thebes, Luxor has a history which goes back to 2000 B.C. Like Babylon and Nineveh, it was considered one of the great cities of the ancient world, but of the three it is only here that the splendor survives. The massive columns and statues are unique and exciting to visit. You can walk down the Avenue of the Sphinxes to the grand ceremonial gateway of the Temple of Amun-Ra. Across the Nile is the Valley of the Kings, sacred burial ground of the Pharaohs.

Sharm El Sheikh

The tip of the Sinai Peninsula hints at the massive granite mountains looming up behind. Among them is the peak of Mt. Sinai itself. St. Catherine's Monastery, a wildly beautiful outpost of faith preserved for more than 800 years, is available on optional shore excursions.

Suez Canal

One of 19th-century engineering's most useful achievements, the 110-mile Suez Canal links the Mediterranean with the Red Sea. Unlike the Panama Canal, this is a sea-level waterway with no locks. Sailing through the canal is a tranquil experience imparting an acute sense of history and place. The first attempt to excavate a canal was recorded in 2100 B.C., and over the years Egyptians, Persians, Romans, and Arabs attempted this project. The British and French did so in a joint undertaking that culminated in the 1869 completion of the canal.

ECUADOR

Esmeraldas

Named for the emerald quality of its luxuriant vegetation, this provincial capital is a favorite of beach-lovers and birdwatchers. Good buys can be found in handicrafts and filigreed gold jewelry.

Galapagos Islands

Renowned as the inspiration for Charles Darwin's theory of evolution, this archipelago is so isolated that many of its creatures cannot be found anywhere else on earth. From the giant tortoises that bear the Galapagos' name to the marine iguanas and "Darwin" finches, the Galapagos Islands afford visitors the chance to observe a living laboratory of adaptation.

Guayaquil (Quito)

Guayaquil is the port for Quito, the beautiful capital of Ecuador. As you stroll the cobbled streets of the city called "Queen of the Andes," rich legacies of art, history and magnificent Spanish colonial architecture surround you.

ESTONIA

Tallinn

Tallinn is the capital of the recently independent republic of Estonia. In the medieval old town, with its winding cobbled streets, there is a marvelous cathedral and Gothic town hall dating from the 14th century. Though lesser known than many other ports in the former Soviet Union, this is one of the most spectacular medieval cities in the Baltic. Walking through Tallinn's streets, you can imagine living there centuries ago.

FIJI

Suva

Suva sits on the southeast shores of mountainous Viti Levu ("Great Fiji"), largest of the over 800 islands that comprise the Republic of Fiji. Local folk traditions remain strong. These include fire walks and welcoming ceremonies, wood-carving and the fabrication of tree-bark cloth. The island's proud history is showcased in the Fiji Museum which has an impressive collection of war canoes and other interesting artifacts.

FINLAND

Helsinki

Finland's capital is known for its impressive architecture, wide boulevards and beautiful harbor. After a devastating fire in 1808, Helsinki was totally rebuilt, mostly in the neo-classical, Empire style. An impressive example of this architecture can be seen around Senate Square, dominated by the exquisite Tuomio Church (Lutheran Cathedral). The city has wonderful museums, displaying everything from art to architectural design, and a colorful harbor front with a lively market.

FRANCE

Ajaccio, Corsica
On the French island of Corsica, Ajaccio is famous as the birthplace of Napoleon. Visit the Bonaparte family home and the 16th-century church where he was baptized. Or, take a tour into the wild and rugged outback countryside they call the maquis.

Antibes
Antibes is a port and a popular tourist Côte d'Azur resort, with sandy beaches, an excellent climate, and luxury hotels. Formerly Antipolis, a trading post founded by Greeks in 340 B.C., the town and port were Roman settlements before being controlled by the powerful Grimaldi family of Genoa between 1384 and 1608. The 16th-century Grimaldi Château remains, serving as a gallery devoted to the work of Pablo Picasso who lived and painted here in 1946.

Cherbourg (Normandy)
Cherbourg is a deep-sea port, famous in the day of the great ocean liners for having given many Americans their first view of France. Walk through the Chanatereyne Marina, through parks and gardens, or travel along footpaths which have historical markers. Visit Emmanuel Liais Park, with its mansion-turned-museum, greenhouses and collections of rare, exotic plants. Or, head for Normandy and Utah Beach, one of the D-Day landing beaches during World War II, approximately 30 miles away.

Le Havre (Paris)
Le Havre is one of the traditional French transatlantic ports, homeport for the French Line in the days of the great liners. In Le Havre itself, cruise visitors can explore at leisure, visit fish and vegetable markets, public parks, walk along a long seaside promenade next to a vast beach. The city is a frequent base for drives along the Seine and visits to Rouen and its medieval cathedral or Paris, without question one of the world's greatest capitals.

Marseilles (Toulon)
Marseille is the country's most important seaport. Two fortresses guard the entrance to the harbor: Fort Saint Nicolas and, across the water, Fort Saint Jean. The city is divided into 16 Arrondissements

fanning out from the Old Port – Vieux Port in French. The intimate, picturesque old harbor, packed with fishing boats and pleasure crafts, is the heart of Marseille.

Nice
Known as the "Queen of the Riviera" this cosmopolitan resort city is abundant in boutiques, nightclubs and museums, including the fascinating Chagall Museum. You can walk along the elegant beachside Promenade des Anglais, or venture to neighboring cities including Cannes, Monte Carlo, Antibes and the medieval town of St. Paul de Vence.

Toulon (Marseilles)
Built around a sheltered bay with 1,700-foot Mount Faron as an impressive backdrop, Toulon is home to a sizeable marina of yachts and pleasure boats. Its large harbor also serves as the French navy's Mediterranean home port. During World War II, the bulk of the French fleet at Toulon's naval base was scuttled by French crews to prevent its acquisition by occupying German forces. The city was liberated in 1944 by French troops.

Villefranche
This village of 7,000 inhabitants is hidden among wooded slopes, above the crystalline waters of the Côte d'Azur. The town itself is delightful, with medieval chapels and an impressive hilltop fortress built by the Duke of Savoy in 1560. The town is located just a few miles from Nice, Cannes, St. Tropez and Monte Carlo.

FRENCH GUIANA

Devil's Island
The most notorious of the three Iles du Salut, off the coast of French Guiana, Devil's Island functioned for generations as a French penal colony and was renowned as the "Dry Guillotine" because so many prisoners died there. The most famous was Henri Charrière, whose numerous alleged escape attempts were chronicled in a 1970 best-selling book, Papillon. In 1973 it was made into a movie starring Steve McQueen and Dustin Hoffman.

FRENCH POLYNESIA

Bora Bora
No name captures the imagination of paradise as well as the French Polynesian island nation of Bora Bora. Majestic mountains sculpted by

ancient volcanoes, a shimmering lagoon and a barrier reef dotted with tiny motu or islets welcome visitors to perhaps the most stunning island in the South Pacific. Generations of travelers, including novelist James Michener, regarded Bora Bora as an earthly paradise. Approximately 4,600 people live a seemingly idyllic lifestyle in the main villages of Vaitape, Anau and Faanui.

Huahine

Located within the Society Islands just over a hundred miles from Tahiti, two islands – Huahine-Nui and Huahine-Iti (Big Island and Little Island) – joined together by a bridge, make up Huahine with its pristine waters and ancient villages. Surfers from all over the globe meet to ride some of the best waves in French Polynesia. Both islands boast white-sand beaches, vanilla and banana plantations, and some of Polynesia's most significant cultural sites.

Moorea

Just 12 miles across the lagoon from Tahiti lies Moorea. Visiting Moorea, you will discover the Polynesia of Melville, Gauguin and Michener. This former haunt of Tahitian royalty is a place where you will still see fishermen paddling outrigger canoes, pareo-clad women strolling along the roads and children fishing from island bridges. It is an island of steep vertiginous mountains where most of its fourteen thousand people live along the narrow coastal shelf, with a backdrop of lush green mountains rushing upwards to fill the sky.

Noumea

Noumea, New Caledonia's capital is a bastion of French culture and often referred to as the St-Tropez of the Pacific. Yet just down the road, the indigenous Kanak people dress in colorful ankle-length dresses and fish the reef with spears for their evening's meal. This stark contrast of modern and ancient cultures illustrates the dichotomy of paradise: the natives who have survived a century of repression, and the French settlers who represent the last surviving stronghold of colonialism in Melanesia. This is still a French territory. It served an important headquarters function for allied forces defending Australia, New Zealand, and the Southwest Pacific, notably during the Guadalcanal Campaign and after.

Papeete

The largest of the Society Islands in French Polynesia, Tahiti held a magical attraction for artist Paul Gauguin and writer Robert Louis Stevenson. To understand why, simply listen to the winds whistling through casuarina trees on a secluded black-sand beach, or stroll through beautiful botanical gardens and marvel at island flora. Coastal drives help you to best enjoy the island's great beauty.

Rangiora

Rangiroa, meaning "huge sky," is the largest atoll in French Polynesia, and one of the four largest in the world. It has more than 240 islets separated by more than a hundred small channels that make up its ring of coral. Divers from all over the world flock to its 42-mile aquamarine lagoon filled with unique marine life and magnificent underwater scenery.

Tonga (Nuku'Alofa)

The Kingdom of Tonga is the oldest, and last remaining Polynesian monarchy. Here is the place where Captain James Cook landed in 1777, along with the now huge tree that was planted on that occasion. There are also the ancient tombs of Tongan kings. Local crafts can be viewed at the Tongan National Centre.

FRENCH WEST INDIES (FRANCE)

Fort-de-France, Martinique

This large, sophisticated island has a distinct French accent, not surprising inasmuch as this is a part of Metropolitan France though separated geographically from the home country. It offers you delicious Creole cooking and Parisian fashions in the capital of Fort-de-France. You can ride head for the beach, join an excursion to Martinique's mountainous interior, or visit St. Pierre, formerly the island's capital, which was destroyed completely by a volcanic explosion of Mt. Pelee that killed 30,000 people.

Pointe-a-Pitre, Guadeloupe

Tropical Guadeloupe is butterfly-shaped. Explore either wing – Grand Terre or Basse Terre – to discover plantations of bananas, lovely waterfalls and rum distilleries. Or visit Pigeon Island, extolled by Jacques Cousteau as one of the world's best underwater sites.

GERMANY

Hamburg

As Germany's principal port, Hamburg surprises its visitors with an amazing expanse of parks, lakes and tree-lined canals. These give the city a refreshing rural feel and a sense of openness. Founded over a thousand years ago as a fortification against Viking attacks, Hamburg grew during the Middle Ages and became a leading member of the Hanseatic League. With its impressive historical background and today's big city ambience, attractions include a great variety of old and modern architecture, historical and art museums, superb shopping and fine dining.

Warnemünde (Berlin)

A small fishing village back in the Middle Ages, Warnemünde today is a fashionable resort with splendid villas along with fishermen's cottages and captains' mansions. It is also a Baltic gateway to Berlin, Germany's capital, among the most exciting cities in Europe. Although much was destroyed toward the end of World War II and the city was divided for 40 years, the reunification of Germany brought on a hive of activities. New building and restoration projects have closed the gaps caused by bombings and Cold War separation. Today you can see a city that dramatically combines palatial Prussian buildings with glamorous new structures.

GHANA

Tema (Accra)

Tema is Ghana's major port and your gateway to Accra, the nation's capital. Europeans descended on Ghana in the 15th century in search of gold. The wealth of the slave trade led them to stay, erecting forts along the Gulf of Guinea and naming the region "The Gold Coast." Today, Ghana is a fascinating destination, and one of the most densely populated countries in West Africa. It has a population of approximately 20 million.

GIBRALTAR (BRITISH CROWN COLONY)

Gibraltar

One of the "Pillars of Hercules," the British crown colony of Gibraltar is an historic landmark with British and Spanish influences. Guarding the entrance to the Atlantic, the great rock still serves as Britain's threshold to the Mediterranean. A cable car will take you to the top of the rock for a spectacular view of two continents as well as a visit with the famous Barbary apes.

GREECE

Aghios Nikolaos, Crete

The port of Aghios Nikolaos is a picturesque village spread around Mirabello Bay. This charming small town has developed into a popular holiday resort thanks to its beautiful beaches and its convenience as a center from which to explore eastern Crete. Crete itself is the largest of the Greek islands, lying at the southern limit of the Aegean Sea.

Corfu

Though once ruled by Venetian doges, Turkish sultans and French invaders, today's Corfiot citizen is as Greek as they come. Marvel at the 17th-century icons in St. George's Church, the Medieval Palace of Phrourio or the 19th-century Achilleion Palace. The greenest of the Greek Isles, Corfu also boasts thriving vineyards and olive orchards among its rugged mountains.

Galasidhi (Delphi)

This is one of the ports for Delphi where pilgrims once trekked to gain wisdom from the oracle. Even now, the ruins are said to work magic for visitors. An amazing bronze charioteer is among the many treasures in the Delphi Museum.

Heraklion, Crete

Heraklion, the capital of Crete and its principal commercial port, is just three miles away from the fantastic ruins of the Palace of Knossos. Discovered in 1899 by Sir Arthur Evans and partially reconstructed, the elaborate palace is believed to be the mythical Labyrinth of King Minos and the seat of ancient Minoan culture. The Archaeological Museum in Heraklion displays many of the treasures found during the excavations.

Hydra

Hydra was once home to seafaring merchants who built Italian-style villas overlooking the harbor. You can enjoy walking along the traffic-free waterfront lined by shops, tavernas and bakeries. You can also ascend the hills on a donkey and enjoy splendid views from the Monastery of St. Constantine.

Itea (Delphi)

This is a port used for access to Delphi, one of the ancient wonders of classical Greece. A short drive there reveals the Sacred Way and the famed Shrine of Delphi, where the mythological Oracle was said to foretell the future.

Katakolon (Olympia)
Katakolon is your gateway to Olympia, where the ancient Greeks gathered every four years for more than a millennium to celebrate the sacred games dedicated to Zeus. You can walk through the ruins of the sanctuary with its athletic quadrangles, stadium-temples and treasuries. There is also the modern Archaeological Museum, a treasure house of Archaic, Classical and Roman sculptures, including the famous Niki "Winged Victory."

Kos
Kos is known as the home of Hippocrates, father of medical science. The town is an archeological repository of Archaic, Classical, Hellenistic, and Roman ruins. Explore ancient Asklepeion and the island's archaeological museum.

Limassol, Cyprus
The southern central coast is home to the port city of Limassol. The city is a convenient starting point from which to explore the island's ancient ruins and lush scenic highlights, including miles of olive, orange and lemon groves, cherry orchards and vineyards that cling to the island's craggy slopes. Wooded mountains create a stunning backdrop to the stretches of picture-perfect beaches rimming the coastline.

Mykonos
The narrow passageways of Mykonos are a twisted maze of whitewashed houses, miniature churches, lazy windmills, and tiny cafes serving up Greek specialties. Sample the freshest squid or lobster just snatched from the blue Aegean Sea, or shop for typical flokati rugs. There is a vibrant nightlife that adds zest to evening port calls.

Mytilini, Lesbos (see also Molyvos and Monemvasa)
The birthplace of Sappho, a famous poet in ancient Greece, Lesbos is a charming island of picturesque villages like Agiassos. The Byzantine Monastery of Leimon (Moni Leimonos) is also of special interest.

Patmos
This island is known as the site of the apocalyptic Revelations of St. John the Divine, written here during his exile from the Roman Empire. The cave where he lived is near the site of the Monastery of the Apocalypse. The Monastery of St. John, built on one of the island's highest points, houses priceless icons and manuscripts in its Treasury.

Piraeus (Athens)
Piraeus is the seaport for Athens, the capital of western civilization, which boasts a fantastic mix of classical ruins and vivacious modern life. In a single day, you can climb the hill of the Acropolis to wonder at the Parthenon, join the lively Athenians in Constitution Square, and then find a welcoming taverna for some spirited Bizouki music, plenty of ouzo to drink, and with any luck, energetic Greek dancing. Piraeus itself has inviting waterfront café's and restaurants. It is fun to watch a non-stop stream of ferries and cruise ships sail into and out of this colorful harbor.

Rhodes (Lindos)
Legend has it that Apollo blessed this isle with sunshine and beauty. True to the myths, the "Island of Roses" is rich in magnificent scenery and umbrella-lined beaches. Many visitors take an excursion to Lindos, where high on a hill rises an ancient acropolis dedicated to the goddess Athena. You will also want to walk through the medieval Old Town, once home to the Crusading Knights of St. John. There is also the Grand Master's Palace, an Italian restoration famed for its superb mosaic floors.

Santorini
With its steep volcanic flanks looming straight up from the sea, and the tiny white village of Thira clinging high atop the cliffs, Santorini is perhaps the most breathtaking and legendary of all the Greek Isles. To the south is Akrotiri, where recent Minoan excavations support the theories that Santorini might be the fabled lost continent of Atlantis.

Thessaloniki (Vergina)
A rich experience awaits visitors to this wealthy, energetic and youthful city. Sophisticated shops, cafes, and markets hidden away beyond historic city squares, as well as the superlative Archeological Museum are but a few. Explore the castle-bound Old City with its fine Byzantine churches. Or, spend the day touring the ruins of ancient Pella, birthplace of Alexander the Great. At Vergina, the intact tomb of Philip II, Alexander's father was recently discovered.

GUATEMALA

Puerto Quetzal (Antigua)
This port was constructed a quarter century ago to provide access to Guatemala's attractions from the

Pacific Coast. The great Maya civilization dominated Central America for centuries. By 250 A.D., great temple-cities were beginning to be built in the Guatemalan highlands. Today Guatemala is the most populous of the Central American republics and the only one largely Indian in language and culture. The country offers Mayan ruins and such picturesque cities as Antigua.

HONDURAS

Roatan Island
The island of Roatan is filled with attractive beaches, jungle-covered hills, and heartwarming people with a unique blend of cultures. The island paradise is renowned for its diving and water activities. Roatan, a mere 28 miles long and an average of four-miles wide, is the most developed of the Bay Islands. It is located just 40 miles northeast of mainland Honduras.

ICELAND

Akureyri
Akureyri is the largest city in Northern Iceland with 16,000 inhabitants. Its location is at the southern end of the 30-mile-long Eyjafjordur, some 60 miles south of the Arctic Circle. A long valley extends southwards from the fjord. This is one of the most fertile agricultural areas of Iceland with many large farms. High mountains on each side of the fjord and valley offer protection from harsh winds.

Reykjavik
The island's settlement dates back to 874 when a Norwegian named Ingolf Arnarson arrived at present-day Reykjavik. In 930, the settlers formed a legislature, the Alting, which was the beginning of the Commonwealth of Iceland. From the 10th through the 14th centuries, Iceland developed a literary form, the Icelandic Saga, which spread throughout the Nordic culture and into the English and German languages. It was used to spin stories of the gods, record historic events and glorify heroes. As Iceland's capital and main center of the country's population, the city of Reykjavik is a fascinating blend of the traditional and modernism.

INDIA

Bombay, see Mumbai

Chennai (Madras)
This thriving port on the Bay of Bengal provides the perfect introduction to the wonders of southern India. Magnificent Dravidian temples compete with monuments from the British colonial past, including the Chepauk Palace and the High Court buildings. Chennai is also a thriving university and cultural center, as well as a leader in Indian film making.

Cochin
The lush Kerala region is the proverbial land of incense and myrrh, from which the world has sought its exotic spices since ancient times. The aromas of ginger, cloves, cardamom, cumin and other key ingredients of Indian curries fill the air. A visit to the St. Francis church reveals the tomb of the Portuguese explorer Vasco da Gama. Guests may also tour Mattancheri Palace, which houses some of India's finest Hindu frescoes and ceremonial costumes. Not far from Mattancheri is a Jewish colony dating back to 1000 A.D. A 16th-century synagogue has hand-painted floor tiles from China.

Goa, see Mormugao

Madras, see Chennai

Mormugao (Goa)
A fascinating blend of India and the West, the mythical kingdom of Goa was conquered in 1510 by the Portuguese, who held it until it joined India in 1962. The Portuguese influence is still clear in the names and Christian faith of the locals, and in Renaissance monuments like the Cathedral, the Basilica Bom Jesu, and the convent of St. Francis, a converted mosque.

Mumbai (Bombay)
Few cities evoke such a wealth of sensations as Bombay. Entering the city under the Gateway of India, which commemorates the visit of King George and Queen Mary in 1911, the sounds and aromas are exotic and the level of activity from the bazaars to the street vendors assaults the senses. Remnants of British rule along oceanfront Marine Drive stand alongside the former home of Mahatma Gandhi, and the cave temple at Elephanta with its second-century Hindu gods. Bombay also serves as the gateway for land tours to Agra, home of the Taj Mahal, and Delhi, the historical center of India.

INDIAN OCEAN ISLANDS

Andaman Islands (Port Blair)
The Andaman and Nicobar islands are spread over a 500-mile area in the Bay of Bengal between India and Malaysia. They are inhabited by about 12,000 aboriginal tribesmen. In addition to the

sociological aspect, a main attraction of these islands are the coral reefs. Cruise ship passengers come ashore at Port Blair.

Colombo, see Sri Lanka

Mahé, Seychelles (Port Victoria)
Port Victoria, the cruise port and capital of the Seychelles, lies on Mahé, the largest island in the chain and where you can explore lush tea, coconut and tropical fruit plantations and enjoy great beaches. One of the world's smallest capitals, Port Victoria is a pretty town with fine colonial Law Courts and a silver clock tower, which was erected in 1903 and modeled on the tower at London's Vauxhall Bridge.

Mauritius (Port Louis)
Located just off the east coast of Madagascar, Mauritius is a tropical paradise. Approximately 10 million years old, Mauritius is thought to be the peak of an enormous sunken volcanic chain stretching from the Seychelles to Réunion. In fact, volcanic lakes and inactive craters can be found scattered throughout the island. Mauritius also boasts a unique marine environment. Surrounded by one of the largest unbroken coral reefs on the planet, conservationists are now campaigning to protect its white coral sand beaches and fragile ecosystem.

Reunion (Pointe des Gallettes)
Réunion is the largest of the Mascarene Islands, which also include Rodrigues and Mauritius. The archipelago was named Mascarenes in 1512 by the Portuguese navigator, Pedro de Mascarenhas. The French made the decision to settle Réunion in 1642, but no one actually lived here until four years later when the French governor of Fort Dauphin in Madagascar exiled a dozen mutineers to the island. In 1649, the king of France officially took possession of Réunion and renamed the island Colbert Bourbon. After the French Revolution, the island took back its original name. It remains an overseas territory of France.

Sri Lanka (Colombo)
Sri Lanka lies 55 miles north of the equator, just off the southern tip of India. With its unique beauty, warm climate and near-perfect beaches, Sri Lanka is one of Asia's most adored island destinations. Since the 16th century, the Portuguese, Dutch and British have all left their architectural and cultural marks in Sri Lanka's capital of Colombo. Yet despite its colonial architecture, Sri Lanka has always remained Oriental in spirit, with colorful bazaars, dancing elephants, graceful women in saris, and many Buddhist shrines and temples.

Zanzibar, Tanzania
For many centuries, traders from Europe, India, the Orient and Arabia were lured to these shores. It was from here that explorer David Livingstone set off on his last expedition into the heart of Africa. Today, as you walk along the winding streets of the old Stone Town, lined with whitewashed-coral rag houses, you can see reminders of this rich history all around you. Among the attractions are the Palace museum, former residence of the Omani Sultans, and the cathedral that now stands on the site of the notorious slave market.

INDONESIA

Bali (Padang Bay)
Known as the "Island of the Gods," Bali is famous for its shimmering beauty and fascinating culture. Hundreds of Hindu temples, towering mountains and verdant rice terraces form a spectacular backdrop to the charm of the Balinese people. Here are mysterious volcanic lakes and jungle-shrouded volcanoes, wondrous ancient temples, fabulously creative painters and wood-carvers, and the legendary dancers who re-enact the stories of their Hindu deities.

Komodo Island
A rare discovery awaits the traveler who ventures onto this remote island of Komodo. Walking through the dense vegetation, hearing and seeing a variety of bird and animal life, you may feel you've landed in another epoch. Indeed, the last vestiges of long-gone dinosaurs survive here, in the form of the legendary giant lizards called Komodo dragons.

Semarang, Java (Borobudur)
Semarang provides access to the remote interior of Java and the astounding temples of Borobudur, the largest Buddhist monument on earth built in the eighth century. Here you can explore a complex of dramatic carved towers that were forgotten for almost 800 years. Topped by graceful stupas, the winding pathways display carved panels depicting the life of Buddha.

Sulawesi (Bitung, Palopo, Pare-pare, Ujung Pandaang)
Visitors will discover the natural wealth of Sulawesi, a fertile land of cocoa and clove

plantations. Tiny off-shore islands harbor coral reefs teeming with hundreds of species of tropical fish. In nearby Gunung Dua Saudara National Park, there is a cross-section of endemic animal life as tarsiers,hornbills, macaques and cockatoos thrive in a geologically fascinating area of hot springs and volcanic craters. The island is well known for its primitive tribes, most notably the Bugis. So feared were they that the word bogeyman, some say a corrupted form of bugis man, was coined to describe these fighters.

IRELAND

Dublin (Dun Laoghaire)
Situated at the wide sweep of Dublin Bay, the capital of the Republic of Ireland enjoys one of the loveliest natural settings in all of Europe. Following centuries of invasions by Vikings, Normans and the English, Dublin became a center of agitation for Irish independence. Today, Ireland's capital attracts scores of visitors from around the globe with its old-world charm and friendly atmosphere. In addition, some of the world's greatest literary figures hailed from here including James Joyce, who based nearly all of his writings in his native city; Oscar Wilde, who attended Trinity College; Jonathan Swift, who served as Dean of St. Patrick's Cathedral; and George Bernard Shaw, born here in 1856. Located only 15 minutes away from Dublin, Dun Laoghaire serves as a gateway for passengers on larger ships that cannot enter Dublin's harbor.

Waterford
Arriving at Waterford is spectacular. It is a big event for this small town and the people warmly welcome you. Available for touring is its famous crystal factory. It is also pleasant to enjoy a drive across Ireland's scenic countryside. Waterford is also conveniently accessible from Cobh.

ISRAEL

Ashdod (Jerusalem, Bethlehem)
Perched on sand dunes, Ashdod is a gateway to the Holy Land. From here, you can journey to Jerusalem and Bethlehem and walk the Via Dolorosa, and visit the stations of the cross. Among the many other sites of interest are the Western or "Wailing" Wall, the Church of the Holy Sepulcher, Mount of Olives and, in Bethlehem, the Church of the Nativity.

Haifa (Jerusalem, Bethlehem)
A lovely seaport in its own right, Haifa is also a departure point for Holy Land sightseeing. Jerusalem, Jericho, Nazareth, Bethlehem, and the crusader city of Acre are also within reach.

ITALY

Amalfi (Positano)
Located roughly between Salerno and Sorrento, Amalfi was already an important maritime republic in the Middle Ages. The port is one of the most popular resorts and stopovers along the famed Amalfi Drive. The coastal road hugs the mountainous coast and carves its way through sheer rock; around every hairpin turn spectacular scenery awaits. Positano, once a small fishing village, is now the star attraction of the entire coast. White Moorish-type houses cling dramatically to slopes around a small sheltered bay. Many of the houses can only be reached via steep staircases.

Cagliari, Sardinia
As Sardinia's capital, Cagliari is both a thriving modern city and a fine example of the varied history of this Italian island. Worth seeing are the Roman amphitheater, Spanish townhouses, and Pisan watchtowers. Antiquities from the native Nuraghi culture and from the Phoenician era onward are well-displayed in the National Archaeological Museum.

Capri
Known as the "Island of Love" since the days of the Roman Empire, Capri offers stunning views, dozens of international cafes, fine Mediterranean restaurants and sophisticated resort shopping. Boat trips around the coast enable visitors to witness the hypnotic beauty of the Blue Grotto. Ana Capri, high atop the island, offers breathtaking views of the Bay of Sorrento below.

Catania, Sicily
Steep, rugged Sicily has bred a race of fierce, funny and passionate people. From this important port, one can drive up the coast to visit Taormina. First Greeks, then Romans used this as a place of worship and reward. Attractions include the temples and the theater, all with Mt. Etna in the distance. You can also take a stroll and shop in the little village of Catania before you leave.

Civitavecchia (Rome)
The port of Civitavecchia is the gateway to Rome, where all roads lead. Mad traffic careens past

monuments of the great civilizations of the past. Mandatory objectives are the soaring inspiration of St. Peter's, the Vatican and the Sistine Chapel; the flow of life along the Spanish Steps; the Coliseum; the Via Veneto; the Trevi Fountain; and many other attractions. It is also fun to spend time in an outdoor trattoria in one of the many small piazzas or village squares.

Genoa

Christopher Columbus hailed from Genoa "the Proud," which enjoys one of the most illustrious maritime histories in all of Italy. It also features the largest medieval city center in Europe as well as Renaissance palaces that once enthralled Rubens and Van Dyck. Although not yet a mainstream destination for North American tourists, those who can enjoy the charms of Genoa's narrow streets, piazzas and galleries will be richly rewarded.

Livorno (Florence, Pisa)

From Livorno, your path leads through the rolling green hills of Tuscany to Florence, the flower of the Renaissance. The creative explosion happened right here, with masterworks by Michelangelo, Brunelleschi and Botticelli now landmarks of daily life. Ufizzi, Academmia, il Duomo: the art treasures of a golden age are commonplace to blessed Florentines. Livorno also serves as a gateway to Pisa, one of Tuscany's great historic gems.

Messina, Sicily (Taormina)

The setting for Shakespeare's Much Ado About Nothing, Messina has much to offer in the way of history. Its dramatic, boulder-filled harbor has challenged navigators since the days of Ulysses. Try to visit the city's Bell Tower at the stroke of noon – the hour when one of the world's largest and most fanciful mechanical clocks springs into action. Messina's museum is also noteworthy for its Renaissance masterworks. Messina also is an access port for Taormina and its ancient Greek theater.

Naples (Pompeii, Capri)

The Bay of Naples is overlooked by the imposing Sant'Elmo medieval castle, high up on Vemero Hill. Many visitors choose to explore the archaeological wonders of nearby Pompeii. Completely buried by the eruption of Mt. Vesuvius in 79 A.D., Pompeii is one of the world's most magnificently preserved ancient cities. Built within curved walls, the excavations unearthed sumptuous private homes that featured colonnaded central courtyards with lavish fountains and interior murals painted in vivid colors. Excursions are also offered to the resort isle of Capri.

Palermo, Sicily

Once regarded as Europe's grandest, most beautiful city, Palermo is still quite impressive. The Four Corners of Palermo, where each 17th-century Spanish Baroque facade is adorned with a statue, is one of the city's most memorable sights. The Fontana Pretoria, often called the Fountain of Shame because of its nude Florentine figures, is also worth noting, as are the famous Norman Cathedral and Capuchin catacombs.

Portofino

Often called the "Pearl of the Riviera," this charming hideaway on the Ligurian Sea is a favorite vacation spot of many wealthy Europeans. Once a quiet fishing village, Portofino is now best known for its chic boutiques, wonderful outdoor restaurants, and beachside cliffs that are speckled with pastel-colored villas. Picturesque neighboring coastal villages include Paraggi and Santa Margherita.

Sardinia (Porto Cervo, Poltu Quatu)

Porto Cervo is in the heart of Costa Smeralda, a vacation retreat situated among the inlets of Sardinia's rugged northern coast. The Costa Smeralda was conceived and implemented by the Aga Khan in 1962 and is still the exclusive resort that he envisioned. A scenic drive into the mountains takes you past elegant private homes and resort hotels that look out over hidden coves and sparkling beaches. The resort of Poltu Quatu Marina dell'Orso is located on the northeast coast of Sardinia.

Sorrento (Capri, Pompeii)

Some of Italy's most romantic villages cling to the dramatic slopes of the ruggedly beautiful Amalfi Coast. Available to the visitor is a drive along the scenic coastal road. Further afield are the amazing ruins of Pompeii, uncovered from the ashes of Vesuvius, and the charming island of Capri, a short boat ride away.

Trieste

A major seaport in the Northern Adriatic, the sights in Trieste include numerous examples of Art Noveau and neoclassical architecture from its Austrian past. The city served as a major port for the Austro-Hungarian Empire. Though seldom visited by cruise ships today, it was a major terminal for the transatlantic liners of the Italian

Line. Through it, many emigrants sailed for the Americas. It is also the home to Italy's foremost shipyard, Fincantiari in nearby Monfalcone.

Venice
Located on Italy's north coast and virtually surrounded by water, Venice is singular among the world's cities. Shakespeare must have agreed, for he selected Venice as the setting for his Othello and the Merchant of Venice. Built over a sprawling archipelago, Venice encompasses 118 islands separated by more than 150 canals that are spanned by some 400 bridges. The many splendid palaces lining the famous Grand Canal, historic St. Mark's Square, and a wealth of incomparable art treasures, make its reputation as one of the world's great cities well justified.

JAMAICA

Montego Bay
The recently renovated "Mo' Bay," as the locals call this town, competes with Ocho Rios as the island's most visited resort town. Montego Bay has great bars and restaurants, renowned shopping, and an endless array of leisure activities. And with the friendly hospitality of the Jamaican people, having a great time is always "no problem." Nearby is Rose Hall Plantation, worth a visit on tour or independently.

Ocho Rios
The town of Ocho Rios, on Jamaica's north coast, is edged with beautiful white-sand beaches and unbelievable landscapes. Contrary to popular belief, its name does not refer to "eight rivers," the literal Spanish translation. It derives instead from the Spanish word "chorreras," meaning waterfalls, of which Ocho Rios has many – including the famous and spectacular Dunn's River Falls.

JAPAN

Beppu
Among Beppu's attractions is Beppu Jigoku (Beppu's Boiling Hell), pools of mineral-colored water and bubbling mud. A circuit of the nine hells, seven of which are located in the old geisha district of Kannawa, discloses their different functions, colors, and mineral properties. Atop Mt. Tsurumi, accessible by aerial tramway, is an observation platform, children's playground, gardens and two take-off platforms for hang-gliders. Though this mountain last erupted more than 1,100 years ago,

slight volcanic activity can still be detected on the far side of the crater.

Hiroshima
Set on a bay in the Inland Sea, Hiroshima was the infamous site of the first atomic bomb explosion in August 1945. But perhaps the best reason to visit Hiroshima is the enchanting island of Miyajima with its famous Itsukushima Shinto shrine, considered one of Japan's most beautiful sights. Its famous torii stands just offshore, a tall, vermilion-colored symbol of Japan, which appears to float during high tide.

Kagoshima (Kyushu)
This large city is an excursion base from which to explore the dramatic coastlines, national parks and volcanic mountains of Kyushu, Japan's third largest island. Mount Sakurajima, an active volcano, can be reached by ferry. To the north, Kirishima-Yaku National Park is a scenic area of smoking volcanoes, craters and lakes. South of the city, Ibusuki, the island's most popular seaside resort, welcomes kimono-clad bathers to its sandy beaches and warm, underwater springs.

Kobe
Famous for its succulent Kobe beef and cosmopolitan flair, this booming port town sits between the Rokko Mountains and Osaka Bay. It contains a remarkable cultural mix of Swiss chalets, Moslem mosques and Russian Orthodox churches tucked between traditional Japanese buildings. A cable car ascends to the summit of Mount Rokko, a national park.

Nagasaki
One of Japan's most historic cities, Nagasaki was a major port, trading with the Portuguese and Dutch in the 16th century. You can still see this colonial legacy in the brick buildings, old forts, canals and curving cobblestone streets. On a hill overlooking the bay, beautiful Glover Mansion, the setting of Madame Butterfly, is typical of the fine homes built by wealthy foreign residents. But Nagasaki's ties with Korea and China are equally apparent in the famous Chinese temple, a large Chinese colony and the numerous fine Korean and Chinese restaurants.

Osaka (Kyoto, Nara)
This large, bustling port is the starting point for tours to Kyoto and Nara, the cultural fountainheads of classical Japan. Kyoto's Old Imperial Palace and the shogunal Nijo Castle

remain glorious symbols of the power the city held for over 1,000 years. Until 1868, Kyoto was the capital of Japan, filled with elegant timber buildings, hundreds of Shinto shrines and over a thousand Buddhist temples, as well as sacred treasure-houses of religious sculpture, painting and exquisite gardens. Nara, City of the Seven Great Temples, lies in an idyllic setting.

Yokahama (Tokyo)

Yokahama is the main gateway to Tokyo, where huge department stores brim with shoppers, neon flashes from dusk to dawn, and the entire world pays heed to fluctuations on the Nikkei Index. From the Imperial Palace and Meiji Shrine to the fabled Ginza district, Tokyo is an intriguing composite of East and West. Yuppies sporting MP3 players bow formally in greeting. Women in kimonos and business suits stroll side-by-side. Geishas play samisens while disc jockeys play rap and pop hits. Japanese houses of wood and paper stand in the shadow of towering steel and mortar. Not far away, Mount Fuji, the majestic symbol of Japan, soars 12,388 feet to its snow-clad peak.

JORDAN

Aqaba (Petra, Wadi Rum)

From Jordan's port on the Red Sea, you can travel to the mysterious lost city of Petra, hidden for centuries. At first it looks like a mirage: rugged sandstone hills seem to melt into windows and doorways, columns and gargoyles. But it is not: all the buildings of Petra, except one, were elaborately carved into the rock hills by a nomadic Arabian tribe in the 6th century B.C. It is a remarkable sight. Also commonly offered are excursions to Wadi Rum, an oasis where Bedouin families set black goat-hair tents at the base of massive, striated "jebels," the sheer-faced hills of the region.

KENYA

Mombasa

East Africa's history is on view in Mombasa. The old Dhow Harbour was a center of trade among the Swahili nations of the Indian Ocean. The Portuguese Fort Jesus looms above, surveying the old town's Arab-style craft bazaars. From here, it's a short flight to Nairobi, the staging ground for one of travel's most exciting and rewarding experiences: an East African game safari. Herds of elephant, giraffe and other game are to be found in reserves like Tsavo East, Taita Hills, Shimba Hills and Masai Mara national parks.

KIRIBATI

Fanning Island

Kiribati is more a sprinkling of far-flung coral atolls than dry land, more ocean than sandy beach, more coconut trees than people, more Catholic church than ancient island beliefs. Kiribati is hard to get, except on boat-days, and mostly undeveloped, but is an excellent example of a small, Pacific atoll before tourism development.

KOREA

Inchon (Seoul)

Inchon is the port of Korea's booming capital, a shopping paradise which vies with Hong Kong. But historic Seoul also brims with treasures. Begin with a bird's-eye view atop Namsan Hill. Visit Kyonbok Gun, the Palace of Bright Happiness, and the 14th-century Changdok Palace, home of the royal family. Stroll through its beautiful Secret Garden, 80 acres of ponds, tea houses and pavilions. Discover the extensive collection of Korean art in the National Museum. Or travel beyond Seoul's ancient gates to the Nanhan Mountain Castle or historic Suwon and its wonderful Folk Village of Minsokchon.

Pusan (Kyongju)

From Pusan, visitors can journey to the ancient Silla capital of Kyongju, a dynasty which reigned in Korea for almost a thousand years. Today this small provincial town is virtually a museum without walls, dotted with many splendid ruins. Nearby, the forested mountains and valleys shelter hundreds of beautiful Buddhist shrines including the renowned Sokkuram Grotto, and Tongdosa and Pulguksa temples. Pusan is also a shopper's mecca and Korea's vital southern link to Japanese and American trade.

LATVIA

Riga

This Latvian city offers mementos of a splendid 800-year-old history in the form of medieval architecture and the greatest number of 20th-century ArtNouveau homes in all of Europe.

LIBYA

Tripoli

Libya's capital, also known as Tarabalus Al-Gharb (Tripoli of the West), dates back to its founding by the Phoenicians in 1000 B.C.

Remains of once regal Greek and Roman cities were buried beneath Libya's sands for eons. Only in the past century, excavation works have brought to light the unbelievable splendor of Libya's artifacts. The country's stunning connection to the past is also depicted in some world-class museums. Tripoli's natural harbor and strategic location on the Mediterranean led to Libya's position as a cross-road of cultures with essential ties to Europe and Africa dating back to ancient times.

MADAGASCAR

Nosy Be (Nosy Komba)
Nosy Be, the largest island in proximity to Madagascar is known as "the perfumed isle" for its profusion of ylang-ylang, patchouli, cinnamon, vanilla, pepper and saffron. It is also a holiday resort with a colonial French atmosphere. Neighboring Nosy Komba, is set aside to protect the small, endearing primates known as lemurs which are indigenous here.

MALAYSIA

Penang
The swirl of Batik in eastern bazaars, the cascade of waterfalls in the Botanical Gardens and jungle-clad hills ringed by golden beaches are among the images you will take from Penang. This lovely resort island and its bustling capital of Georgetown are the picture of Malaysian diversity. Visit the Temple of the Reclining Buddha and Kek Lok Si, one of the most beautiful temples in Southeast Asia; see the ornate Khoo Kongsi, an old Chinese clan house; or marvel at the Penang Bridge (third longest in the world).

Port Kelang (Kuala Lumpur)
This port is used as an access point for Kuala Lumpur. Malaysia's capital rises like a vision from the deep jungles. Its fascinating array of architectural styles includes Malay stilt villages, Islamic minarets, Hindu temples, Chinese shop houses and the indescribable opulence of the Royal Palace. In the background rise the world's tallest buildings, the Petronas Twin Towers completed in 1996.

MALTA

Valetta
Malta's capital city of Valletta has been designated a World Heritage City by UNESCO. The Phoenicians, Romans, Arabs, Normans, Castilians, the Knights of St. John, the French and the British all left their mark. Controlling the island was a prerequisite to domination of the Mediterranean by the British in World War II. Malta's location at the crossroads of Europe made it a center of cultural, social and political activity over the centuries. Among the sites are the impressive Palace of the Grand Masters and the baroque masterpiece that is St. John's Co-Cathedral. Be sure to also save time for walking along the colorful streets of the old town section of this extraordinary port.

MEXICO

Acapulco
Beaches and whitewashed villas ring magnificent Acapulco Bay, making this an especially beautiful port whether viewed from shore or ship. Acapulco is Mexico's premier Pacific playground. Enjoy the view from the scenic highway above the harbor, then stop to enjoy Acapulco's most famous attraction: the daredevil cliff-divers of La Quebrada. The divers pray at a nearby chapel before plunging from the 130-foot-high cliffs.

Cabo San Lucas
Sail past Los Arcos, the soaring rock archway at the extreme southern tip of Baja California that guards Cabo's perfect harbor. This idyllic bay once sheltered both treasure ships from the Orient and pirate brigs bent on those treasures. Now Cabo caters to an international vacation set and has a strong artistic tradition famous for its black-coral jewelry.

Cozumel
Lying just off Yucatan's coast, Cozumel revels in its mythic white-sand beaches and world-class coral reefs. Yet Cozumel was also the last stronghold of the Mayas who settled the island in 300 A.D. Residents still speak Maya, and sometimes wear traditional Mayan clothing. On the mainland, an easy day-trip away, are the Mayan ruin sites of Tulum and Coba.

Ensenada
Ensenada is located 70 miles south of the international border and only a 90-minute drive from San Diego. Visitors are drawn to Ensenada's warm Mediterranean climate and friendly atmosphere, making it Mexico's second-most visited port of call for cruise lines and pleasure boats.

Huatulco
In addition to snorkeling and diving, Huatulco offers ecotourism attractions such as river rafting, rappelling and jungle-trail hiking. The town boasts an 18-hole golf course and some of the best resort hotels on the southern Mexican coast.

Ixtapa
Ixtapa and Zihuatanejo lie 150 miles northwest of Acapulco. Although a mere three miles of geography separate the two towns, they are in fact poles apart. In the 1960's, Mexico's tourism chose sites for future development. They selected Cancun and Ixtapa. Today, Ixtapa is an internationally renowned tourist destination with luxury resorts. Zihuatanejo, on the other hand, remains a relatively unspoiled fishing village graced with golden beaches and a relaxed air.

Mazatlán
Mexico's largest Pacific ocean port, Mazatlán, has been called the "Pearl of the Pacific" for its splendid beaches and island-strewn harbor. The resorts of the Zona Dorada ("Golden Zone") deserve their fame, as does the sport-fishing which is known the world over. Yet somehow, the city maintains much of the simplicity and peace of its fishing village past.

Playa del Carmen
A charming Mexican port town on the Yucatan Peninsula, Playa del Carmen is the dropping-off point for excursions to the ancient temples and tombs of Tulum, the only Mayan city over-looking the ocean, and to the coral lagoon of Xel-ha and the Xcaret eco-park.

Progreso
This is a seaside retreat located about 25 miles north of Merida along the Gulf Coast of Mexico. Progreso is quickly becoming an important gateway for cruise ship passengers. Founded in 1872 by Juan Miguel Castro and heavily influenced by the Mayan culture, Progreso enjoys a very simple and relaxed lifestyle. Its white-sand beaches, emerald green waters and cooling gulf breezes are a natural draw for vacationers from all over the world.

Puerto Vallarta
Hollywood discovered this little fishing village back in the 1960's, and since then luxury resorts and bougainvillea-covered villas have flourished in the delightful seaside climate. Yet hints of past tranquility remain: cobbled courtyards where the locals hold their markets, and superb sport-fishing just offshore. Broad sandy beaches offer a view of sea and low-lying mountains.

Zihuatanejo
This lovely, unpretentious fishing village of "Zihuat" curves around a protected bay, lined with golden beaches. When you've had enough sunning and swimming, wander the market stalls laden with Mexican arts and crafts, try a delicious tuba drink in the nearby coconut plantations, or make a quick trip to the superb resorts of neighboring Ixtapa.

MONACO, Principality of

Monte Carlo
An intimate enclave of castles and mansions perched high on a sun-washed ledge above the blue waters of the Mediterranean, this mile-wide principality is the glittering jewel of the French Riviera. At its heart is the glamorous city of Monte Carlo, playground of the rich and famous. World-renowned for its chic gambling casinos, luxurious hotel and beach resorts, and elegant restaurants and boutiques, Monte Carlo rose to fairy tale stature in the 1950's with the romance and wedding of its sovereign ruler, Prince Rainier II, to Hollywood movie star Grace Kelly, the much beloved Princess Grace of Monaco.

MOROCCO

Agadir
Across the river from the gleaming new town of Agadir is ancient Taroudant. Here you can explore within old city walls and see merchants selling handicrafts fashioned by centuries-old methods. Caravan trails lead south along the coast. Down them, a view of Berber life awaits in the pink-walled town of Tiznit.

Casablanca (Marrakech)
The economic capital of Morocco and the second-largest city in Africa, Casablanca is a blend of African, Arabian and European cultures. White-washed houses and peaceful mosques line the narrow streets of the ancient Medina, the original Arab section. Nearby, souks hum with the activity of contented shoppers bargaining for fine leather and handicrafts. For a glimpse of the old Morocco, go to the mysterious "pink" city of Marrakech with its famed market and snake-charmers.

Tangier
The "Gateway to Africa," located at its northwestern tip, Tangier is a fashionable resort that retains all of its age-old mystery and excitement. French and Islamic influences meet and merge in this fascinating old city. Mosques and minarets overlook the shadowy streets of the bazaar while the higher part of town, with its broad boulevards and lovely parks, looks down on the ocean.

MYANMAR (Burma)

Yangon (Rangoon)
Myanmar, known as the "Golden Land" for its rich soil and the wealth of minerals and precious stones, was called Burma by the British. In 1852, the British annexed Myanmar and gradually transformed Yangon into a booming trading center for rice, oil and teak. Their colonial rule lasted until 1948, interrupted only by the Japanese occupation during World War II. Yangon's cosmopolitan air dissipated after the country achieved independence in 1948. When General Ne Win seized power in 1962, Myanmar closed its doors to the outside world. After suffering decades of neglect, Yangon has begun to awaken and today it is possible once again to experience this country's unique culture, relatively untouched by Western influences.

NETHERLANDS

Amsterdam
One of Europe's leading cities, Amsterdam's rings of canals and traditional Dutch architecture are unmistakable. Rich in art, history and culture, Amsterdam is home to the Van Gogh museum, Anne Frank's house, and the Rijksmuseum, which houses many works by Rembrandt and Vermeer. This is an excellent walking city, and those so inclined can reach many attractions on foot.

NETHERLANDS ANTILLES

Aruba (Oranjestad)
Blessed with a non-stop breeze, neat little Oranjestad reflects the Dutch passion for cleanliness. Stroll the town's chic shops, venture out to see the wind-formed divi-divi trees, or visit an undersea garden of brilliant corals on a semi-submersible craft.

Bonaire
Spectacular underwater beauty prevails, along with white beaches and a breathtaking collection of ocean-carved rock formations. Bird watching is at its best here. You can see one of the loveliest and largest flamingo colonies in this hemisphere as well as Caribbean parakeets and Bonairean "lora." Outstanding opportunities for snorkeling and diving abound here, amid one of the Caribbean's richest collections of marine life.

Curaçao (Willemstad)
Curaçao is the largest of the Netherlands Antilles, 38 miles long and seven miles wide. Its varied landscape is filled with rolling hills, pastures, towering cacti, divi-divi trees and salt flats. Today, Curaçao is noted for the easygoing tolerance and harmony of its people. Curaçao is still closely tied to the Netherlands. Dutch and the local Papiamento (developed from a mixture of African, Portuguese, Jewish, Spanish, Dutch and English) are the official languages.

St. Barts (Gustavia)
St. Barthelem, its proper name, has a chic French style that appeals to the rich and famous. There are ruins of four guardian fortresses as you stroll Gustavia's few streets. You could travel a short way to Corossol to shop for hand-woven fabrics made from fan palm fronds, or head out to one of the beaches for some fashionable relaxation.

St. Maarten (Phillipsburg)
St. Maarten and St. Martin share a single island of only 40 square miles in size. In 1649, this island split in two, with the Dutch inhabiting the southern portion of the island and the French inhabiting the north. There are two capital cities, one for the Dutch side, and one for the French. Phillipsburg, St. Maarten, is the largest city on the island, and among the top destinations for cruise-ship passengers. On the French side of the island is Marigot, St. Martin, which is reminiscent of a small French seaside village.

NEW ZEALAND

Auckland
Sprawling across a narrow isthmus, Auckland and its far-flung suburbs are divided by two magnificent harbors. At the city's downtown doorstep lies Waitemata Harbour, separated from the Hauraki Gulf and Pacific Ocean by Rangitoto Island. West of the city, the shallow, turquoise waters of Manukau Harbour funnel into the Tasman Sea. As a dramatic backdrop, numerous cones of extinct volcanoes protrude from Auckland's landscape. With a population of one million, Auckland is New Zealand's largest city. The "City of Sails," as Auckland is often called, boasts more boats per capita than any other city in the world.

Dunedin/Port Chalmers
Dunedin is a little sliver of Scotland, set on the tropical shores of New Zealand's South Island. Founded by Scottish emigrants in 1848, Dunedin (the Gaelic name for Edinburgh) has fine Victorian and Edwardian architecture including the Olveston, stately home and majestic Larnach

Castle. There is also New Zealand's only scotch distillery and kilt shop.

Lyttleton (Christchurch)

Wooden houses cling to steep streets above the harbor bustling with cargo vessels, freighters, sailing yachts and sightseeing launches. Quaint Lyttelton serves as the gateway to Christchurch, South Island's premier city, just 20 minutes by car north. Often described as "the most English city outside England," the busy capital of the province of Canterbury is known for its spacious layout and distinctive English-style buildings in elegant grey stone. The River Avon winds through the city, along parks and gardens that cover one third of the municipality.

Tauranga (Rotorua)

The founders of Tauranga, 19th-century missionaries, left a legacy of well-planned parks and gardens for today's residents and visitors to enjoy. The area is blessed with a good climate and fine beaches. Tauranga also plays an important role as gateway to one of New Zealand's most famous tourist attractions: Rotorua. Inhabited by the Maori since the 14th century, the area's bubbling mud pools, spouting geysers and geothermal waters are used daily for cooking, heating and washing.

Wellington

From the top of Mt. Victoria, New Zealand's capital lies at your feet. It is a stunning vista of forested peninsulas, with a bustling waterfront, dramatic cliff-side homes and fine Victorian architecture. Wellington is also home to many museums, gardens, winding streets and even a cable car. There is a fine botanical garden. Many travelers compare this port to San Francisco. The harbor is one of the most beautiful anywhere. You can discover and enjoy the city's maritime heritage by visiting the maritime museum.

NORWAY

Bergen

This is a classic Norwegian town full of colorful charm. You can wander up narrow streets into the surrounding hills or enjoy Gamte Bergen, the old town, with cobbled streets and wonderful little shops and bakeries. You can also view this wonderful collage of sea, sky and mountains by taking the funicular to the top of Mount Fløien then walk along good paths to enjoy the area.

Honningsvag (North Cape)

The remote fishing village of Honningsvag is situated on the treeless island of Magerøya,

Europe's northernmost point known as the North Cape. Sheer cliffs rise 1,000 feet above the Arctic Ocean and there are some 200 different types of plants that grow here. An eerie light casts a 24-hour glow, a phenomenon that makes this the "Land of the Midnight Sun."

Oslo

Norway's political and cultural capital, Oslo was recently selected as the city with the highest quality of life in Europe. It's not surprising, considering the city's treasures: beautiful Frogner Park filled with modern sculpture, the emotional power of the Munch Museum and the Viking Ship Museum, together with forested mountains and secluded coves, all within the city limits.

Tromso

The most northern of Norway's rugged islands, Tromso possesses the true wonders of the polar environment: glistening glacial ridges, the icy clear waters of Lake Prestvatn, even windswept valleys where reindeer roam free. Amidst the beauty, there is fascinating history to be found as well, from ancient northern settlements to signs of sacrificial sites and cults that pre-date Christianity.

PANAMA

Balboa (Panama City)

Mostly known for its association with the Panama Canal, this is the port for Panama City on the canal's Pacific side. Balboa is a fine place to enjoy American tropical architecture in what was an important administrative center for the operation of the Canal. In Panama City, you will find a blend of centuries-old ruins and modern skyscrapers as well as the beauties and ruins of Colonial Panama.

Cristobal (Colon)

Situated at the Caribbean entrance of the Panama Canal is the port of Cristobal (Spanish for Christopher), your stopping off point for Colon (Spanish for Columbus). Colon, founded in 1850 by the Americans working on the Panama railroad, is today Panama's second-largest city. Colon underwent a massive redevelopment program for the new millennium and is now a fantastic place to shop, as well as a great base for exploring the rest of Panama.

Panama Canal

This is one of the world's great engineering masterpieces. It represented and symbolized United States' coming of age and entering the arena of world powers. It takes most of a day to transit the canal. Experiences range from witnessing the raising and lowering of your ship through locks, to an idyllic sail across the large open expanse of Gatun Lake. Good preparatory reading is David McCullough's The Path Between the Seas.

San Blas Islands
The friendly Cuna Indians live quietly on these primitive islands off Panama's Caribbean coast. Your visit to their home is still a special occasion for these isolated island dwellers. They are happy to let you photograph them in their colorful attire for a small tip. You can bargain for one of their fancifully designed handmade reverse appliqués called molas.

PAPUA NEW GUINEA

Rabaul, New Britain Island
Rabaul is the capital of New Britain, the largest of Papua New Guinea's islands. Covered by tropical rain forests and surrounded by a colorful coral reef, Rabaul is also is also the last resting place for many Japanese warships. It was one of their most important bases in the area.

PERU

Callao (Lima, Machu Picchu, Cuzco)
Callao is a port of entry to the elegant city of Lima. Founded by Pizarro and the Conquistadors, the capital city today offers priceless collections ranging from the Museum of Gold to the Museum of Anthropology and Archeology. Pizarro's remains can be found in the Cathedral, built in 1746. From Lima, you can also take a tour to Machu Picchu, the mysterious lost city of the Incas high in the Andes, or to Cuzco, the capital of the Incan Empire.

San Martin (Pisco)
Named after the liberator General San Martin, this area on the Paracas Peninsula is significant in Peruvian history as the birthplace of Peru's struggle for independence. San Martin is also one of the gateways to the ruins of Machu Picchu and Cuzco.

PHILIPPINES

Cebu
Cebu is the Philippines' oldest city, first discovered by Ferdinand Magellan in the 16th century. Historic sites include Magellan's Cross where the explorer baptized the first Christian Filipinos and Fort San Pedro, the oldest fortification in the islands. You'll find that Spanish influence lingers in the island's staunch Christianity, the names of the Cebuano people, and in their cuisine. Today, Cebu attracts scuba divers and beachcombers alike with its fascinating marine life and white-sand beaches.

Manila
Bustling Manila is the second-largest city in Southeast Asia with its towering skyscrapers and remarkable joie de vivre. Yet amid the big-city turmoil are oases of calm: lush tropical parks, magnificent cathedrals, and dramatic Spanish forts. Intramuros, Manila's famous walled city, was founded by the Spanish in the 16th century. A "must see" is the Malacanang Palace with its opulent displays of Ferdinand and Imelda Marcos' decadent indulgences.

POLAND

Gydnia (Gdansk)
Once a tiny fishing village, today Gdynia is Poland's most important port and the gateway to Gdansk. With its origins going back to the 10th century, prewar Gdansk – or Danzig as it was known then – was forged by years of Prussian and Hanseatic domination. The battles to liberate the city in 1945 resulted in almost total destruction. Gdansk's historic center was rebuilt with great respect for the past. Today, it represents one of the richest and most lavish complexes of architectural relics in Poland. Entering the historic quarter is like walking straight into a Hansa merchants' settlement.

PORTUGAL

Lisbon
Lisbon, the capital of Portugal, is a city open to the sea and carefully planned with 18th-century elegance. Cruising up the Tagus River to the ship's berth, you can already spot three of Lisbon's famous landmarks: the Monument to the Discoveries, the Tower of Belém and the Statue of Christ. The city is divided into two areas: the Baixa, or lower section, with its shops and spacious boulevards; and Barro Alta, or upper city, with its teeming nightlife and other attractions. You can connect between the two areas via the public elevator designed by Gustave Eiffel. Lisbon also serves as a good starting point for picturesque nearby towns such as Sintra and the medieval village of Obidos.

Ponta Delgada, Azores
A hidden treasure, the remote Azores island group lie 900 miles west of Portugal and 2,110

miles east of New York. Ponta Delgada's stunning Portuguese architecture and luxuriant, flower-filled parks make this city a joy to visit. The scenery outside of the city is equally spectacular. Dramatic rocky cliffs descend to pristine bays where you may find a virtually deserted stretch of gorgeous beach. Extinct craters are filled with turquoise waters, and surrounded by gardens of hydrangeas and greenery that thrive in the rich volcanic soil.

PUERTO RICO

San Juan
The fortress of El Morro guards the harbor against long-gone Sir Francis Drake and his British privateers. The colorful streets of Old San Juan retain the Latin flavor of its seafaring past when this was the heart of the Spanish Main. Sample the many varieties of rum made here, or indulge in an icy treat made from fresh tropical fruit.

RUSSIA

St. Petersburg
Peter the Great styled this to be his Venice of the North. Strategically, this city would become for Russia an ice-free port through which its citizens could trade and communicate with the world in all seasons. Italian architects created baroque facades to line the banks of the Neva River. Long, arched bridges join the city's halves. You'll want to see the spires of the Saints Peter and Paul Fortress, the blue domes of the Ouspensky Cathedral and, of course, some of the million masterworks of art contained in the Hermitage galleries of the Winter Palace. Especially notable are the partially restored palaces of Russian czars, among the most popular visitor attractions.

SAMOA

Apia, Western Samoa
After years of wandering the South Seas, Robert Louis Stevenson chose this paradise as his home. If you like, visit his house and Aggie Grey's hotel. After touring the island, you'll come to understand why the Reverend John Williams, the first European to visit Apia, dubbed Samoa the "Friendly Islands."

Pago Pago, American Samoa
Pago Pago Bay – pronounced "Pango Pango" – is one of the most dramatic harbors in the South Pacific. Eons ago, the massive seaward wall of a volcano collapsed and the sea poured in. Today, dramatic mountain peaks encircle the deep harbor. The capital of American Samoa, Pago Pago is more village than city. The town is dominated by looming Mt. Pioa, whose summit draws moisture-bearing clouds, earning it the nickname of The Rainmaker. Indeed, Pago Pago draws more than its fair share of rain; the island of Tutuila is a vision of deep, verdant green. Explore the ancient volcanoes and thriving coral atolls or get a taste of village life with a tour of the town.

SENEGAL

Dakar
The capital of Senegal, on the tip of Western Africa, is a modern town with a charming colonial center known for its handicrafts, textiles, silver-work and beaches. Watch the local fishermen or take an optional excursion into the beautiful African hinterlands.

SINGAPORE

Singapore
One of Asia's great success stories, this island republic has merged diverse cultures into a dynamic and thriving nation. Clean, modern and full of green gardens, its neighborhoods reflect the Chinese, Malay, Indian, Arab and European backgrounds of its past. After sampling the legendary shopping, retire to Raffles Hotel's famous bar and toast Maugham, Kipling and Noel Coward with a Singapore Sling.

SOUTH AFRICA

Capetown
One of the world's most scenic harbors, the "Mother City" has welcomed sailors since Portuguese navigators first rounded the Cape of Good Hope in the 15th century. Take a cable car ride to the summit of massive, flat-topped Table Mountain, the city's dominating landmark, for a panoramic view of the Cape from 3,300 feet. Browse in shops and restaurants in the redeveloped waterfront area or head for nearby Stellenbosch, the university town famous for its Cape Dutch architecture, where you can sip crisp local vintages at one of the well-known wine estates.

Durban
In addition to golden beaches, the cosmopolitan city of Durban offers a fascinating mélange of

African and Asian cultures. Zulu rickshaw drivers beckon passengers along Durban's Marine Parade, a harbor-front esplanade. Silks and gold-threaded saris tempt visitors at the bustling Oriental Arcades. It is also a gateway to Zululand, where the drumbeat of tribal dancing is testimony to the enduring traditions of the Zulus.

Port Elizabeth

Port Elizabeth is the third-largest port and the fifth-largest city in South Africa. The center, spread over steep hills overlooking Algoa Bay, boasts a wonderful city museum, a must-see Oceanarium with a very scary snake park. One of its closest game reserves is Addo Elephant Park. Here you will find more than 300 Cape Elephants – so relaxed you can really get up close and personal, even to mother elephants with babies in trunk-to-tail tow. There are ostriches, antelope, 200 species of birds, and a few shy rhino, too.

SPAIN

Alicante (Madrid)

The bustling resort of Alicante serves not only as the port for Madrid, but is also a lovely vacation spot along Spain's sunny Costa Blanca. This is primarily due to the pleasant climate. Various civilizations have flourished along these shores. Early records indicate that the city dates back to a Carthaginian settlement established in 325 B.C. These settlers were followed by the Romans who equally found the area inviting. Then the Moors ruled this region for five centuries and named the city Al-Akant. Today's name probably stems from this origin. The city's occupation by Roman and Moorish forces accounts for a notable and varied heritage. In fact, much of this cultural impact is still apparent today in numerous buildings, names and the cuisine.

Barcelona

Barcelona is the cultural heartland of Spain, yet its first language is Catalan, the native tongue of the proudly independent Catalonia region. Among its many attractions are shady, tree-lined streets and the major central artery, Las Ramblas, where you will find street musicians, elegant bistros, tapas bars and exuberant nightlife. Visitors enjoy exploring the venerable Gothic cathedral, the Picasso Museum, or Antonio Gaudi's still-unfinished Sagrada Familia. Be sure to sample paella in the seaside city, said to be among the tastiest in Spain.

Bilbao

As the cultural heart of Spain's celebrated Basque country, the shining city of Bilbao is filled with Gothic architecture and landmarks that herald its centuries-old history. But the more modern additions to this port – namely, the spectacular Guggenheim Museum of Modern Art – seem to be drawing the most attention these days. Designed by architect Frank Gehry, the museum is made of undulating strips of titanium and limestone, creating the building's unique shape. Inside, works by Picasso, Braque, Sera and Warhol offer glimpses into the minds of some of the greatest artists of modern time.

Cadiz (Seville, Jerez)

Whitewashed houses line narrow streets that lead into lovely squares. The magnificent baroque cathedral and impressive mansions were built with the gold brought back from the New World. The port of Cadiz also provides a convenient starting point for trips to Seville, Spain's capital during the discovery and exploration of North America. From Cadiz, you can also explore the rolling hills of Jerez de la Frontera, 30 minutes to the north. Here the production of the liquid gold, as the famous sherry is often called, ensures a booming economy.

Ibiza

Spain's jetset playground of Ibiza rocks to a late-night dance beat, but when the sun rises it draws sleepy international sun-worshippers out to the island's many beaches. Twisting streets in Dalt Vila (High Town) lead up to the 14th-century cathedral and magnificent views of the city. Shop for Spanish handicrafts and souvenirs, sip Sangria at a beachfront bar or enjoy freshly prepared seafood specialties at an open-air bistro.

Lanzarote, Canary Islands (Arrecife)

Lanzarote astounds visitors with its amazing landscapes. Due to a massive volcanic eruption in 1730, one third of the island was covered by a sea of lava. The eruption lasted for six years. In 1824, a new volcano thrust out of the earth's crust and once again molten lava poured over a good part of Lanzarote. This left a lunar landscape of more than a hundred craters, lava fields, and layers of cinders and pebbles. View this bizarre scenery at Timanfaya National Park. Wander in the well-preserved colonial town of Tequise, the island's former capital. Or visit the unusual house of the island's famed artist, the late Cesar Manrique, who designed it as part of the volcanic landscape.

Las Palmas, Gran Canaria, Canary Islands
The capital of Gran Canaria is a delight for strollers with areas such as Ciudad Jardin, where beautiful gardens surround the Canarians' homes, and the old quarter of Vegueta, where Christopher Columbus stopped in 1492. The island's landscape is beautiful. Visitors also often venture to the Guanches' caves where the island's primitive inhabitants once dwelled.

Malaga (Granada)
Situated on Spain's Costa del Sol, Malaga is the region's capital and a popular holiday destination. The city is known as the birthplace of Pablo Picasso and for the sweet Malaga dessert wines that come from the hilly vineyards just outside of town. Other points of interest include impressive Gothic architecture, the remains of a Moorish castle and several interesting museums. A pleasant town to explore, Malaga also serves as a popular starting point for trips to Granada and the famed Alhambra, the region's most outstanding attractions.

Palma, Mallorca
The heart of Mallorca hums with activity in its casinos, shops and beaches, but calmer pleasures also abound. Palma, the capital of the Balearic Islands, is a cosmopolitan city with sophisticated boutiques and restaurants; it also offers buildings of spectacular Moorish and Gothic architecture. Tour the 13th-century Gothic cathedral and hilltop Bellever Castle, or head for the geological wonders of the Caves of Drach and the majestic estate of Valldemosa.

Seville
According to legend, Seville was founded by Hercules and its origins are linked with the Tartessian civilization. It was called Hispalis under the Romans and Isbiliya by the Moors. Situated on the banks of the Guadalquivir, Seville is one of the largest historical centers in Europe. Part of its treasures include the minaret of La Giralda, one of the largest cathedral's in Christendom; Alcázar Palace; Casa de Pilatos; the Town Hall; Archive of the Indies, where the historical records of the American continent are kept;, the Fine Arts Museum, the second-largest picture gallery in Spain; plus convents, parish churches and palaces.

Tenerife, Canary Islands (Santa Cruz)
Tenerife, approximately 790 square miles, is the largest of the seven Canary Islands. Called the "Island of Eternal Spring" by the locals, Tenerife offers idyllic weather, fragrant fruit trees and charming locals. The port of Santa Cruz has colorful markets and fine museums. However, many visitors are tempted by the drive to the summit of Mount Teide, the highest peak on Spanish territory.

SWEDEN

Gothenburg
Located at the mouth of the Göta River, Gothenburg is Sweden's second-largest city and the busiest port in Scandinavia. Arriving by ship, your first impression of this immense port and shipyard may be somewhat misleading, but beyond this development you will soon discover one of Sweden's prettiest and friendliest cities. Its town center, crisscrossed by canals, allows pedestrians to enjoy the many traffic-free streets.

Stockholm
Founded in the 13th century, Stockholm is Sweden's strikingly elegant and beautiful capital, spread out over many islands. Entering through its archipelago, you will be greeted by yachts. Moreover, one third of the city's total land area is devoted to parks. Guided by a strong belief in individual freedom, Sweden is governed by a constitution that is the oldest in use in Europe. The country's neutrality has allowed it to avoid wars for more than 150 years. Its cities and industries remained intact during both World Wars. An absolute must is the Vasa Museum, containing the salvaged remains of a huge wooden warship that is virtually intact.

Visby, Gotland Island
The island of Gotland, with its magnificent walled town of Visby, is one of Sweden's most popular summer destinations and an outstanding tourist attraction. Already settled in the Stone Age, Visby reached prominence in medieval times when it was annexed by the powerful Hanseatic League. There are medieval fortifications encircling the entire settlement. The actual purpose of these massive walls, built at the end of the 13th century, was not to protect from enemy attacks, but rather to isolate the local population from the city's foreign traders.

TAIWAN

Keelung (Taipei)
Across the Formosa Strait from mainland China is the bustling port of Keelung. Just 20 miles inland

is Taipei, the national capital and one of the most prosperous cities in Asia. Attractions include the Chiang Kai-shek Memorial Hall, the Grand Hotel, and the National Palace Museum with its art treasures from Beijing's Forbidden City.

THAILAND

Bangkok
A mirror of Venice in Asia, this "City of Angels" is a bustling place with a maze of extensive waterways constantly in motion. In between the office towers and royal palaces are beautiful parks, boulevards and gardens. Bangkok is a city with more than 400 Buddhist temples. The most famous of these is the Temple of the Emerald Buddha, containing a statue carved from a single piece of jade. Gaze at one of Bangkok's best-known landmarks is Wat Arun, the Temple of the Dawn. Spend time in the city's oldest and biggest monastery, Wat Pho, where you'll be awed by its famed Reclining Buddah. Shoppers will enjoy the excitement of the floating markets.

Laem Chabang (Bangkok)
For most cruise vessels the port of Laem Chabang is the gateway to Bangkok, a lustrous city of immense Oriental charm, festooned with ornate temples, shrines and a lacework of canals. Shining through this dream-like setting is the hospitality and warmth of the gentle Thais. These talented people have raised folk dance to high art, created mouth-watering cuisine and built a splendid capital, unique in all the world.

Phuket
Set like a jewel in the Andaman Sea, Thailand's largest island has great expanses of sandy beaches that lure sun-seekers to their shores, and a unique culture combining influences from China and Portugal. Visit the fabled monastery of Wat Chalong, the Orchard Garden and the Thai Village where examples of the country's culture are presented in a tranquil lakeside setting.

TUNISIA

La Goulette (Tunis)
Tunisia's capital lies at the western end of the shallow Lake Tunis which opens to the sea at La Goulette. The city's port, La Goulette, is located at the first of a string of beach suburbs that stretches away to the north. This coastal area attracts more visitors than Tunis itself. You will be awed by the Roman baths, cisterns, and basilicas of ancient Carthage. The theater and amphitheater are worth a visit as well. The capital city of Tunis has an easy-going, unhurried air about it. It is very liberal by Islamic standards and certainly leading the way in Western trends for the rest of the country.

TURKEY

Canakkale (Troy)
Canakkale lies at the narrow (3/4 of a mile) entrance to the Dardanelles that connects the Sea of Marmara and the Aegean. The area is known for two battles, one of them legendary and one all too real. The first is the mythological war surrounding Troy, which Homer immortalized in his Iliad. Archaeological digs in Troy have proven that there have been nine separate settlement periods on that site. The other battle, Gallipoli, took place during World War I when a British Expeditionary Force sought to take Istanbul in order to remove Turkey from the war as a German ally. 500,000 from both sides gave their lives here. The peninsula has been made a national park of remembrance, and monuments can be seen from ships sailing through this waterway.

Istanbul
Istanbul has dominated the Straits of Bosphorus for 25 centuries. As Constantinople, the city was the capital of the Eastern Roman Empire, a metropolis of stunning splendor when the great capitals of Europe were mere villages. The religion of Christians and Moslems, and the culture of Europeans, Persians and Asians have all found their way into daily life. Landmarks worth visiting include Hagia Sophia, the Blue Mosque, the Sultan treasures in Topkapi Palace, and the Grand Bazaar featuring carpets, beaten brass and spices from afar. Be sure to also sample the culinary delights of a meze, a spectacular array of Turkish hors d'oeuvres, at one of Istanbul's many reasonably priced restaurants.

Izmir (Smyrna)
Little was left after a fire ignited at the tail end of the War of Independence destroyed all traces of the cultural melting pot that was once Smyrna. Seventy-six years after the reconstruction began Izmir has been reinvented as a prosperous, cosmopolitan, commercial city, more livable than Istanbul, less sterile than Ankara, and filled with wide boulevards and swaying palm trees.

Kusadasi (Ephesus)
This charming, picturesque resort where Antony and Cleopatra used to vacation is best known as the port for the ancients ruins of Ephesus, one of

the world's most wondrous archaeological sites. Explorations should include such masterpieces as the Great Amphitheatre, where St. Paul addressed the Ephesians, the Library of Celsus, and the temples of Athena and Apollo. These are all connected by marble streets rutted by the wheels of countless chariots.

UKRAINE

Odessa
Known for its cultural and historical attractions, Odessa is often referred to as the "Pearl of the Black Sea." Founded by Catherine the Great in the late 18th-century, it later thrived under refugee Cardinal Richelieu. This Ukrainian town is now a center of industry and shipping as well as a popular coastal resort where visitors come to experience its "curative" mud. Many visitors head to the top of Potemkin Steps for the magnificent harbor view. Another point of interest is the Odessa Opera Theatre where famous Russian ballets are performed.

Yalta
Yalta and its surroundings are protected on three sides by mountains. This accounts for the region's exceptionally mild climate and its reputation as a favored vacation destination. Situated on the southern tip of the Crimean Peninsula, this is the area's largest and most important resort and as such has catered to pleasure lovers and health seekers for more than a century. Here at the Golden Riviera, Russian aristocracy built their elegant summer palaces and palatial villas that rivaled those of Nice and Cannes. Livadia became the summer residence of the tsars and earned fame as the site of the 1945 Yalta Conference.

UNITED ARAB EMIRATES

Abu Dhabi
Just a few decades ago, Abu Dhabi, the island capital of the United Arab Emirates, was a small fishing village with houses made of mud-brick and palm fronds. Today, as a result of revenue from oil, Abu Dhabi is one of the world's richest cities, with wide tree-lined boulevards, lush green parks, gushing fountains and imposing skyscrapers. Somewhat of a dichotomy, Abu Dhabi is a combination of ultra-modern sophistication and Arab mystique.

Dubai
Despite the primeval desert that surrounds it, spirited Dubai has spent its oil income on modern architecture based on soaring Islamic spires.

Explore the souk bazaars for gold and silks, Persian and Afghani rugs, and one or two of the glamorous new hotels that are so architecturally spectacular that they are destinations in themselves.

UNITED KINGDOM

Belfast, Northern Ireland
Capital of Northern Ireland, Belfast was a big industrial city in the 19th century, famous for its linens and shipyards. It was city of great pride that had been transformed by the Industrial Revolution. Belfast curls around the west bank of the River Lagan. Among the sights are its grand public buildings and a natural geological feature known as the Giants Causeway. Belfast was home to the great Harland & Wolff shipyard that built the Titanic and many other famous ocean liners.

Dover, England (London)
The white cliffs of Dover are famous in song and story. This has become a major cruise terminal and remains a departure point for France for those still preferring cross-channel ferries even following completion of the Chunnel. From here you can visit nearby Canterbury and its cathedral. Dover is also a gateway to the sights of London, including Westminster Abbey, Trafalgar Square, Big Ben, Buckingham Palace and more.

Falmouth, England
Falmouth is located on the Cornish coastline in England's southwest corner. It is best known for its romantic past of pirates and smugglers. The town boasts a superb natural deepwater harbor, the third-largest in the world and is a bustling commercial port which is strongly influenced by its maritime history. There is a wide range of amenities for the visitor including maritime attractions, beautiful sheltered beaches, quality restaurants, pubs, cafes and shops.

Glasgow, Scotland
About 30 miles east of Greenock, Glasgow is known as the "Second City of the Empire." One of Britain's liveliest cities, a recent rejuvenation along with many priceless art collections draws visitors to the city center. From Glasgow, venture out into the rich farmland and salmon streams of the lowlands for the scenic lochs. You can also spend time in the city's shopping districts and art galleries.

Greenock, Scotland (Glasgow)
Here on the shores of central Scotland is some of the most dramatic scenery in Europe. Stretching

before you are the scenic lakes and lowlands around Greenock. This is also a convenient departure point for Glasgow (see entry above).

Edinburgh, Scotland (Leith)
Dominated by the ramparts of Edinburgh Castle, this picturesque city offers shopping on Princes Street, the grandeur of the Royal Mile, St. Giles Cathedral and historic Palace of Holyrood House where Queen Mary lived and many Scottish kings were wed. If you have visited Edinburgh previously, you can venture across the moors of Scotland and visit the scenic highlands.

London, England (via Southampton and Dover)
Only the smallest cruise ships can sail beneath the Tower Bridge and dock in the heart of London. Most go to Dover, Harwich, Southampton or Tilbury, which can accommodate large vessels. Stretching for more than 30 miles on either side of the River Thames, London is Europe's largest city with a diverse population of about eight million and all the cultural and gastronomic attractions you'd expect from a world capital.

Southampton, England
Rich in maritime history, Southampton's attractions include good restaurants and pubs, conservation walks in the lush, open Common, viewing art that dates back six centuries, and musical as well as theatrical performances. If you have just an hour or two to spare, visit the city's superb maritime museum which vividly illustrates the port's glamorous role as one of the leading terminuses for the great ocean liners sailing to North America, South Africa, Australia, and wherever Britons needed to sail.

UNITED STATES

Anchorage, Alaska
Cosmopolitan Anchorage is a city that has its own symphony and ballet yet offers rugged wilderness only minutes away. Art enthusiasts will enjoy the Anchorage Museum of History and Art and the many galleries. Shoppers will discover excellent native Alaskan arts and crafts.

Baltimore, Maryland (Annapolis; Washington, D.C.)
When Francis Scott Key wrote "The Star Spangled Banner" during the siege of Fort McHenry in 1814, no one knew that the little town would become a great American seaport. Baltimore has a unique turn-of-the-century flavor enhanced by such attractions as the Streetcar Museum,

its revitalized Inner Harbor and the new/old Camden Yards, home of the Baltimore Orioles. Nearby, discover 18th-century Annapolis and the U.S. Naval Academy. Just an hour away is the nation's capital and a treasure-trove of U.S. history, including The White House, Jefferson and Lincoln memorials, and the many, outstanding Smithsonian museums.

Bangor, Maine
From shipbuilding to steamships and lumberyards, this picturesque port has proven its resiliency and flourished in the last century into a city once described by Henry David Thoreau as "a shining light on the edge of wilderness." Today Bangor proudly displays a touch of modern culture with museums and revival architecture forever encapsulating a fascinating history.

Bar Harbor, Maine
Tucked into a cove in the shade of the Acadian National Park, Bar Harbor is the quintessential New England coastal town. Enjoy the great outdoors with a bike ride or kayak adventure. Participate in a lobster bake. Savor hand-stretched taffy from a local candy shop.

Boston, Massachusetts
The history and brick-adorned beauty of Boston is easy to enjoy. Discover landmarks of America's birth along the Freedom Trail, past the Old North Church, Paul Revere Park, Faneuil Hall, Old Ironsides and the Boston Common, the oldest city park in the United States. Across the Charles River is Cambridge, home to Harvard University. Further afield is Lexington and Concord to the north. Be sure to enjoy New England clam chowder near the wharf, or great Italian food in the city's North End.

Brooklyn, New York (New York City)
The new Brooklyn cruise terminal, located in this city's Red Hook section, is one of three cruise ship terminals serving New York City. The 180,000-square-foot facility opened in the spring of 2006. Most visitors make the short trip to the island of Manhattan to catch a Broadway show, go to the top of the Empire State Building, to explore one of New York City's renowned museums or to shop Fifth Avenue's glamorous department stores.

Cape Liberty, Bayonne, New Jersey (New York City)
When it was opened in 2004, this became the first new cruise port in New Jersey in 40 years. It is on

the site of the Bayonne Military Ocean Terminal. Bayonne is just 45 minutes by car or coach from New York City and its many world-famous attractions (see New York City below).

Catalina Island, California
Santa Catalina Island has been inhabited for more than 7,000 years, ever since the Pimungan tribe settled there, attracted by the island's rich marine life. Yet Catalina's popularity dates from 1919 when chewing gum tycoon William Wrigley purchased the island. Overnight, Catalina secured its reputation as a playground for magnates and movie stars. Since 1975, the Santa Catalina Island Conservancy has held most of Catalina in trust. Buffalo, imported for a 1924 movie, roam the island's arid uplands. Offshore, kelp beds shelter brightly colored Garibaldi fish, barking sea lions, playful seals and dolphins. It's no wonder Catalina still woos yachtsmen, deep-sea fishermen and divers.

Charleston, South Carolina
Aristocratic, stately, and gracious, Charleston personifies the flavor of the Old South. Tour the town's many historic homes and gardens by coach or by horse-drawn carriage. Boone Hall Plantation recreates the antebellum grandeur, and the Isle of Hope recalls the Low Country past. Tour Fort Sumter where, on April 12, 1861, local troops opened fire beginning the Civil War.

Fort Lauderdale, Florida (Port Everglades)
Originally a fort built by the U.S. Army in 1838, the Greater Fort Lauderdale area welcomes visitors with 23 miles of broad, palm-fringed beaches. Shoppers will enjoy fashionable boutiques along Las Olas Boulevard and upscale department stores at The Galleria mall. There are also sightseeing cruises through the city's 300+ miles of waterways, boasting more canals than Venice. If you have more time, venture to the wildlife sanctuary of the Everglades, or to Sawgrass Mills, Florida's largest outlet mall, with more than 350 name-brand stores.

Galveston, Texas (Houston)
Texans flock to sandy barrier isles like Galveston Island to frolic in the warm waters of the Gulf of Mexico. Visitors can do this, or absorb the atmosphere of Galveston itself. Stately homes grace the island. There is also the chance to visit mainland Houston and the impressive NASA Space Center.

Haines, Alaska
Alaska's heritage comes alive in the handcrafted artistry of the Tlingit (pronounced "Klink-it")

Indians and in the lively performances of the Chilkat dancers with their brightly painted tribal masks. Take a walking tour of Haines and get a glimpse of the town's gold-rush history in local museums. You can also visit the Chilkat Bald Eagle Preserve. Haines boasts the world's largest concentration of the magnificent birds, drawn to the area by the salmon-rich waters.

Hilo (Island of Hawaii), Hawaii
The "Big Island" of Hawaii is the youngest and largest of the Hawaiian Islands, and the most varied in landscape – with striking black- and green-sand beaches, tropical rain forests, ancient Hawaii heiau ruins, alpine terrain, and surreal lava-rock landscapes. Green gardens and cascading waterfalls encircle Hilo, the eastern side's port city, where the seat of the Big Island's government resides. Hilo is also a launching point for many Big Island attractions, including Volcanoes National Park.

Honolulu, Hawaii
Diamond Head, Waikiki Beach, Pearl Harbor – these names evoke magic, mystery, drama, and history, and they are all located in Honolulu. The capital of Hawaii, this city not only offers some of the best beaches alongside big-city skyscrapers but also parks, shopping, the only royal palace in America, the Polynesian Cultural Center and more. A highlight of any visit to Honolulu is a visit to the Arizona Memorial and the Missouri, a preserved battleship at anchor. The two provide a counterpoint involving the defeat and tragedy at Pearl Harbor and the triumphant signing of the Japanese surrender which took place on board Missouri.

Juneau, Alaska
Alaska's capital can't be reached by road. You fly or sail here to enjoy its greeting of dockside flags and flowers. It is surprisingly urban and cultured for being so remote. Visit the museum for insights into Inuit culture and crafts. Drive up to Mendenhall, the only glacier inside city limits! Or get an aerial view from a helicopter. Fish for silver salmon, or just enjoy some at a local restaurant – then kick back at the Red Dog Saloon.

Ketchikan/Misty Fjord, Alaska
Ketchikan is the salmon capital of the world. The canneries are busy, and the stream below Creek Street's rustic boardwalk bustles with life. Visit the ancient grove of Totem Bight, the largest collection of authentic totem poles anywhere. If you like, you can also fly to nearby Misty Fjords, a breathtaking vista of Alaska's unspoiled wilderness and

America's newest national monument. Salmon fishing is also available.

Key West, Florida
Located 155 miles south of Miami, Key West is the best known and southernmost spot in the continental U.S. It is a tropical blend of exotic foliage, beautiful waters and history-rich attractions. Since its founding in 1822, the town has gone through many phases. Over the years pirates, smugglers, writers and revolutionaries have made the Conch Republic their home. Ernest Hemingway, Tennessee Williams, Robert Frost and Thornton Wilder are among the most noted who came here to enjoy the idyllic setting and casual, relaxed atmosphere.

Kona (Island of Hawaii), Hawaii
Located on the leeward side of the Big Island and best known for its coffee, Kona was once the playground of Hawaii's royalty. You can visit both coffee and macadamia nut plantations, Kealakekua Bay where Captain James Cook first landed (and was later murdered) in 1779, and The Sacred City of Refuge, a haven for ancient lawbreakers. There is also Parker Ranch, the largest cattle ranch in the world with over a quarter of a million acres.

Kauai (Nawiliwili), Hawaii
This quaint port was named for the wiliwili trees that grow here in profusion. Known as the Garden Isle, Kauai claims the wettest spot on earth – Mount Waialeale – with 486 inches of rain per year. All this rain makes for lush vegetation, taro, pineapple and sugar plantations. Among the attractions: Fern Grotto, a huge variety of native flora, Waimea (the Grand Canyon of the Pacific), and Sprouting Hole, a blowhole that sends a geyser 50 feet into the air. You can also swim at the very beach where the movie South Pacific was filmed!

Maui (Kahului), Hawaii
Located on the north side of Maui, known as the Valley Island, Kahului is the principal seaport and the best "jumping off point" for this island's attractions. You may visit the old provincial town of Wailuka and its museum; or the Valley of the Kings, with its towering rock monolith, Iao Needle – dramatic, beautiful and isolated. You'll also find fabulous beaches, and Lahaina, an old whaling town and the first capital of the islands. Maui also boasts the largest dormant volcano in the world.

Maui (Lahaina), Hawaii
Historic Lahaina was once a rough-and-tumble whaling town in days gone by. Today visitors come to watch, not hunt, the humpbacks in Lanai Channel. You can ascend through waving sugar cane fields to the summit of Haleakala for sweeping views over its vast dormant crater and of this beautiful island. Another activity is a tram ride through the Tropical Plantation on its slopes.

Miami, Florida (Miami Beach/South Beach)
Cosmopolitan Miami serves as a gateway to the Caribbean, Central and South America. Visitors can stroll through quaint Coconut Grove, with its art galleries; tour Vizcaya, a National Historic Landmark built by agricultural industrialist James Deering; or discover over 50 diveable wreck sites, including ships, oil platforms, army tanks and a Boeing 727 jet, sunk to provide artificial reefs for marine life. Miami Beach, just a short drive away, is home to the trendy South Beach neighborhood, with its carefully preserved Art Deco architecture and plentiful cafés. Inland, at Everglades National Park, visitors can spot alligators and other wildlife.

Midway Island, Hawaii
Located near the geographical midpoint of the Pacific Island, Midway Atoll is the last of the volcanic sea mounts that form the Hawaiian Islands. It was also the site of the most decisive naval battle of World War II. Today, Midway is an internationally acclaimed wildlife refuge. The peaceful beaches are home to terns, albatrosses and myna birds. Over 250 species of fish frequent Midway's unique fringed reef, and Hawaiian monk seals and Hawaiian spinner dolphins frequent the azure waters. For World War II buffs, Midway still bears the marks of war, including the original 1941 seaplane hanger.

New Orleans, Louisiana
Unique in all the world, the lacy Creole look and carefree atmosphere of the "Big Easy" set it apart. In spite of the devastation caused in August 2005 by Hurricane Katrina – the costliest and one of the deadliest hurricanes in the history of the U.S. – the city's irrepressible spirit came through the storm unscathed. Whether you take time to savor authentic Creole cuisine, browse through quaint antique shops in the French Quarter, or tour historic mansions that date back over a century, you're sure to find dozens of other things to delight you in this high-spirited city that pulses with the beat of Dixieland jazz.

Newport, Rhode Island
A posh summer resort with a vivid history dating back to colonial times, Newport is home to fabulous summer "cottages" of the turn-of-the-century wealthy. You can tour The Breakers, a 70-room

estate surrounded by magnificent grounds and pounding surf or Marble House, patterned after Versailles, or Belcourt Castle, a 62-room mansion resplendent with treasures from 32 countries.

New York City, New York
This vibrant metropolis is actually a rich mosaic of many neighborhoods. Feel the excitement of Broadway with its plays and musicals. Explore Little Italy and the Wall Street financial district. Walk the streets of Chinatown, stopping for dim sum along the way – and don't forget Soho's art galleries and artsy Greenwich Village. Visit the Empire State Building for a panoramic city view. Pop into the glamorous department stores and designer boutiques. Visit any number of world-renowned museums. It truly is a wonderful city!

Norfolk, Virginia
Steeped in naval lore, Norfolk got its start shortly after Jamestown was founded in 1607. Its deep-water harbor is now the site of the largest naval base in the world. On an excursion, discover 18th-century Virginia in Colonial Williamsburg, restored by John D. Rockefeller as a gift to all Americans. See the Governor's Palace and the House of Burgesses, where Patrick Henry, George Washington and Thomas Jefferson served prior to the Revolution.

Philadelphia, Pennsylvania
No city reflects America's birth and colonial beginnings better than the "City of Brother Love." From Revolutionary War battlefields and the Liberty Bell, to once serving as our nation's capital, Philly, itself, is an historic site. Visit the Liberty Bell, with its famed cracked lip; the 160,000-square-foot National Constitution Center, dedicated to one of our most important documents; and Independence Hall, where our nation declared its independence from England in 1776. You can also travel through the scenic countryside to the Pennsylvania Dutch country.

Port Canaveral, Florida (Orlando)
Port Canaveral is home of the Kennedy Space Center, featuring exhibits and an IMAX theater which takes you through the entire history of America's space program. From here you can also visit nearby Orlando, home to more theme parks than anywhere else on earth – including Walt Disney World® Resort, Universal OrlandoSM and SeaWorld® Adventure Park.

Portland, Maine
Long ago, ships relied on the steady glow of a lighthouse to guide them from rough waters to port and safety. Today, visitors to Portland can visit the oldest lighthouse in Maine, one of a swiftly, dwindling number left in North America. You will also find a lively city with a broad range of architectural styles and a charming section known as Old Port, where visitors can walk through quaint, lantern-lit streets. You can also visit Longfellow's boyhood home.

Providence, Rhode Island
The state capitol of Rhode Island is known as the "Renaissance City." Over three centuries of fascinating history are preserved and celebrated here, from Benefit Street's "Mile of History" to immaculate examples of Colonial, Federal, Greek Revival and Victorian architecture. There are plenty of historic landmarks to discover, such as the Rhode Island State House, the John Brown House and the Meeting House of the First Baptist Church in America.

San Diego, California (Coronado)
Father Junipero Serra journeyed from Spain and settled San Diego in 1769 in order to Christianize the local Indians. Blessed with a sunny climate and a fine natural harbor, San Diego has grown from a Spanish mission into California's second-largest city. Visitors enjoy a host of attractions, including a world-class zoo and safari park, museums and 70 miles of beaches. Nearby is Coronado, a small island in San Diego Bay, which is home to the famous Hotel Del Coronado, a National Historic Landmark built in 1888.

San Francisco, California
Sailing under the Golden Gate Bridge and into San Francisco's broad bay will surely be a highlight of your cruising life. Once docked along the Embarcadero, you're within a cable car ride of Fisherman's Wharf, Chinatown, North Beach, the Castro, Alcatraz and other attractions that make this one of the world's favorite cities. Acclaimed Sonoma and Napa valley wine estates are nearby, too.

San Pedro, California (Los Angeles, Hollywood)
This city serves as the port for Los Angeles, one of the world's most exciting cities, and Hollywood, the movie-making capital of the world. Compare your footprints and handprints with those of your favorite celebrities at Mann's Chinese Theatre on Hollywood Boulevard, shop the fashionable boutiques along Rodeo Drive in Beverly Hills, visit Disneyland in nearby Anaheim, or join a movie studio tour to learn the history of motion pictures and how films are made.

Savannah, Georgia

This genteel Southern city is an excellent example of urban historic preservation, with approximately two square miles of downtown granted landmark status and thereby protected from modern development. A pleasant walk will take you to some of the city's most important old buildings for a glimpse into her gracious past, and through the spacious squares and the mansion-museums that mark this district. A little further afield, there is historic Fort Pulaski and also Wormsloe, an eloquent example of Southern plantation life.

Seattle, Washington

Situated on Puget Sound, surrounded by the Olympic and Cascade mountain ranges, the Seattle city skyline is impressive with shimmering glass high-rises and hundred-year-old buildings standing side by side. This beautiful port city came into its own after gold was discovered in the Klondike and 100,000 people passed through the Northwest in 1897 and 1898 on their quest for wealth in Alaska.

Sitka, Alaska

When Alaska belonged to Russia, Sitka was the capital and center of its fur trading empire. Today, Sitka's Russian heritage and magnificent setting make it an enchanting destination. The city features a harbor studded with islands, a backdrop of mountains, and spectacular Mt. Edgecumbe, a volcano often compared to Japan's Mt. Fuji. Sitka displays its past in such attractions as St. Michael's Cathedral, with its striking onion-shaped dome; the Russian Blockhouse, and Historic Park, where Tlingit Indians battled Russian settlers in 1804.

Skagway, Alaska

Skagway was born during the great Alaska gold rush. Those were the days when Skagway had 80 saloons and was known as "the roughest town on earth." The city's rip-roaring past will come alive when you walk down Broadway, a main street so authentic it is part of the Klondike Gold Rush National Historical Park. This is also the starting point for train trips up White Pass, and flights that take you over Glacier Bay National Park.

Tampa, Florida

Florida's third-largest city, Tampa is a lively Gulf Coast port that still hints of its Spanish heritage. In the Latin Quarter stands Ybor City, site of the once flourishing cigar industry. Hugging Tampa Bay and near Tampa is St. Petersburg. Some of the attractions found in the area include Busch Garden's The Dark Continent and Adventure Island, a water theme park.

Wilmington, North Carolina

Wilmington was the only open seaport in the Confederacy from 1863 until the last months of the war – nearly two years. Fort Fisher kept the port open to blockade runners. Another attraction is the Bellamy Mansion Museum of History and Design Arts. In 1865, it was commandeered as headquarters for the Union forces.

U.S. VIRGIN ISLANDS

St. Croix

Old plantation windmills dot the landscape, and the island's Dutch heritage can be found in the towns of Christiansted and Frederiksted. One of the most spectacular attractions is Buck Island, home to the only underwater U.S. National Monument. There are also the shops of Christiansted. With beautiful beaches, distilleries making Cruzan rum and one of the Caribbean's finest golf courses, St. Croix has much to offer the cruise passenger.

St. Thomas

St. Thomas and its capital, Charlotte Amalie, is the busiest shopping center in the Caribbean. More than 10 cruise ships a day steer into the port at St. Thomas. In addition to the busy shopping and cultural center located in and around Charlotte Amalie, more than half of the island is located within the environmentally protected Virgin Islands National Park. The island's Magen's Bay has been rated as one of the 10 most beautiful beaches of the world.

URUGUAY

Montevideo

With its population of 1,362,000, Montevideo is home to nearly half of Uruguay's population. The relatively small capital is the nation's only major city, yet visitors do not come here in search of the hustle and bustle of a large metropolis. As Uruguay's cultural, political and economic center, the city boasts a good number of monuments, museums and impressive architecture, in addition to sidewalk cafés, fine restaurants, chic shops, casinos and miles of clean beaches.

VENEZUELA

La Guaira (Caracas)

This is the major gateway to Venezuela. When line voyages were common, this was the port of arrival for passengers from Europe. From La Guaira, there is easy access to the energetic capital city of Venezuela. Both modern and tropical, Caracas is an entirely exotic metropolis that lies in the shadow of lush Avila Mountain. It boasts towering skyscrapers, a central park, public sculptures and murals of the city's historic figures.

Los Roques
Venezuela's largest archipelago, Los Roques, lies 92 miles due north of Caracas. It comprises about 340 islets and reefs and constitutes one of the country's loveliest national parks. Its main attraction are long stretches of white-sand beaches, miles of coral reef with crystal-clear water and many bird nesting sites. Small lizards, iguanas and cactus vegetation on some of the islands add to the atoll's variety.

Margarita Island
Located off the north shore of Venezuela, Isla Margarita boasts year-round sunshine. Known as the "Pearl of the Caribbean," the name is a reference to the Spanish conquest of 1498 when discoverers found the waters full of pearls and baptized the location La Margarita or "The Pearl." Among its attractions: long stretches of unspoiled beaches, friendly locals, and water so clear that snorkelers can easily spot lobsters frolicking beneath the waves from 15 feet above.

Puerto Ordaz (Canaima/Angel Falls)
Located 180 miles up the Orinoco River, Ordaz is a growing port city. From here visitors can take a flight-seeing excursion over Angel Falls and visit the jungle camp of Canaima in Canaima National Park. Located in a spectacular natural setting, Angel Falls is the highest waterfall in the world. It is 15 times higher than Niagara Falls. The rushing torrent falls 3,200 feet in a matter of seconds. The falls were named after American aviator and explorer Jimmy Angel who reported their existence in 1935.

VIETNAM

Cai Lan (Hanoi)
From Cai Lan visitors can traveler through the stunning landscape of the Red River Delta to the Vietnamese capital of Hanoi. Lush parks and beautiful wooded lakes lend a delightfully civilized air to the city. The One Pillared Pagoda, built in the 11th century during the reign of Emperor Ly Thai Tong, is constructed of wood and designed to resemble a lotus blossom, the symbol of purity. The Temple of Literature also dates to the 11th century and is a fine example of traditional Vietnamese architecture.

Da Nang (Hue, Hoi An)
Today this lovely town on the South China Sea reflects the peaceful era of pre-war Indochina. Up the coast, the grand Thien Mu Pagoda and stately Tu Duc Tomb welcome you to Hue, Vietnam's ancient royal capital on the banks of the Perfume River. Nearby, visitors can also explore the historic commercial seaport of Hoi An, which preserves colorful buildings from the 16th century onward in picturesque riverbank streets.

Haiphong (Hanoi)
Haiphong is a gateway to the Vietnamese capital of Hanoi, where you can see the Du Hang Pagoda, a fine example of the country's traditional architecture, and the Hang Kenh House, famed for its intricate wood carvings. The city is considered an architectural museum piece with a rich history dating to Neolithic Times. Ho Chi Minh's final resting place, his mausoleum, is near the Citadel and is open to the public. The Old Quarter is an especially fascinating area, reflecting the country's French colonial past.

Ho Chi Minh City (Saigon)
After 20 years of isolation, this history-laden Vietnamese capital will charm and fascinate you with her vibrant sights. Formerly Saigon, Ho Chi Minh City is a blend of magnificent French colonial architecture set against spacious boulevards thronged with trishaws, motorcycles, bicycles and pedestrians. Leave time to shop in the Ben Thanh Market or wander in the landmark Reunification Hall. The more adventurous may opt for an excursion to the Cu Chi Tunnels, a network of underground tunnels used by the Viet Cong in hiding from Allied troops.

YEMEN

Aden
Strategically located at the southern entry to the Red Sea, the Land of the Queen of Sheba is a mosaic of desert sheikdoms and was for years the primary British outpost in Arabia. From Aden you can travel to the ancient city of Sana'a – a little-known capital of long ago and now a UNESCO World Heritage Site. Mud and stone tower houses stand that are more than 400 years old. Tour the National Museum and the Summer Palace of Imam Yahya.

YUGOSLAVIA

Montenegro (Kotor)

Montenegro is a country with a lovely coast on the Adriatic, crystal clear rivers, mountains that reach the sky, dense forests, and beautiful lakes. It is bordered on the southeast by Albania. On the south, it is separated from Italy by the Adriatic Sea. Its western neighbors are the republics of Croatia, Bosnia and Herzegovina. The old town of Kotor is one of the best-preserved medieval towns in this area of the Mediterranean. It has succeeded in maintaining its original form, typical of towns from the 12th through the 14th centuries.

GLOSSARY

A

Advertising Promotion that costs money.

Affinity group A group of people who have some psychographic trait in common.

Air/sea package A package that includes airfare, the airport-to-dock transfer, and perhaps lodging.

Alumni rate See **Past passenger rate**.

Atrium A multistory space on ships.

At-sea day A day when the ship is traveling a long distance and doesn't stop at a port of call.

B

Bare boat charter A yacht charter without a crew.

Basis two (also called **Double occupancy**) Pricing per person, based on two passengers sharing a stateroom designed to accommodate two or more.

Berth A bed on a ship; also can refer to the docking space of a ship.

Bow The front of the ship.

Bridge Place on the ship from where it's controlled.

C

Cabin See **Stateroom**.

Cabin steward The person who maintains staterooms.

Circle itinerary (also called **Round-trip itinerary**) Itinerary with the ship leaving from and returning to the same port.

Closed-ended question Question that requires simple, factual responses.

Closed-jaw itinerary (also called **Round-trip itinerary**) A flight to and from the same city.

Consumer research (also called **Market research**) Research that tries to discover who the public is, how they think, and what they like to buy.

Cross-selling Offering the client something in addition to the cruise itself but related to it.

Cruise-only trip Cruise with no need for air transportation.

D

Database An organized collection of customer profiles.

Debarkation See **Disembarkation**.

Deck The equivalent of a story in a building.

Deck plan Ship's floor plan, showing cabins and public spaces.

Disembarkation (also called **Debarkation**) Exiting the ship.

Double occupancy See **Basis two**.

Draft Measurement from waterline to lowest part of the ship's frame.

E

Embarkation Boarding the ship.

F

Fam See **Familiarization cruise**.

Familiarization cruise (also called a **Fam**) A cruise offered at a very reduced price to travel agents by a cruise line.

First seating (or **sitting**) The earlier of two meal times in the ship's dining room.

Front desk See **Purser's office**.

G

Galley Area on ship where food is prepared (the kitchen).

Gangway Walkway that connects the ship with the dock.

Gross registered tonnage (GRT) Size determined by a formula that gauges the volume of the public spaces on a ship.

GRT See **Gross registered tonnage**.

Guaranteed share A single passenger who is willing to share a cabin with a stranger (of the same sex) may book at the per-person double occupancy rate. Offered by some cruise lines.

H

High season The time of year with the highest demand and the highest prices.

Hot button Anything that powerfully entices a buyer.

Hotel desk See **Purser's office**.

I

Incentive program A program to motivate people to perform better through potential awards.

Information desk See **Purser's office**.

Inside stateroom (also called **Interior stateroom**) Stateroom that has no windows.

Intangible product Product or service that has no physical form.

Interior staterooms See **Inside stateroom**.

L

Lido deck Pool deck area that offers informal, buffet-like dining, both indoors and outdoors.

Lower bed A bed that's on the stateroom's floor.

Low season The time of year with the lowest demand and the lowest prices.

M

Magrodome A glass skylight that can slide to cover the pool area in cold weather.

Market research See **Consumer research**.

Meet-and-greet A company representative meets cruise passengers at the airport.

Megaship Giant-sized ships, 70,000 GRT and above, that can accommodate at least 2,000 passengers.

Multiline rep An independent salesperson who represents two or more noncompeting travel suppliers.

N

Niche A narrow segment of consumers who have something in common.

O

One-way itinerary Itinerary with the ship starting at one port and finishing at another.

Open-ended question Question that elicits complex and telling responses.

Open-jaw itinerary An air itinerary featuring a return from a different city than from the one first flown to.

Open seating (or **sitting**) Passengers may sit anywhere in the dining room; tables are not assigned.

Outside stateroom Stateroom that has windows.

Override commission A commission over and above the standard commission rate.

P

Past passenger rate (also called **Alumni rate**) Discounted rate given to people who have sailed a cruise line before.

Pax Industry abbreviation for "passengers."

Pied piper A member of an organization who is especially respected and admired by its members.

Port Facing forward, the left side of the ship.

Port day A day when the ship stops at a port of call.

Port charge What ports charge the cruise lines to dock their ships.

Post-cruise package Package that includes lodging at the cruise arrival port after the cruise.

Pre-cruise package Package that includes lodging at the cruise departure port before the cruise.

Preformed group A group of people who belong to a club, association, or other pre-existing organization.

Product research Research that focuses on the elements of what is to be sold.

Promotional group See **Speculative group**.

Prospect A potential buyer of a product.

Publicity Promotion that is nearly or completely cost-free.

Purser's office (also called **front desk, hotel desk, reception desk,** or **information desk**) The direct equivalent of a hotel's front desk.

R

Reception desk See Purser's office.

Repositioning cruise A cruise during which the ship moves from one general cruise area to another.

Round-trip itinerary See **Circle itinerary** or **Closed-jaw itinerary**.

S

Second seating (or **sitting**) The later of two meal times in the ship's dining room.

Shore excursion A port-based tour or activity.

Shoulder season The time of year between high season and low season, when prices are somewhat lower than in the high season.

Single occupancy One passenger booking a stateroom designed to accommodate two or more.

Single supplement The additional price one passenger must pay for single occupancy of a stateroom designed for two or more passengers.

Spa Facility on the ship that offers massages, facials, saunas, whirlpools, aromatherapy, and other beauty or relaxation-related services.

Space ratio Figure determined by dividing GRT by passenger capacity.

Speculative group (also called **Promotional group**) A group of individuals who probably do not know each other.

Stabilizers Underwater wing-like devices that reduce a ship's roll.

Starboard Facing forward, the right side of the ship.

Stateroom (also called **Cabin**) A guest room on a ship.

Stateroom category The price that a certain kind or level of stateroom represents.

Stern The back of the ship.

Suite The most expensive accommodation on a ship, typically featuring, in the same rectangular space, both a sitting area and a sleeping area, often divided by a curtain.

T

Tangible product Product that has physical form.

Tender A small boat that ferries passengers between port and ship.

Travel incentive A program to motivate people to perform better through the potential award of an exceptional travel experience.

U

Upper bed Similar to an upper bed in a bunk bed. It's recessed into the wall or ceiling during the day and is pulled out for bedtime, above floor level.

Upselling Offering the client something that costs a little more than they expected to pay.

Y

Yield management The practice of adjusting price to supply and demand.

Z

Zodiac boat A large rubber boat, mainly used on adventure cruises.

INDEX